D0866732

Please return to:

The Kernodle Center for Service Learning
and Community Engagement
CB 2999, Elon, NC 27244
(336)278-7250

PRAXIS I

A Faculty Casebook on Community Service Learning

Edited by
Jeffrey Howard

Series Editors: Joseph Galura and Jeffrey Howard

OCSL Press
University of Michigan
Office of Community Service Learning
2205 Michigan Union
Ann Arbor, Michigan 48109
(313) 763-3548
(313) 763-1388 (fax)

1993

The OCSL Press
2205 Michigan Union
Ann Arbor, Michigan 48109
(313) 763-3548

First Printing

Printed in the United States of America

ISBN   0-9638136-0-9   (the series)

        0-9638136-1-7   (Praxis I)

        0-938136-1-5   (Praxis II)

Dedication

To my children,

Adam Miller-Howard
and
Rachel Miller-Howard,

who I cherish beyond words,

and from whom I have learned
life's most important lessons.

And to my wife,

Janet Montonye Miller,

who I love deeply,

and who continues to be
my most important teacher.

Table of Contents

Acknowledgments   iii

Foreword   *Wilbert McKeachie*   v

Part One   **Generic Issues**   1

Chapter 1   Community Service Learning in the Curriculum   3
             Jeffrey Howard
Chapter 2   Preparing Students to Learn from
             the Experience of Community Service   13
             Allen Menlo

Part Two   **Undergraduate Course Models**   25

Chapter 3   Community Service Learning as
             Innovation in the University   27
             Mark A. Chesler—Sociology
Chapter 4   Creating Spaces:
             Two Examples of Community-Based Learning   41
             Buzz Alexander—English
Chapter 5   Integrating Service-Learning into a
             Course in Contemporary Political Issues   57
             Gregory B. Markus—Political Science
Chapter 6   Detroit Summer:
             A Model for Service-Learning   67
             Bunyan Bryant—Urban Studies

Chapter 7   Community Service Writing in an
             Advanced Composition Class 75
             Karis Crawford—English Composition
Chapter 8   Field Research:
             A Complement for Service-Learning 85
             Kathleen Daly—Sociology
Chapter 9   Women in the Community:
             A Course in Social Change 97
             Christina Jose Kampfner—Women's Studies
Chapter 10   Taking Over the Reins:
             Service Projects in Environmental Studies 111
             Lisa Bardwell and Shannon Sullivan—Environmental Studies
Chapter 11   Psychology in the Community 123
             Jerry Miller—Psychology
Chapter 12   Adapting Drama Activities for
             Individuals with Disabilities 135
             Hilary U. Cohen—Theatre and Drama
Chapter 13   Environmental Action Projects as
             Community Service Learning 139
             Peter B. Kaufman and Mari Ziegler—Biology

Part Three   Graduate Course Models   149

Chapter 14   Contradictory Missions of a
             Tempered Radical's Teaching 151
             Sharon E. Sutton—Architecture and Urban Planning
Chapter 15   Student Workshops as
             Community Service Learning 163
             Barry Checkoway—Social Work and Urban Planning
Chapter 16   The Social Work Practicum as Service-Learning 173
             Lily Jarman-Rohde and John E. Tropman—Social Work
Chapter 17   Linking Community Service
             with Independent Studies 181
             Toby Citrin—Public Health

Bibliography   187

About the Contributors   195

Acknowledgments

First and foremost, we wish to thank all the authors of this book for stimulating our thinking about the integration of community service into academic courses.

We are grateful for the confidence communicated by the Michigan Campus Compact in accepting our grant proposal to publish these two volumes on service-learning, and express our thanks to the Commission on National and Community Service for providing the funding. We also acknowledge our great indebtedness to the W. K Kellogg Foundation, for the credibility and legitimacy that accompanies their grants, and under whose auspices we have developed these publications.

We would be remiss not to express our deep gratitude to Mark Chesler, who has never flinched from his commitment to service-learning and to our Office, and who will always be our primary source for stimulation on service-learning pedagogical issues.

We wish to thank our Student Affairs leaders—Frank Cianciola, E. Royster Harper, and Maureen Hartford—for their continuing confidence in our programs. And, a warm thank you is extended to David Schoem for allowing us to utilize his book on multicultural teaching as a model.

To our colleagues at the Michigan Campus Compact—Julie Busch and Nancy Ironside—and at the Michigan Community Service Commission—Diana Algra—a heartfelt appreciation for your colleagiality and friendship.

To Cris Zerkel-Shankleton, thank you so much for serving as our graphic designer; we will be forever in your debt.

To Venus Sage and Tamara Agnew a sincere thanks for the typing and editing that must have seemed never-ending to you. We could not have met our deadlines without your commitment.

Last but not least, great gratitude is extended to the staff of the Office of Community Service Learning—Anita Bohn, Margaret Elias, Joe Galura, and Joan Scott—for being my community service learning partners. I care about all of you.

Jeffrey Howard

Foreword

Wilbert McKeachie

Recently a friend asked me if students had changed much over the 47 years since I began teaching in the Psychology Department at the University of Michigan. I replied that fundamentally they still seem to me to have some of the same characteristics of curiosity and anxiety, as well as values that are fundamental to human nature. I went on to describe some of the different cohorts as I have experienced them.

When I began teaching, many of the students were older than I, since both they and I had returned from several years in the Armed Services during World War II; today we once again have a sprinkling of older students—albeit much younger than I. The students of the 1960's and 70's were sometimes difficult to teach and aggressively anti-authority, but I do miss the degree to which they were committed to the values of peace and service to humanity. Students of the recent past have seemed more materialistic and concerned about jobs, but I attribute that primarily to the difficult job market.

Students today, despite their concerns about surviving economically, may again be characterized as having strong service values. When they are given opportunities to gain experience in serving other people, they find great satisfaction.

But in serving other people, beyond great satisfaction there is also great learning to be mined. We know from our research that active learning leads to better retention and use of knowledge. So when community service is integrated with academic learning it has great capacity to multiply student learning outcomes. Add to this its additional capacity to encourage civic and social responsibility, and one sees how community service learning can be instrumental in helping students to become our future educated citizenry.

With a new national administration calling people to return from the emphasis upon accumulating greater individual wealth to an emphasis on greater human welfare, community service learning opportunities seem once again to be timely and continue to be valuable both in terms of impact upon student values and upon traditional educational objectives.

This book, and the volume which succeeds it, will contribute greatly toward both stimulating more faculty to incorporate community service learning into their courses as well as to increasing the effectiveness of those of us who use community service learning in our courses today.

PART ONE

Generic Issues

Chapter 1

COMMUNITY SERVICE LEARNING IN THE CURRICULUM

Jeffrey Howard

Much of the attention and support for college student involvement in community service has focused on students' contributions to the community and on the development of students' lifelong civic responsibility. These are essential outcomes of a community service program. But there is more.

Community service learning, or service-learning as it is more commonly called, is a first cousin of community service. It, too, engages students in service to the community and contributes to the development of students' civic ethic. Where it differs is in its deliberateness about student learning. Though learning necessarily occurs in the act of serving in the community, with community service learning there is an *intentional effort made to utilize the community service experience as a learning resource.*

A number of possible avenues enable students to intentionally learn from their community service experiences. One option is for students to self-direct their learning, for example by keeping a reflective journal or by reading germane materials. A second option is for the campus community service program to provide a learning structure, such as a reflection guidebook or periodic seminars, for students placed in the community. Any of these intentional learning interventions would transform the community service to community service learning.

A third option is to have the community service integrated into an academic course. In this model, the community service experiences of the students are not just a sidebar but an integral component of the course. When used in this way, community service learning may be conceptualized as a *pedagogical model that connects meaningful community service experiences with academic course learning.*

Why Integrate Service into Academic Courses?

There are some educationally-sound reasons for integrating community service experiences into academic courses:

- faculty are well equipped to design effective assignments that enable students to capture the learning from their community service experiences

- students are more likely to intentionally learn because they are more accustomed to, and accountable for, learning in academic courses than in co-curricular activities

- community service experiences enhance academic learning[1]

- community service experiences are important sources of knowledge and scholarship

- faculty can play a role in reducing the chances that students' stereotypes and preconceived notions about under-served populations are perpetuated

In addition, integrating service into the curriculum strengthens the prospect for the institutionalization of community service learning because:

- faculty are more likely to perceive community service as educationally valuable if the service occurs within, rather than outside of, the curriculum

- curricular efforts are a higher funding priority than co-curricular efforts

About This Book

This book, then, is about the third alternative—integrating community service experiences into university academic courses. Each chapter, written by a University of Michigan faculty member, describes a community service learning course, discusses relevant pedagogical issues, evaluates the course, and assesses student learning. Though each instructor's motivations, interpretations, and priorities are unique, the common thread is the utilization of students' service in the community as a learning resource in the service of the academic learning in the course. Each instructor views the students' community service experiences as important for the provision of service and for the development of students' civic responsibility as well as for the study of the particular academic field.

We have broadly interpreted the parameters of community service learning courses so as to provide the reader with the greatest variety of models. Included in this book are internships (Jose Kampfner), workshops (Checkoway), studios (Sutton), field research (Daly), practicums (Jarman-Rohde/Tropman), summer programs (Bryant), and independent studies courses (Citrin), as well as the more traditionally-defined service-learning courses (Chesler, Alexander, Markus, Crawford, Bardwell/Sullivan, Miller, Cohen, Kaufman/Ziegler). There are also chapters that describe research on student outcomes (Markus, Crawford), and chapter appendices that include course syllabi and course assignments.

Why a Faculty Casebook?

Curriculum-based community service learning is experiencing a major growth spurt. More and more faculty are coming into the community service learning fold. Record numbers of students are enrolling in service-learning courses. Many prominent education stakeholder groups are supporting the integration of service into the formal academic curriculum. A teaching/learning model that prepares young people for their role as community members while better engaging them with their studies is difficult to oppose.

But to successfully blend service and learning in a course involves a pedagogy with which most instructors (and most students) have had little prior experience. In fact, in many ways service-learning pedagogy stands in contrast to traditional academic principles and values. And, though the literature is replete with discussions on co-curricular community service and community service learning, we found the literature to be wanting in materials that provide models for, and address pedagogical issues relevant to, community service learning courses.

Therefore, this casebook is written primarily for faculty: to encourage and inform those who have hesitated to join the community service learning movement, to dispel the negative perceptions held by those who have been averse to incorporating service into the curriculum, and to stimulate course innovations and refinements for those already involved in this field.

Principles of Good Practice in Community Service Learning Pedagogy

The field of community service learning has a number of outstanding sets of principles of good practice, most notably the Johnson Foundation/Wingspread "Principles of Good Practice for Combining Service and Learning."[2] However, these sets of principles have mostly focused on non-curricular community service learning programs. And though these prior principles have application to community service learning courses, they are insufficient for developing and implementing what is for many faculty a new kind of course. Therefore we offer the following set of principles of community service learning pedagogy, subscription to which will enable students' community learning to be fully integrated with, and utilized on behalf of, course learning.

The 10 principles below are derived from a host of sources, most notably the models depicted in this book, my 16 years of involvement with curriculum-based service-learning, and the candid responses of 10 University of Michigan academic leaders as part of the evaluation of our Kellogg Foundation grant.[3]

None of these 10 principles are antithetical to, or inconsistent with, previously disseminated principles of good practice, and none of these will compromise the service that students provide in the community. On the contrary, these principles not only complement previously generated lists, but a number of them enhance the student's capacity to be of service in the community.

Principle 1: Academic Credit is for Learning, Not for Service

Credit in academic courses is assigned to students for the demonstration of academic learning. It should be no different in community service learning courses. Academic credit is for academic learning, and community service is not academic in nature. Therefore, the credit must not be for the performance of service. However, when community service is integrated into an academic course, the course credit is assigned for both the customary academic learning as well as for the utilization of the community learning in the service of the course learning. Similarly, the student's grade is for the quality of learning and not for the quality (or quantity) of service.

Principle 2: Do Not Compromise Academic Rigor

Academic standards in a course are based on the challenge that readings, presentations, and assignments present to students. These standards ought to be sustained when adding a community service learning component. Though experience-based learning is frequently perceived to be less rigorous than academic learning, especially in scholarly circles, we advise against compromising the level of instructor expectation for student learning. The additional workload imposed by a community service assignment may be compensated by an additional credit, but not by lowering academic learning expectations. Adding a service component, in fact, may enhance the rigor of a course because, in addition to having to master the academic material, students must also learn how to learn from community experience and merge that learning with academic learning, and these are challenging intellectual activities that are commensurate with rigorous academic standards.

Principle 3: Set Learning Goals for Students

Establishing learning goals for students is a standard to which all courses ought to be accountable. Not only should it be no different with community service learning courses, but in fact it is especially necessary and advantageous to do so with these kinds of courses. With the addition of the community as a learning context, there occurs a multiplication of learning paradigms (e.g. inductive learning, synthesis of theory and practice) and learning topics (e.g. the community, the population). To sort out those of greatest priority in the service of the course goals, as well as to best take advantage of the rich bounty of learning opportunity offered by the community, requires deliberate planning of the course learning goals.

Principle 4: Establish Criteria for the Selection of Community Service Placements

To optimally utilize community service on behalf of course learning requires more than merely directing students to find a service placement. Faculty who are deliberate about establishing criteria for selecting community service placements will find that the learning that students extract from their respective service experiences will be of better use on behalf of course learning than if placement criteria are not established.

We offer three criteria as essential in all community service learning courses. First, the range of service placements ought to be cirumscribed by the content of the course; homeless shelters and soup kitchens are learning-appropriate placements for a course on homelessness, but placements in schools are not. Second, the duration of the service must be sufficient to enable the fulfillment of learning goals; a one time two-hour shift at a hospital will do little for the learning in a course on institutional health care. And, third, the specific service activities and service contexts must have the potential to stimulate course-relevant learning; filing records in a warehouse may be of service to a school district, but it would offer little to stimulate learning in a course on elementary school education.

We also offer three guidelines regarding the setting of placement criteria. First, responsibility for insuring that placement criteria are established that will enable the best student learning rests with the faculty. Second, the learning goals established for the course will be helpful in informing the placement criteria. And, third, faculty who utilize the volunteer services office on campus or in the community to assist with identifying criteria-satisfying community agencies will reduce their start-up labor costs.

Principle 5: Provide Educationally-Sound Mechanisms to Harvest the Community Learning

Learning in any course is realized by the proper mix and level of learning formats and assignments. To maximize students' service experiences on behalf of course learning in a community service learning course requires more than sound service placements. Courses assignments and learning formats must be carefully developed to both facilitate the students' learning from their community service experiences as well as to enable its use on behalf of course learning. Assigning students to serve at a community agency, even a faculty approved one, without any mechanisms in place to harvest the learning therefrom, is insufficient to contribute to course learning. Experience, as a learning format, in and of itself, does not consummate learning, nor does mere written description of one's service activities.

Learning interventions that instigate critical reflection on and analysis of service experiences are necessary to enable community learning to be harvested and to serve as an academic learning enhancer. Therefore, discussions, presentations, and journal and paper assignments that provoke analysis of service experiences in the context of the course learning and that encourage the blending of the experiential and academic learnings are necessary to help insure that the service does not underachieve in its role as an instrument of learning. Here, too, the learning goals set for the course will be helpful in informing the course learning formats and assignments.

Principle 6: Provide Supports for Students to Learn how to Harvest the Community Learning

Harvesting the learning from the community and utilizing it on behalf of course learning are learning paradigms for which most students are under-prepared. Faculty can help students realize the potential of community learning by either assisting students with the acquisition of skills necessary for gleaning the learning from the community, and/or by providing examples of how to successfully do so. An example of the former would be to provide instruction on participant-observation skills; an example of the latter would be to make accessible a file containing past outstanding student papers and journals to current students in the course.

Principle 7: Minimize the Distinction between the Student's Community Learning Role and the Classroom Learning Role

Classrooms and communities are very different learning contexts, each requiring students to assume a different learner role. Generally, classrooms provide a high level of learning direction, with students expected to assume a largely learning-follower role. In contrast, communities provide a low level of learning direction, with students expected to assume a largely learning-leader role. Though there is compatibility between the level of learning direction and the expected student role within each of these learning contexts, there is incompatibility across them.

For students to have to alternate between the learning-follower role in the classroom and the learning-leader role in the community not only places yet another learning challenge on students but it is inconsistent with good pedagogical principles. Just as we do not mix required lectures (high learning-follower role) with a student-determined reading list (high learning-leader role) in a traditional course, so, too, we must not impose conflicting learner role expectations on students in community service learning courses.

Therefore, if students are expected to assume a learning-follower role in the classroom, then a mechanism is needed that will provide learning direction for the students in the community (e.g community agency staff serving in an adjunct instructor role); otherwise, students will enter the community wearing the inappropriate learning-follower hat.Correspondingly, if the students are expected to assume a learning-leader role in the community, then room must be made in the classroom for students to assume a learning-leader role; otherwise, students will enter the classroom wearing the inappropriate learning-leader hat. The more we can make consistent the student's learning role in the classroom with her/his learning role in the community, the better the chances that the learning potential within each context will be realized.

Principle 8: Re-Think the Faculty Instructional Role

Regardless of whether they assume learning-leader or learning-follower roles in the community, community service learning students are acquiring course-relevant information and knowledge from their service experiences. At the same time, as we previously acknowledged, students also are being challenged by the many new and unfamiliar ways of learning inherent in community service learning. Because students carry this new information and these learning challenges back to the classroom, it behooves service-learning faculty to reconsider their interpretation of the classroom instructional role. A shift in instructor role that would be most compatible with these new learning phenomena would move away from information dissemination and move toward learning facilitation and guidance. Exclusive or even primary use of the traditional instructional model interferes with the promise of learning fulfillment available in community service learning courses.

Principle 9: Be Prepared for Uncertainty and Variation in Student Learning Outcomes

In college courses, the learning stimuli and class assignments largely determine student outcomes. This is true in community service learning courses too. However, in traditional courses, the learning stimuli (i.e., lectures and readings) are constant for all enrolled students; this leads to predictability and homogeneity in student learning outcomes. In community service learning courses, the variability in community service placements necessarily leads to less certainty and homogeneity in student learning outcomes. Even when community service learning students are exposed to the same presentations and the same readings, instructors can expect that the content of class discussions will be less predictable and the content of student papers will be less homogeneous than in courses without a community assignment.

Principle 10: Maximize the Community Responsibility Orientation of the Course

If one of the objectives of a community service learning course is to cultivate students' sense of community and social responsibility, then designing course learning formats and assignments that encourage a communal rather than an individual learning orientation will contribute to this objective. If learning in a course is privatized and tacitly understood as for the advancement of the individual, then we are implicitly encouraging a private responsibility mindset; an example would be to assign papers that students write individually and that are read only by the instructor. On the other hand, if the learning is shared amongst the learners for the benefit of corporate learning, then we are implicitly encouraging a group responsibility mentality; an example would be to share those same student papers with the other students in the class. This conveys to the students that they are resources for one another, and this message contributes to the building of commitment to community and civic duty.

By subscribing to this set of 10 pedagogical principles, faculty will find that students' learning from their service will be optimally utilized on behalf of academic learning, corporate learning, developing a commitment to civic responsibility, and providing learning-informed service in the community.

Introduction to Chapters

This book is divided into three sections. The first section offers two chapters that cut across disciplines and have generic value for the design and implementation of community service learning courses. The present chapter has introduced curriculum-based community service learning and delineated principles of good practice therefor. In chapter 2, Allen Menlo discusses four competencies—reflective listening, seeking feedback, acuity in observation, and mindfulness in thinking—that are needed by students to capture the learning from their community service experiences. These initial chapters will serve to ground the newcomer and to refresh the veteran.

The second section offers eleven models of undergraduate courses in which service and learning are combined. Though each chapter in this section is about a discipline-based course (as identified in the Table of Contents), the pedagogical descriptions and the issues raised are pertinent to all community service learning courses. In chapter 3, Mark Chesler segues from his description of an eighteen year old service-centered course to an analysis of the counter-normative nature of community service learning courses and the concommitant challenges facing service-learning faculty, students, and institutions. The fourth chapter is Buzz Alexander's captivating description of two English courses committed to "creating spaces" for students and service acquirers to each achieve both their service and learning potentials. In chapter 5 Gregory Markus describes his political science course, and argues that preparation for partici-pation in the polity does not necessarily occur through the act of service alone. Bunyan Bryant waxes philosophic in chapter 6, admonishing us for our dislocation and disengagement from each other, from our communities, and from Nature, followed by a review of "Detroit Summer '92," a program that enabled young people to begin to recapture these lost relationships. Karis Crawford, in chapter 7, describes her incorporation of community service writing into an English Composition class. In chapter 8, Kathleen Daly's description of a field research assignment for her criminology class serves as a model for how students may concurrently conduct research and serve in the community.

A Women's Studies service internship course is described by Christina Jose Kampfner in chapter 9, and includes an organizational analysis paper assign-ment that may be of interest to service-learning faculty in other disciplines. Lisa Bardwell and Shannon Sullivan describe in chapter 10 their experience with incorporating a community service project in their environmental studies course and its capacity to move students from despondency about the magnitude of environmental problems to the optimism and hopefulness that accompanies working for change. Jerry Miller, faculty coordinator of the Psychology Department's very large service-learning course, Project Outreach, packs chapter 11 with thirty years of lessons learned. In chapter 12, Hilary Cohen describes a course in which University students utilize drama to help disabled youth learn. And Peter Kaufman and Mari Ziegler, in chapter 13, discuss their Botany course, born in the beginning of the environmental movement, and how they involve students in community action projects.

The third and final section offers four graduate level models of community service learning courses. Here, too, the models are discipline-based, but the issues raised and the models described have broad value. In Chapter 14, Sharon Sutton describes an inter-disciplinary master's level studio, followed by a discussion of the contradictory roles inherent in instructing a community service learning course and the influence of student traits on student evaluations of her studio. This is followed by Barry Checkoway's model of workshops as community service learning, describing in chapter 15 substantial community improvement efforts co-developed by social work and urban planning students with members of underserved communities. In chapter 16, Lily Jarman-Rohde and John Tropman describe what is tantamount to a community service learning immersion course—the social work practicum—in which community agency staff serve as adjunct educators. And, in chapter 17, Toby Citrin of the School of Public Health describes a number of different independent studies course formats initiated either by a student's educational interest and/or by a need in the community, and interprets the students' role as connecting the resources of the University and the faculty with needs in the community.

Though, regrettably, a number of disciplines are absent from this volume, the pedagogical models offered and the issues raised have application to courses situated in many of the unrepresented fields.

The Praxis Series

This book is the first of a two volume set. The reader's attention is directed to the complementary second volume, *Praxis II: Service-Learning Resources for University Students, Staff, and Faculty*, written by University of Michigan students and service-learning educators. In the process of preparing volumes one and two, we have generated new material and new ideas for materials that, contingent upon funding, we plan to publish as the next volume in the *Praxis* Series.

Final Note

As is depicted in each chapter of this book, community service learning is a comprehensive educational experience. In addition to contributing to the community, furthering students' social responsibility, and their general learning about the community, it is a teaching-learning model with a myriad of other learning benefits. It enhances academic learning. It offers students new learning paradigms as well as a chance to try on new learner and instructor roles. It renews investment in learning. It offers an opportunity to reconsider prior values, ethics, and attitudes. It offers an experience that counterbalances the curriculum's predisposition for theory. It provides experience with ambiguity and with variance in data significance, both of which in turn foster critical thinking. It encourages student self-direction and learning about self. It brings books to life and life to books. And, it provides opportunities for developing real world skills and real world knowledge.

Is there any other kind of educational experience that can boast such a litany of outcomes? Please read on and join us on an educational voyage that opens new learning paradigms for students and new pedagogical vistas for faculty. Come discover how community service learning is a comprehensive and satisfying educational experience for both students *and* faculty.

Notes

1. Markus, Gregory B., Jeffrey P.F. Howard, and David C. King. "Integrating community service with classroom instruction enhances learning: Results from an experiment," *Educational Evaluation and Policy Analysis*, Winter 1994.

2. The Wingspread Principles of Good Practice for Combining Service and Learning are as follows:

    An effective program ...
    1. engages people in responsible and challenging actions for the common good
    2. provides structured opportunities for people to reflect critically on their service

experiences

3. articulates clear service and learning goals for everyone involved
4. allows for those with needs to define those need
5. clarifies the responsibilities of each person and organization involved
6. matches service providers and service needs through a process that recognizes changing circumstances
7. expects genuine, active, and sustained organizational commitment
8. includes training, supervision, monitoring, support, recognition, and evaluation to meet service and learning goals
9. insures that the time commitment for service and learning is flexible, appropriate, and in the best interests of all involved
10. is committed to program participation by and with diverse populations

3. Jeffrey Howard's proposal received $156,000 from the Kellogg Foundation for three years beginning July, 1990. One of the goals of the grant was to enhance the valuing and support for community service learning at the University of Michigan. To assess progress on this goal, the external evaluators of the grant conducted pre-grant and post-grant interviews.

Chapter 2

PREPARING STUDENTS TO LEARN FROM THE EXPERIENCE OF COMMUNITY SERVICE

Allen Menlo

Introduction

This chapter begins with a brief reflection on the nature of service-learning. It then addresses the question of what major competencies students need to have in order to engage the service-giving experience in ways which increase the likelihood of their successfully extracting and realizing learnings about self, others, and the multi-level social-political environment. Four teachable-learnable competencies are identified and described as priorities among whatever the full range of those necessary and near-sufficient conditions of the learner are that help assure success in this type of venture. What the exact theoretical linkage is between each of these competencies and specific learning outcomes is not addressed.

About Service Learning

I recently had an occasion on which the idea of learning from the experience of giving service was operationalized and made especially vivid to me. I happened to be informally observing a University of Michigan student serving in the community as part of a service-learning course. This student was working with senior citizens—sharing companionship and helping with day-to-day and special tasks and occasions. On this particular occasion, he was with an elderly man at the check-out counter of a large store. The man was trying to exchange a non-working item he had purchased earlier in the week for one which was in good working order. The price had been raised during the week and the college-age clerk was telling the man he now had to pay the higher price for the same item the store had just recently sold him in a damaged state. The man objected and he and the clerk continued their disagreement, until the clerk finally called the manager on the inter-com and told her semi-publicly that an older man was wanting to evade paying for the present price of an item. After some phone discussion, the clerk was informed that the transaction should be treated as an even exchange. On turning back to face the man, the clerk said that they should start all over again and, with a facial expression of displeasure and impatience, threw onto the older man's side of the counter the $20 bill he had given her earlier for the purchase of an additional item. After a few moments of apparently uncomfortable hesitation, the man partially looked up and said he would prefer to settle for accomplishing just the item exchange and not bother with the additional purchase. The encounter ended, the clerk began to wait on the next person in line, and the man left with his exchanged item and no interest in risking the receipt of another piece of the store's assistance. The student had been supportively at the senior citizen's side throughout the event and left the store in conversation with him.

I have pondered over this event numerous times, and have done so with special interest since I was so kindly invited to contribute this chapter to *Praxis*. I have wondered about the nature of the student's and elderly person's conversation following the event, what was going on in the student's mind while the in-store interaction was happening, and how the student reflected on both of these brief but potentially learning-loaded encounters. The more I wondered, the more fascinating and serious questions emerged in my mind for the student's possible exploration. Here are just a few: What is the meaning of helpfulness to another person? How can one person try to help another during that other's negative interpersonal encounter without being intrusive on the other's own needs? Was what the student observed a case of interpersonal violence? How do age discrepancies influence seller-consumer interactions? How can people emerge strengthened rather than weakened from such encounters? What is the role of organizational staff development and training in dealing with clients? How should advocacy groups, and legal protection agencies function for older persons as consumers? How well are we doing on the care and utilization of the wisdom resources of our older population? What is my role and responsibility in all of this, and what does that imply for the education I should seek in order to think about these issues in the service of society as well as for my own development?

I have also wondered what the complex of knowledge, skills, attitudes, and values are for learning from experiences of the kind just described. When embraced by the college teacher, the precise issue becomes: What competencies can I teach students that will help them explore the foregoing and other such questions in ways which assure that the learnings from their community service experiences will be productive and creative?

I believe it is particularly important to distinguish between two levels of learning here—learning how to give service, and learning how to learn (i.e., learning how to extract learnings) from the giving of service. The range of intended learnings in the former is usually restricted to enhancing the process of service-giving. The array of learnings intended in the latter may include the same learnings as in the former, but high priority is also placed on learnings about self, relationships and social responsibility; knowledge, appreciations and awarenesses about humanity and the environment; and becoming a self-initiating life-long learner in almost any context. Put in this perspective, the facilitation of this level of learning is exciting, profound, and complex. Some of its complexity arises from the number and depth of the aspects of the learner that are often touched, and some relates to the fact that in the service-giving setting it is not unusual for service-givers to be unaware of discrepancies between their intentions and their behavior, and, furthermore, to be unaware of their own unawareness. Thus, it can become quite a struggle to access some of the intra-personal information needed for learning.

In what follows I will identify and describe what I view as the four most essential competencies college teachers can help students acquire in order to prepare them to maximally tap the kinds of learnings available from the experience of giving service. While I do not propose a particular curriculum or methods for teaching these competencies, I do describe several aspects of each competency in order to communicate its meaning and develop an image of it in action. I also suggest one or more instructional tools which teachers can use to facilitate students' understanding of each competency. I view these competencies as generic and generally applicable for the extraction of learnings relevant to most any course of study. Thoughtful teachers will probably want to add their own special "twist" in facilitating their students' acquisition of these competencies so as to focus their potential for extracting experiential learnings which are most applicable to their own subject matter.

Reflective Listening

The image I have in mind for reflective listening is the service-giver making an authentic, honest inquiry of someone in the experiential setting as to whether or not the service-giver's expressed understanding of that someone's concern, position, or idea accurately represents that concern, position, or idea as it is held by that person. The importance of this understanding rests in the fact that it is difficult to provide service in response to another's needs if one does not truly comprehend the nature of the need. Without this comprehension, much service is given that is not helpful, and the service-receiver, sensing the lower power position in the transaction, is more ready to depart from a mutual learning relationship than to contribute toward it.

In reflective listening the information one acquires and the struggle to reach an empathic understanding of the other person's internal frame of reference provide remarkable sources of learning and development for the service-giver. The service-giver and the service-receiver cease to be two individuals representing private worlds which cannot quite get into a shared position. They slip into a common stream of communication and the service-giver begins to more clearly understand what the other person is saying—not just the words, but the meaning and feeling behind the words. As a result of this understanding, a mutual appreciation is initiated for each other as individuals and as persons of value. The service-giver begins to see the other almost as an entirely different person than before. The service-giver asks questions to clarify uncertainties, and, in the process, helps both parties clarify their own thoughts. The service-receiver grows in security about what she/he is saying and, over time, discloses more authentic perceptions and feelings. There is no need to do otherwise since the person knows the service-giver is accepting and trying to understand, not evaluating or judging. It gradually becomes clear to the other person that in this engagement the service-giver has no intentions of trying to influence the person toward any particular views or behaviors, but only wishes to have a more complete understanding of the person's situation. In return, though, the person becomes more desirous of hearing the service-giver's views and much more receptive to considering those views and ideas. A person is decidedly more amenable to the acceptance of new and different ideas, attitudes, and ways of acting when the person has had ample opportunity to first express her/his own feelings about an issue at hand

and when the person's feelings are accepted as being just as reasonable and valid in her/his particular situation as are anyone else's.

The open-endedness of reflective listening and its accompanying authentic question-asking can provide much psychological space for the free movement of the service-receiver. In this sense, the service-receiver moves from being a presented, not-self person, constrained to roles perceived as required by the situation, toward sharing a more real presence. The person becomes much more accessible as a source of learning to the service-giver. At the same time, the service-receiver moves freely in the psychological space provided, telling more about her or himself and making more visible the issues, problems, concerns, aspirations, sources of enthusiasm and discouragement, and life views of her/his community. These begin to comprise a new window of cultural understanding for the service-giver. The extent and richness of learning from service-receivers and the process of service-giving in the experiential setting is strongly related to service-givers having within their verbal and non-verbal repertoires the confirmation-seeking, non-judgmental, reflective listening response and the associated questions and question-asking processes of authentic, interested inquiry.

Listening holds several personal and interpersonal benefits. One finds out more information, one increases his or her influence, and one extracts more learning from experience. But, listening has its risk; as you listen authentically to others you become vulnerable to changing your own opinions—or losing your opinions in favor of the opinions of others. For some persons this possibility can become quite threatening, and even devastating. Also, it is interesting that in our mainly competitive society, persons are more likely to compete for who talks the most rather than for who listens the most; and in the daily win-lose context, the one designated as social or political winner is usually the one who talks the most, and had the most to say. So listening often takes an abundance of courage which is often unrecognized socially. Service-givers can be helped to learn and exercise this kind of courage.

An instructional tool that can help students appreciate the difficulty in fully understanding another person is the following heuristic device portraying how one person's (A) intended message is usually accompanied by elements of unintended message. The two, together, produce noise and result in message distortion for the receiver (B). Reflective listening can then be viewed as an intervention that reduces the influence of unintended message or as an antidote for noise, and, in so doing, increases clarity and mutual understanding.

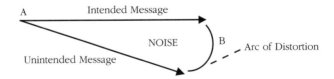

Another type of instructional tool is a small group exercise in which students practice the use of reflective listening. This is available from the Office of Community Service Learning.

Seeking Feedback

It is very difficult for a service-giving person to truly know the extent to which service efforts are helping to bring about results which are consistent with the service-giver's intentions, unless that person has developed some formal or informal means of receiving information on how the efforts and their results are being experienced by service recipients and seen by observers of service efforts. Additionally, it becomes difficult to make reliable modifications in one's efforts to "hit the intended mark" with very limited information on the relationship between one's efforts and their resulting consequences.

Feedback, information about one's behavior and its consequences, when thoughtfully reflected upon, can also be an essential ingredient for learning about one's self, for discovering the nature of one's own motives, values, beliefs, and views and how these shape, sometimes unknowingly, one's own behavior. Further, it provides insight into how one's own inclinations can impact the behavior of others. In this latter sense, one can begin to learn about and become sensitive to oneself as a stimulus to others, rather than only as a responder to the behavior of others. This realization may arouse a service-giver's interest in working on a change in his or her own stimulus value as a means of influencing others rather than always focusing on the service-recipient as the direct target of change. Engaging in this kind of activity usually moves the service-giver to a personalized consideration of several important interpersonal and social issues, such as the tension between individual rights and organizational authority, the rightful locus of power for change, the function of diversity in individualizing efforts toward change, and the ideological conflict between freeing the capacity and voice of community members as against repairing their perceived deficiencies.

Feedback that is authentic in both its nature and its substance is not usually a readily available commodity, and seeking it can be a rather precarious venture. Many wish to have it, but few seem to be ready to risk giving it—partially because of their misunderstanding of what it actually is. Therefore, it is important for service-givers who desire feedback to understand its true social science meaning, rather than the meanings which have been popularly attached to it over the years.

Feedback is a communication process which involves the non-evaluative observation of behavior, the non-judgmental citing of the behavior's consequences, and the inquiry to the behaver as to whether the observed consequences are in line with the behaver's intentions. The following schematic portrays this sequence of components:

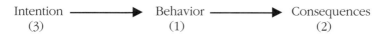

Intention ⟶ Behavior ⟶ Consequences
(3)   (1)   (2)

By its nature, feedback is comprised of neutral information. In this sense, there is no such thing as "positive feedback" or "negative feedback." The former is *praise* and the latter is *criticism*. Praise has the potential of arousing a "shaping of self" response in order to maintain the praise of the praiser, and criticism has the potential of generating an expectation of loss of personal and/or social esteem and power, as well as promoting feelings of resistance, and a deterioration of the feedback-receiver's interest in being influenced by the criticizer.

It is very reasonable that a gap may exist between a service-giver's intention and the consequences of the behavior executed in order to actualize the intention. Additionally, it is understandable that the service-giver may be unaware of this gap. Furthermore, the service-giver may also be unaware of this unawareness. Patient, thoughtful, non-presumptuous, discussible feedback can be a most valuable tool to help untangle this complexity and assist the service-giver to more ably "hit the desired mark." So, in seeking feedback, the service-giver may wish to establish ongoing arrangements with particular members of the service-receiving community and selected co-workers who then arrive at a shared image of the giving and receiving of feedback and an agreement on the need for its discussibility as well. Seeking feedback from more than a single source can provide the service-giver either a consensual validation of received information or it can present the opportunity to explore how persons of different age, gender, ethnicity, personality, and values may vary in the predominance of what they notice and do not notice in the behavior of others.

In addition to the preceding schematic which identifies the components of the feedback process and the sequence of addressing them, the following instructional tool may assist service-givers in their understanding of the personal learning which can become theirs through feedback processes.

	What you know about me	What you do not know about me
What I know about me	Shared between us (3)	My hidden areas (2)
What I do not know about me	My "blind spots" (1)	Undiscovered territory of me (4)

(Adapted from J. Luft (1969) *Of Human Interaction.* Palo Alto, CA: National Press Books.)

The intended message of this heuristic device is that, as the feedback seeker and the feedback giver become more able to risk seeking and giving information about the seeker's efforts and its consequences, "blind spots" and hidden areas begin to get reduced for the feedback seeker, shared information about the feedback seeker increases, and new self discoveries unfold which the feedback seeker can use toward her or his ongoing development. As service-givers refine this competency of extracting self-related data from those who experience or witness their efforts, they enrich the repertoire they need for continuing as a life-long learner. As with many other things, seeking feedback serves the learner best as a calculated learning tool rather than as a preoccupation with acquiring external information for self-validation.

For college teachers who wish to facilitate their students' learning of the competency of seeking and receiving feedback and translating it into learnings about self, there are small group practice activities available from the Office of Community Service Learning.

Acuity in Observation

Two persons who travel similar paths at the same time through a same setting can each emerge with different quantities of observed phenomena—from being saturated with sightings to being empty-handed. The person who is more successful at learning and personal development through the process of giving service is likely to be one who sees more of the separate and interacting elements in the situation and identifies them as ponderable grist for the learning mill. They generate a more extensive agenda of things to talk about and understand. These things usually have implications for learning of knowledge and life outlook within and across different system levels: self, group, organization, and community. College teachers can help their students develop their abilities to actually see more in the same environments they have been looking at for years, and thus prepare them to be heightened extractors of meaning from their experiences in service learning and in their future day-to-day activities.

A good deal of this competency to see more than one has seen before derives from an increased *patience* in order to slow down and take the time to observe, an increase in *optimistic curiosity* for finding the kind of things for which one is looking, and an expansion in one's repertoire of *frameworks for increasing the visibility of phenomena* occurring at the macro-, meso-, and micro-system levels. Many of these frameworks and their dimensions for observing and recording information are applicable to all system sizes and types. For instance, one can observe and even record happenings and behavioral-attitudinal elements that indicate whether persons, groups, organizations, or communities are mainly cooperative, competitive, or individualistic in their relationships with each other. To do so, one would look for signs of *positive interdependence* (persons acting in the service of other member's good performance as well as in the service of their own performance), *face-to-face interaction, individual accountability* to each other for one's own performance and for the provision of mutual assistance, possession of *interpersonal and small group skills* for effective cooperation, and having the time and procedures for *processing* or analyzing how well the persons, groups, organizations, or communities are functioning and then determining what they can do to enhance their working together. A service-giver can also draw inferences about the extent of psychological health within and between these human systems by observing for indicators of acceptance vs. rejection, openness vs. closedness in communication, trust vs. suspicion, involvement vs. withdrawal, comfort vs. anxiousness, mutual respect vs. disregard, feelings of closeness vs. distance, and awareness vs. unawareness of the others' resources—to mention just a few. Of course, the struggle to define and develop concrete imagery of these initially abstract concepts and then test one's own ability to operationalize them in field observation moves one toward greater sensory awareness of elements of the living environment. In their observations, service-givers often become interested in speculating and personally inquiring about the human antecedents and consequences of psychological health conditions and how living systems interact with non-living systems of a geological, geographical, and economic nature. Questions of personal identity, one's own function as stimulus and response to others and the environment, and moral and ethical issues in the introduction of change are bound to arise.

College teachers can also help student service-givers sharpen their observational acuity though attention to vocal and non-vocal expression. For instance, acquisition of individual, sub-cultural, and cultural understandings and appreciations can come from observing what persons do not talk about as well as what they do talk about, the pace of their verbal expressions, and the postures they assume under various conditions. The metaphors people use often contain message about the nature of their occupations, socio-economic background, and leisure activities, and, in turn, draw the observer's attention to her or his own habits of speech and movement. Thus, a major force toward the increase in observational acuity is the provision of "new glasses" for viewing the elements of the context one witnesses or occupies at any time. It may also be true, at times, that one may wish to enhance the chances of seeing something of note or learningfulness through their new glasses by increasing the density of things to be seen. Service-giving observers can sometimes accomplish this by acting upon the setting (e.g., doing or saying something provocative) and then watching for what happens.

While patience and optimistic curiosity are largely attitudinal in nature, they can be promoted through the learning of ways to look and inquire beyond, around, underneath, and behind phenomena and then having occasions of success when taking the time to do this. An example of patience and optimistic curiosity are illustrated in a recent experience of mine. I have a colleague who would always hurriedly bypass the first level of the university parking structure and whiz up the ramp to upper levels, figuring that no spaces would be available to him at lower levels. I told him of the several surprises that came my way when I drove slowly around the first level, looking exactingly and allowing time for others parked on that level to leave. He told me later that one day he surprisingly located a less-obvious parking spot that, because of the way a non-parking sign was hung, it was perfectly legitimate to park there. He parked there each day until his daily ecstasy was exploded by an official shifting the non-parking sign to its proper position. Despite the latter disappointment, he says he can no longer convince himself to drive by the first level without at least a minimal "look-see" in order to satisfy his optimistic curiosity.

An instructional tool that can function as a framework to help student service-givers identify (increase the visibility) and record forces that are hindering and helping a person, group, organization, or community in its efforts toward bringing about a change in itself, and even allow the service-giver to assist the persons involved in developing strategies for bringing about the change, is the following diagram.

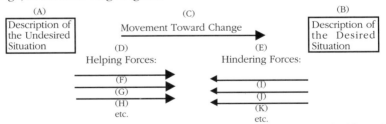

This is one representation of the Force Field Analysis developed by Kurt Lewin (1948) *Resolving Social Conflicts*. New York: Harper and Brothers.

A is the persons' agreed-upon description of the situation about which they are unhappy and which they would like to change. *B* is the persons' agreed-upon description of the situation if it were the way they would like it to be. *C* depicts the movement that must take place if the persons are to bring about the change from *A* to *B*. *D* is a listing of the forces which the persons and the service-giver have identified as driving the movement toward change, and *E* is a listing of the forces identified which are resisting the desired change. Length of vectors represents the power of each force to help or hinder the change. *I-K* are strategies for reducing the power of each hindering force or eliminating each of them. *F-H* are strategies for increasing the power of each helping force or adding new helping forces.

Still another instructional tool is a brief small group activity in which students have an opportunity to observe verbal and non-verbal behavior of their peers, advise their peers of what they observed, and share their speculations about the meaning of these behaviors. This is available from the Office of Community Service Learning.

Mindfulness in Thinking

In order to effectively extract, from the giving of service, both the direct and indirect learnings described here, one must be able to think in rather sophisticated ways. The process of identifying data within the moving stream of experience of which one is a part, and analyzing that data so as to formulate real life meanings, requires one to develop advanced mental processing equipment of an abstract nature.

It is interesting to note that one of the six National Governors Conference goals for education reform by the 21st century is to ensure that all students learn to use their minds well, so that they may be prepared for responsible citizenship, further learning, and productive employment in our modern economy. Taking this perspective, the mind is viewed as a part of a person which the person can learn to use well, like any other body part under some extent of conscious or voluntary control of the person. This would seem to mean that, if students are to become better users of their minds, they must learn how to think in productive ways about how they think in the many encounters of living and working. Thus, the mind is called to act upon itself, in the service of itself, in a subject-object relationship. So, mindfulness in thinking, here, means helping oneself think about how one thinks and will think, so as to help oneself think effectively and creatively, in order to purposively preclude or set aside premature or poorly grounded cognitive commitments.

Good thinking and good meta-thinking (thinking about thinking) involve broad-range inclinations toward thinking which are unlikely to be contingent upon the particular characteristics of different subject matters. There is a flexibility and a comfort in moving off customary paths and an open-ended state of mind that encourages the development of non-usual cognitive arrangements and a readiness and interest in exploring novel and alternative perspectives. At the same time, and somewhat paradoxically, good thinking involves the use of a variety of formal, facilitative structures to guide the process of thinking. These structures can be schemas which have an abstractness due to their generalizability and yet serve as cognitive tools which can help translate abstract notions into more concrete terms. They are heuristic devices which are sometimes referred to as epistemic forms because they can assist in the reformulation of pieces of information and experience into representations of knowledge. They can be useful in thinking directly about experience because they are chooseable formats in which to put one's thoughts. They can be useful in meta-thinking because they may function as an inventory of thinking format types against which to differentially "diagnose" one's own customary types of thinking, from which to selectively augment one's repertoire when such is advised, or from which to build new departures in format for one's own use.

One such heuristic device is the *equation* which, while not intending to be mathematically accurate, can portray the variables involved and their relationship to each other. An example of one such equation which depicts the sources of feelings of security in a group is as follows:

A group member's feeling of security $=$ The member's perception of own value $+$ $\dfrac{\text{The member's perception of friendly forces within the group}}{\text{The member's perception of unfriendly forces}}$

Another device is the *conceptual configuration* in which concepts can be identified and placed in causal, influence, antecedent-consequence, or associative positions or interactions with each other. One such two-part diagram displays the concepts of openness (O) in communication between persons and mutual understanding (U), and the opposite situation of closedness (⊗) in communication between persons and misunderstanding (M) and hostility (H), and the circular influence of these concepts in both cases.

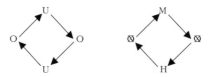

Below is a second example of a *conceptual configuration*. It advises that responses (R) do not usually result directly from a stimulus (S), but are received and processed by an organism (O) before it responds. This format for thinking about behavior is likely to lead a service-giver to ask a person, group, organization, or community in the experiential setting how it was that a choice was made to respond the way it did. The format has equal potential for helping the service-giver reflect on the service giver's own thinking about why she or he chooses to think the way she or he does in certain stimulus situations.

S ⟶ O ⟶ R

Still another device is the *stepwise outline* in which a set of phases of an occurrence is laid out. The phases may be sequentially ordered or contingently alterable. One such device is the set of steps for the occurrence of decision-making:

- Define the question.
- Share all relevant information.
- Prepare answers to the question.
- Evaluate each answer.
- Summarize the feasible and most attractive possible answers.
- Select one answer or a set of answers as the best decision at the time.
- Determine the steps need to be taken to implement the decision.

Yet another device is the *propositional statement* in which there is a declarative presentation of a piece of experiential reality. The reality may be asserted as speculation, hypothesis, or experience-based consensual knowledge. The reality is captured by the positing of causal, influence, or associative relationships between observed concepts, variables, or factors. How the words of the statement are put together is strongly determined by such best-fit formats as if....then, when....when, when....then, the more....the more, the more....the less, the less....the more, etc. One example of a propositional statement is:

The more persons are included in the planning of a change,
the more likely they are to be receptive to that change.

This particular heuristic device provides an excellent means for service-givers to translate their experiences into statements of personal knowledge which, when discussed with many associates, can gradually be raised to the higher level of certainty of consensual knowledge. Such activity allows the practice of service-giving to be viewed as a form of study through which the rich ground of experience is mined for the knowledge that is begging to be discovered within it.

Needless to say, there are many other tested and yet-to-be-formulated heuristic devices for helping student service-givers think systematically about how they will think about their experience. One source of heuristic devices is G.L Lippitt, (1973) *Visualizing Change: Model Building and the Change Process.* San Diego: University Associates.

In addition to having a flexible, developmental perspective and using facilitative structures, the ability to use and manipulate language in fine detail is essential to mindfulness in thinking. For instance, one way to think about extracting learnings from a happening is to view the extraction process as having three phases. The first phase is saturating the field of thought about the happening with as much textual and contextual information of the event that seems necessary to understand it and have a full image of it. The second phase is reducing the amount of information by abstracting it into a description at a more general level. The third phase is forming these abstract terms into statements of relationships between them. In other words one constructs a thick, rich description of what happened and then examines the description to discover and draw out its concepts or broader meanings, and then inter-relates these concepts into statements of speculative propositional knowledge. This is a weighty task which can be accomplished more effectively if the student service-giver has both extensive vocabulary and refined vocabulary-seeking skills, and sensitivity to the alteration in meanings by small grammatical shifts and word placements. It is these kinds of capabilities and inclinations in language that allow student service-givers to think about and describe what they experience in ways which capture the particular character (e.g., sequence, texture, tone, climate) of a situation and then accurately translate that into understandings for more widespread use. Where words that most truly describe phenomena seem to be unavailable in order to think productively about them, the creation of placeholder (itself a placeholder) terms can be encouraged. This would seem to have the exciting potential of exploring aspects of reality that are not immediately obvious, as well as helping students acquire the tolerance for ambiguity and uncertainty needed in creative thinking. Gradually, these students may break free from the constraints of conventionally perceived one-down roles in the teacher-student relationship and begin to frame rich, novel, and well-grounded formats for their own and others' thinking.

Closing

I have proposed and described four competencies which forty years of university teaching and an acquaintance (although ever-incomplete) with relevant behavioral science knowledge advise me are essential for students to have in order to learn broadly and deeply from the experience of giving service. My own observations suggest that as these competencies mature, they begin to overlap, intersect, and interact with each other and become less discernible as separate entities. This would seem to be as it ideally should be; that as healthy growth and development occur and the more fully functioning state unfolds, all systems move toward integration and inter-dependence. One schematic portrayal for thinking further about this phenomenon follows below.

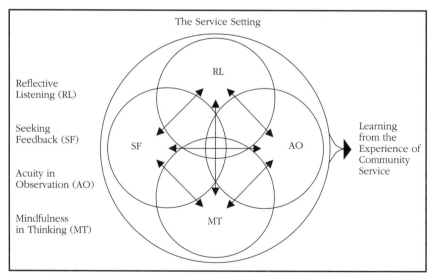

As a final note, it would seem that these competencies are both antecedents and consequences of learning from the experience of giving service, since they are posited as both less matured prerequisites and more matured outcomes. Thus, the above schema is already in need of modification.

PART TWO
Undergraduate Course Models

Chapter 3

COMMUNITY SERVICE LEARNING AS INNOVATION IN THE UNIVERSITY

Mark A. Chesler

The Sociology Department and the Office of Community Service Learning, University of Michigan, have been partners for over 15 years in an experiential learning program. In the Michigan campus vernacular it is called "Project Community," and in the course catalog it reads "Sociology 389: Practicum in Sociology." Our goal is to combine student service in community institutions, with experiential learning, with academic growth. In this article, I describe the processes involved in this program and some of the problems encountered in its ongoing implementation.

The Rationale

There is a wide range of formal definitions and field examples of community service learning (CSL). The core, however, seems to rest on three elements:

1. A viable service to community institutions or constituencies, preferably service that improves peoples' lives or creates change in institutional activities and outcomes. This involves seeing and participating in WHAT is happening.
2. A high potential for students to have new experiences, ones that challenge their prior understandings about themselves and the society, and that lead to new insights. This involves seeing and understanding HOW things happen.
3. A serious process of intellectual reflection and analysis that integrates field experience and academic exploration. This involves asking and answering WHY things happen the way they do.

This enterprise is particularly relevant to Sociology, since students are having experiences with community forces, people and agencies that are the normal focus of much sociological research and teaching. Students' field experiences can lend a real-life perspective to their classroom work, and permit students to "test" their academic insights in the field, and vice versa.

Sociology also is particularly relevant to this enterprise. Encounters with the world do not guarantee student learning and growth, and certainly do not guarantee high quality learning. Service activities and experiential encounters can just as well confuse students, reinforce prior myths and misinformation, and confirm common sense stereotypes. Sociological information and analytic frameworks can help students "look upstream" and identify the structural and institutional sources of the individual and social problems they encounter. For instance, if students tutoring in schools see a great deal of student failure and apathy among students of lower class backgrounds, if students working in hospitals see inadequate staff responses to patients, if students counseling in prisons see disproportionate numbers of African-Americans, Sociology can and does help them identify:

1. Why does such failure, incarceration and illness occur?
2. Whether such phenomena are unique to the situation they are observing, or whether they are representative of major patterns in our society? And are there pattern breaks in some societal sectors?
3. Why is there unequal failure, incarceration and illness among people of different races and economic classes? Or, why is there unequal delivery of basic educational, health, safety services and socioeconomic opportunities throughout our society?
4. How do formal organizations operate in ways that maintain or alter these patterns of failure, recidivism and illness?
5. Why is student service (under the provisions of community service learning) needed? Why do these agencies not have sufficient service resources without the addition of students?
6. How else might human service systems such as these operate?
7. How is each student, in varying ways depending upon their background and life situation, personally involved in the problems of unequal health and educational services in the U. S. society?

Our goal is not simply to help students respond to the individual human tragedies they encounter, but to help them analyze these experiences, and themselves in the process, so they may understand the social and sociological dimensions of their own and others' experience.

The Operation

These goals are implemented through a partnership between the Sociology Department and the Office of Community Service Learning. Over the years student enrollment has increased; currently approximately 700 students a year elect this option. It is staffed by 3 service-learning educators in the CSL office, 1 one-fourth time faculty member in Sociology (the equivalent of one regular course), 4-5 Sociology teaching assistants (at .40 time fraction each), and approximately 40 students who facilitate weekly seminars with their peers.

Students spend several hours a week providing service in community agencies, generally schools, hospitals or prisons, but also including day care centers, drug rehabilitation agencies, half-way houses, homeless centers, literacy programs, etc.

In addition, students meet once a week in a seminar setting, led by a specially-trained undergraduate or graduate student facilitator. Since the locus of much of students' learning occurs outside the classroom, the learning process at the site and in the seminar occurs without the presence of a faculty member. A peer—a student facilitator—guides the learning process. The seminar evokes discussion of and reflection on students' field experiences, and links these experiences with reading material in the Sociology of education, criminal justice, health care, formal organizations, human service systems, etc. The staff of the Office of Community Service Learning and the Sociology faculty member help train seminar facilitators in how to guide an instructional group process. They provide seminar facilitators with reading material (e.g., Freire, 1970; Freire, 1973; Shor & Freire, 1987) and some of these students analyze and write about their seminar and site leadership experience for Sociology credit (see Appendices IA and IB).

In addition, Sociology Department teaching assistants provide facilitators with reading lists to use with their seminar members (see Appendix II, for an example involving hospital sites), help facilitators plan how to engage students in analyzing this material, and design and read student papers that self-consciously seek to conduct a sociological analysis of their field experience and site operations (see Appendix III, also focusing on the hospital sites).

Credit for this community service learning activity is provided on a pass-fail basis. Thus, there are no competitive or ranked grades.

In several ways, then, the pedagogy of this effort is quite unlike typical university efforts. There is no teacher present in a position of power and authority, providing information in a predigested manner, to passive students —a process described by Freire (1970) as "banking education". Rather, immediate authority is located in the student and her peers and seminar facilitator. More distant authority is exercised at selected times in the semester, when the CSL staff verifies (or not) students' site attendance and participation, and when the Sociology teaching assistants evaluate and react to (pass or send back for rewriting) student papers. The students' posture toward the material is active and often occurs external to the classroom. And aside from a baseline for performance there is no grade pressure. The effort to construct a semi-"liberationist pedagogy" (Freire, 1970) is quite challenging to students and staff alike.

The process of combining subjective student experience and more objective sociological information, individual student encounters in the field and collective student experiences, active fieldwork and reflection/analysis, is captured in the two models presented in Figure 1.

Figure 1.

Two Models of the Theory and Practice of Community Service Learning:
A Process of Experiencing, Understanding and Acting

MODEL A

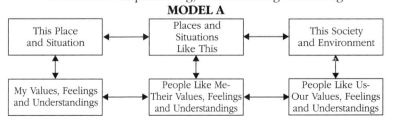

Figure 1 continued.

MODEL B

	Feeling/Sensing Acting/Data Gathering	Reflecting/Explaining Conceptualizing/Data Analyzing
I/ME/WE		
YOU/THEY		

We start seminar explorations with discussion of students' field experience in the site or situation where service is delivered, toward the left side of these figures. We include in this discussion students' own values, feelings and understandings. Since these personal reactions are affected by the site experience, and also affect this experience, we treat the students' reactions, and indeed, their selves, as data.

We then move discussion toward the right hand side of these figures. This involves discussion of other sites like the ones served (e.g., other schools, other hospitals), focusing on a more general analysis of these situations, and a more general discussion of the realities of the lives and reactions of students like the individual student (e.g. the class of students). Thus, we move from the individual (person and site) to the collective, from the "micro" to the "macro" level of phenomena and analysis. The goal is for students to be able to see how their reactions and views often are representative of (or different from) those of other students of their race and class and gender, and how their site reflects (or differs from) the larger class of such sites.

Finally, we try to focus discussion and analysis on the role and operations of the class of sites like the ones students are serving in, compared and contrasted with others in the society at large. This includes examination of the similarities and differences among schools and prisons and hospitals as institutions, the interconnections among these institutions, as well as the links between the political-economic system and these sites and institutions. Moreover, we examine how people other than those represented by members of the students' own class and race and gender may encounter and be affected by these situations.

The seminar is a small group activity, and like other parts of this enterprise it, too, is subject to sociological analysis. Efforts are made to utilize knowledge about small group dynamics and the leadership of instructional groups to create a "little learning community" in each seminar. Dialogue is the central pedagogical and learning tool; it is the crucial link between subjective experience and objective analysis, between the field and the academy, between description and conceptualization, and between thinking and acting in service.

To summarize these operations, a wide variety of inputs and resources are used in the community service learning enterprise. They include, in addition to the students' service at a site, participating in seminar discussions, reading sociological articles, keeping a log of their personal observations and reactions, and writing analytic papers that integrate field experience with sociological literature. This mix of resources and inputs is illustrated in Figure 2.

Figure 2.

Community Service Learning Inputs and Resources

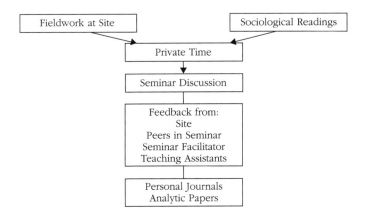

This field experience with service-learning, this pedagogy, and this dialogic approach, of course, exists within and must deal with the surrounding bureaucracy of the CSL Office, the Sociology department, the University and the structure and culture of other classes, accrediting arrangements, faculty norms, student peer relationships, etc. As such, certain problems occur, and I now turn to a discussion of some of these problems.

Problems

This sort of community service learning is oppositional to many of the dominant norms and practices of the University; it is counter-normative in several ways.

CSL's pedagogical orientation toward liberationist rather than banking education sets it apart from most other university courses. Even relatively small courses that emphasize discussion usually focus on a pre-established set of inquiry questions or curricula, and are led and evaluated by a single teacher.

CSL's closely related redefinition of teacher-learner roles, such that learners often operate rather independently from designated teachers, and often teach each other, is a departure from the university tradition whereby most faculty members (or teaching assistants) direct student learning and closely monitor individual performance. Indeed, student collaboration around learning is, in some courses, treated as "cheating" or plagiarism. The situation wherein teachers attempt to facilitate rather than direct learning by following students' leads reverses the source of initiative in curriculum generation and classroom activity found in most university courses.

CSL's sense that what is "real", and what is important to students, often lies outside the classroom, in the community and community agencies, stands in marked contrast to the in-classroom focus of most university courses. Much of what students focus on in traditional university courses is far removed from their daily lives and experiences, but close to the disciplinary focus of the academic curriculum; in community service learning this orientation is reversed. Even those university courses that depart from the norm somewhat to encourage some fieldwork usually do so in response to a pre-established agenda and set of learning materials. Thus in most situations the discipline drives the curriculum, and the curriculum drives the fieldwork, rather than the fieldwork driving the curriculum.

CSL's promise that, within broad limits, students can decide for themselves what it is that they will learn, places more trust and initiative in the hands of students than is typical in university courses. It also places much greater responsibility on students for managing their own learning.

CSL's integration of study with service/action suggests a connection that seldom is made deliberately in university courses. The traditional separation of curricular from "co-curricular" activities, and the emphasis on distance as a key element in intellectual analysis, are two examples of this dislink.

These counter-normative tendencies in community service learning raise a series of institutional dilemmas for those of us involved in such work.

First, they raise a series of personal dilemmas for faculty members and teaching assistants.

1. Standard academic values that are rooted in the "banking" educational mode, such as teacher unilateral control of the teaching-learning process, must be at least partially surrendered.

2. Teaching in these settings requires different pedagogical skills (in negotiating authority, in acting as a co-learner, in group dynamics, in knowledge of field settings, in the integration of action and reflection) than do typical course designs, classroom lectures or discussion leadership. It may be difficult for faculty or teaching assistants who have been socialized in, and who have practiced, only one mode of pedagogical authority, to work comfortably and successfully in such settings.

3. Responding to students' leads, rather than presenting pre-packaged academic material, takes a great deal of time. It also calls for constant re-preparation as the semester and events unfold, and many momentary and weekly adjustments to the course content and materials. It also requires spontaneous adaptation to often unpredictable events, crises, or "teachable moments" that occur in the field and must be analyzed in seminar.

Second, they raise a series of dilemmas for students.

1. Many students are unaccustomed to this pedagogy, do not know how to be active or independent learners, and are uncomfortable when not directed by teacher authority. Thus, some may have difficulty adapting, and may not be able to do their best service or learning within this pedagogical approach.

2. Some students see this experience as a "blow-off" opportunity for easy or cheap academic credit. This is a version of "Gresham's Law" applied to learning credit: these students have been so effectively socialized into the dominant norms of the university pedagogy that they do not value

what they are not forced to undertake, what is not graded, and what is not closely monitored by a legitimate authority figure. CSL does not operate without authority, but it utilizes a different source of authority; nor does it operate without structure, but it utilizes a different kind of structure. Under these conditions, once again, students may not put their best energies into this endeavor, and may not do good service or good learning.

3. Some students find themselves truly confused by what they see in the field, or really excited by their service experience, and need much more attention than our staff can provide.

4. Some students are not comfortable working in a group, or sharing their experiences and reflections in a seminar, and wish for the anonymity of a large classroom or the individual attention of an instructor. The lack of a ranked and competitive grading system also may make it difficult for some who are used to depending upon instructors' standards, or "psyching out" the instructor, as a way of making their grade. Students' general inexperience with a variety of learning modalities makes it difficult for them to know how to negotiate the peer-led nature and group-orientation of the seminar.

5. Some sites are interested in students' labor and assistance, but not necessarily in providing students with a good service experience, and seldom in helping students learn from their service experience. The agencies' own resource problems make true collaboration in this enterprise very difficult.

Third, they create a series of dilemmas for the student seminar facilitators.

1. The CSL learning model, and especially the seminar discussion, calls for a high level of interaction among students, and raises issues of diversity in backgrounds, values and worldy experiences. Seminar facilitators often do not know how to manage or process issues of racism, sexism, classism, or political correctness, in students' views of their field experiences, in their seminar reflections, or in their interpersonal encounters in the seminar.

2. Most seminar facilitators are unskilled in their task and, despite training and preparation by the CSL staff, Sociology faculty member and teaching assistants, some fail to exercise competent leadership with and support of their seminar members. They often are uncomfortable and unskilled in dealing with the mix of authority and democracy present in the peer-led and liberationist approach of the seminar. This issue is heightened especially when the facilitators' friends or fraternity/sorority members are participants in the seminar, or when some students fail to meet their site attendance or seminar attendance commitments. It is clear that seminar facilitators make great progress on these issues over the course of a semester, but their early semester work often is fraught with anxiety and tension

Fourth, they raise some dilemmas with regard to the relation between community service learning and the academic organization of the University.

1. The supervision and accreditation of what is seen by the College as "cheap credit" is problematic for all committed to the CSL enterprise. This credit assessment is reflected in the College's assignment of pass-

fail rather than letter grades to this learning option, and the general lack of high regard within the academic community for the academic value of CSL. As a result, the CSL activity and agenda becomes marginalized by the larger educational apparatus and norms.

2. Advocacy of the position that student learning may occur without faculty teaching occurring, and that sometimes the best thing that faculty can do is to temporarily get out of students' way, suggests to some that the faculty is irrelevant. Nothing could be further from the reality of CSL, but for a university with limited knowledge or practical experience with pedagogical alternatives, this often seems like a "yes-no" issue.

3. Suggesting that learning can be field-driven (or perhaps student-driven) rather than instructor-driven, requires the de-standardization of academic content and the use of alternative pedagogies. This often places those involved in community service learning in contest with an academic administration that increasingly seeks to standardize course offerings, pedagogies, grading systems, evaluative mechanisms, etc.

4. Operating without appropriate rewards, and often without adequate resources, places the burden of innovation and risk on the backs of (generally overloaded) faculty, staff and students committed to community service learning.

5. Challenging the prevailing notion of an action-reflection or service-learning dislink places a difficult burden of "proof" of intellectual viability on advocates of the community service learning enterprise. Seldom is the traditional university conception of this (dis)link similarly called to the test.

These problems may be generic to all service activities and all learning encounters...and even to many traditional university classrooms. But they are escalated here because of the counter-normative character of community service learning within the academic community of the University of Michigan. As such, they necessitate a variety of bargains and contradictions by everyone involved in the operation of CSL, and require constant innovation and risk-taking by students, staff and faculty. That requires all those students, faculty and staff who are engaged in this enterprise to think of themselves as change-agents and as instruments of innovation and reform in the University.

Appendix IA

Sociology 395
Guidelines for Project Community coordinator's papers

The requirements for fulfilling this independent study course are twofold:

1. That you do a good job of facilitating your students' learning, of learning about educational facilitation and leadership, organizing students' field efforts, etc. This requirement will be assessed and graded by the Project Community staff and they will make input to your course grade.
2. That you undertake a serious written intellectual effort to review, reflect upon and generate a conceptual understanding of the role of experiential learning, of your role in facilitating such learning, and of the problems and opportunities in doing so. This requirement will be met by a paper, described below, that will be handed in to me and will determine your grade for the course.

The LSA college is quite clear that course credit (and grading) for facilitating other students' learning is not to be based upon such activity, per se, but upon demonstrated learning and intellectual exploration of such learning processes.

THE PAPER should be rooted in a review and application of P. Freire's concepts of consciousness raising and liberationist education, as spelled out in *Education for Critical Consciousness* and *Pedagogy of the Oppressed*, as well as other works. You are asked to:

1. Describe his concepts of banking and liberationist education, noting how these concepts do or do not fit your experience with pedagogies at the University of Michigan and in Project Community.
2. Analyze or theorize about why the University pedagogy and/or the Project community pedagogy is the way you have described it.
3. Describe some of your dilemmas, problems and/or successes in facilitating experiential learning in Project Community.
4. Analyze the roots of these dilemmas (e.g., why do they occur or where do they come from), in yourself (ideology, skills, fears, hopes), your students (their ideology, skills, expectations, habits, hopes), the Project Community structure and culture (staff relations, sites resources), and/or the surrounding University setting (Sociology staff, LSA curriculum, University pressures, etc.).

An outline of this paper should be shared with me. This is not required, but suggested as a way of increasing the level of dialogue and exchange between us and advising you of my expectations. Note that an acceptable outline or draft is no guarantee of an acceptable final product...one does not subsume the other.

I would be delighted to meet and talk with you about your ideas, problems, outlines or drafts at any time throughout the semester.

Appendix IB

Sociology 395
Special guidelines for Project Community coordinators who are writing for credit and have already writtin the Freire-based paper

The groundrules for credit are already clear to you. Since you have already written the basic paper we are ready to take the next step.

Closely related to the field-site work you and your students are involved in are four closely related terms that often are used carelessly and ambiguously. They are:

> Social change
> Individual change
> Education
> Service

Freire focuses most of his concern on SOCIAL CHANGE, and his notion of EDUCATION as a strategy to get there is quite different than the ways in which most of us discuss EDUCATION, including those of us involved in Project Community who talk about Freire.

Our society, rooted in Western traditions of individualism and voluntarism, usually focuses on INDIVIDUAL CHANGE as a strategy to solve most individual and social problems. But there is no necessary connection between INDI-VIDUAL CHANGE (e.g., in information, attitudes, values, behaviors, feelings), even the changing of many individuals, and SOCIAL CHANGE (e.g., in patterns of resource distribution, allocation of wealth, structures and cultures of major institutions, etc.).

Many organizations, groups and people who are involved in delivering SERVICES to others consider themselves in the business of SOCIAL CHANGE, but there are contradictions between the acts of delivering SERVICES within a stable system and creating SOCIAL CHANGE of that system.

And finally, the tradition of INDIVIDUAL CHANGE often rests on a base of the strategy of EDUCATION as a way to achieve its objectives. But even massive EDUCATION programs, which may or may not lead to meaningful INDIVIDUAL CHANGE, do not necessarily lead to SOCIAL CHANGE.

Write about the following questions:

1. Where are we and what do we do in Project Community...SOCIAL CHANGE (of what), INDIVIDUAL CHANGE (of whom), EDUCATION (of whom), SERVICE (of what, to whom)?

2. If your site work were to seriously address SOCIAL CHANGE as a goal, what would have to be different (in the site, in the students' activities, in your role and knowledge and skills, in the structure of Project Community and its location and relationship to the larger University)? Be concrete and specific about the "how's" and "what's" of this inquiry.

An outline of this paper can be shared with me, and I would get it back to you within 48 hours. This is not required, but suggested as a way of increasing the level of interaction and dialogue between us. I would be glad to meet with you (preferably in small groups rather than one-on-one) at our mutual convenience.

Appendix II

Syllabus
Hospital Sections
Project Community

Editor's note: The syllabus has been included to convey to the reader the range of academic as well as informal kinds of readings that students in this course are required to do.

Topic	**Readings**
1. Background Readings	Kahn, Michael Mills, C. Wright Freire, Paulo
2. Overview	Stages of Dying When someone dies in the hospital, M. Gold, *Aging* June-July 1984 pp. 18-22.
3. The Institution of Medicine	Medicine as an institution of social control, I. Zola, *Contemporary Critical Debates* pp. 511-525. *Vignettes from a hospital stay*, 1985.
4. Perspectives on Hospitals	*Conflicting perspectives in the hospital*, E. Freidson, 1970, pp. 292-296. *The necessity and control of hospitalization*, J. Roth, 1972, pp. 416-441.
5. Access to Care by the Poor and Minorities: Victim Blaming vs. Structural Constraints	The art of savage discovery, W. Ryan, (condensed from *Blaming the Victim*, 1971, pp. 30-39). The use of health care services by the poor, C. Riessman, *Social Policy*, Spring 1984, pp. 30-39. Concepts and Statistics on Discrimination/ Inequalities. Study finds Blacks in Detroit face higher cancer death rates, from *Detroit Free Press*. Socialized medicine, in *Consider*, UM, March 30, 1987. Conceptual Framework for Ism's.

6. Gender Issues	More women physicians: Will it mean more humane health care? J. Lorber, *Social Policy*, Summer 1985, pp. 51-54.
	The doctor-nurse game, L. Stein, *Down to Earth Sociology*, pp. 70-77.
7. Political and Economic Issues	Gut issues, B. Keller, *New Republic*, March 9, 1984, pp. 15-17.
	Medicare, S. Leader, *Ms.* May, 1986, pp. 106-110.
	The revolution in medicine, *Newsweek,* Jan. 26, 1987.
	Hospitals are hawking their wares, *National Journal*, Sept. 28, 1985.
	Some public hospitals are going private, *National Journal*, Sept. 28, 1985.
	Not-for-profits up against for-profits, *National Journal*, Sept. 28, 1987.
	Texas adopts stringent rules on rights of poor to medical treatment, *Ann Arbor News*, Dec. 25, 1985.
8. Ethical Issues	*Patient selection and the right to die*, R. Fox and J. Swazey, 1974, pp. 527-534.
	The prostitute, the playboy and the poet, G. Annas, *American Journal of Public Health*, No. 2, 1985, pp. 187-189.
	Dead on arrival, D. Sudnow, 1967, pp. 173-180.
	Who knows this patient?, P. Klass, *Discover*, June, 1985, pp. 14-16.
	Transplant recipient selected objectively?
	Why won't the doctors let her die? A.R. Feinstein.
	Health care burden in last year of life too high, M. Gates, *Ann Arbor News*, May, 1985.

Appendix III

Paper Assignments

Begin as early as possible exploring paper topics: on site, with your peers and your coordinators, using coursepack readings, using your own site experiences, feelings, reactions and journal entries. Narrow in on a problem or topic of interest to you. You will then be asked to write a 3-5 page prospectus and a 5-7 page final paper.

Prospectus Requirements

1. A BRIEF description of the site and program with which you are involved, including the stated goal of the organization.
2. A statement of the problems you observe—what is happening that causes a problem (or what isn't happening that should be)? Why do YOU consider this to be a problem? What does your choice of topic say about your own values?
3. A statement about the actors involved—who is especially affected by this situation, whether positively or negatively, and in what way(s)?
4. A statement about why things might be this way—what goals are reached, who benefits, and where do those who benefit fit within the organization?

Final Paper Requirements

As you become more involved in the field experience, you will become familiar with the workings of the organization; you will learn who the important "actors" are both inside and outside the site or agency (clients, service providers, administrators, legislators, other community agencies, etc.). You may also observe situations or attitudes that cause problems for all or part of the actors or organization. This is where you may choose to focus your attention. Choose a problem that interests you, and analyze it SOCIOLOGICALLY. This goes beyond description alone. Use sociology rather than psychology-based analysis. If no specific problem is apparent at your site, select a general topic from the coursepack readings/discussions and examine how this may or may not apply to what you or the other actors are experiencing at site. Then write your paper by addressing the following:

1. THE SOURCE OF THE PROBLEM. Use your sociological imagination to look at the factors within the organization that are helping to maintain the present system. Which groups benefit, which groups do not? Are there hidden goals or benefits you could explore? Concentrate on one or two sources that you see as most important. This part should take up no more than half your paper.
2. YOUR SOLUTION TO THE PROBLEM. Be as creative as possible. Could the problem be alleviated through relatively simple organizational changes? Is larger legislation needed? Be sure to be specific about how the changes you propose would impact the problem and its sources that you described in the first section.
3. BARRIERS TO IMPLEMENTING YOUR SOLUTION. Time to be realistic.

There is often great resistance to change within an organization. If your idea is so good, why can't it take effect tomorrow? Identify those actors or groups who might oppose your suggestions, and WHY they might object. What resources would your solution require (financial and otherwise), and to what extent are they already available?

Chapter 4

CREATING SPACES: TWO EXAMPLES OF COMMUNITY-BASED LEARNING

Buzz Alexander

Beginnings

Since I came to the University of Michigan in 1971, I have consistently assigned texts that show my students an economically and socially troubled world their experience has for the most part hidden from them. I have sought to make my pedagogy facilitative and empowering: I have created learning spaces where they can engage with each other over those texts, and I have urged final projects (films, dances, poetry, paintings, social action, etc.) that have allowed them to express what has moved them. This has been the center of every course, and in the 70s it was most catalytic in my large film courses on the Holocaust and the War in Vietnam and on Latin American Cinema. At the end of that decade this pedagogy took a new turn.

In 1978-1979 I spent eight months in the Peruvian Andes and some of that time in two peasant communities. Inspired by Latin Americans, Europeans, and North Americans who were training peasants to be paramedics, agronomists, and carpenters in their own communities, I became very aware of the limits of my own on-campus teaching. Back in Ann Arbor I began to feel my way toward something different. In 1981 I received permission to begin a January 1983 course in which twelve university students, workers in the labor movement, and I would make video tapes which the workers could use as organizing tools. For three winters we worked in Detroit, Pittsburgh, Toledo, and South Bend and produced seven tapes, one of which, "QWL: Nothing to Lose But Your Job" [QWL = Quality of Work Life], continues to be distributed to unions and labor study institutes.

By 1984 I had realized the obvious: the workers in a tape who have shared their experience, risk-taking, and ideas, are absent from the ensuing discussion. Although I had always been shy about performance, I saw that theater had to be my next step, because there the actors remain present. In winter term 1985 I inaugurated "Theater and Social Change," my version of English 319, a Department course on literature and social change. That term and in the winter terms of 1987 through 1991, English 319 students formed into small groups to perform, in non-traditional spaces, street, action, and guerrilla theater pieces advocating social change. In several cases they collaborated with community members. In 1985 one group, "the Pinkertons," conspired with union members to perform short pieces at three local and several other Michigan theaters and to organize a boycott of twenty-one Michigan theaters owned by the Kerasotes corporation, in support of projectionists who had been fired and replaced by minimum wage workers. Two other groups later collectively created and performed plays with homeless Ann Arborites and with a staff person at Vida Latina, an AIDS outreach organization in Detroit.

Most of the 319 groups, however, worked without such community connections, and I found myself wishing for deeper, more consistent engagement in community-based cultural work, both formyself and for my students. January 1990 brought a new phase. Five students and I began a volunteer project (several students received independent study credit) at the Dewey Center for Urban Education, a K-8 magnet school on the edge of Detroit's Cass Corridor which serves mainly children from the nearby Jeffries Homes (housing projects). By late April, working within the school curriculum, we had enabled three "clubs" of 4th-8th graders to produce four video tapes about their community. Every term since then until January 1993, when we moved to Henry Ford High School[1], we continued the project, expanding to include theater and photography. Late in 1990 I requested course credit, and by fall term 1991 310 was on the books, an English Department outreach course, possibly one of very few of its kind in the country. I taught it also in fall term 1992, and during the winter terms, my students and I continued to work on a volunteer and overload basis.

January 1990 also led to the transformation of English 319, when a student requested that two inmates at the Florence Crane Correctional Facility who were enrolled at the university be permitted to enroll in the course. Throughout the term three students and I traveled every week to Coldwater for theater exercises, improvisations, and discussions with inmates Mary and Joyce. After an intense April session, these two women decided we should open the workshop to the entire Facility. Thus was born what eventually became the Sisters Within Theater Troupe, which performed "The Show" for 80 inmates in April of 1991 and Martha Boesing's "Junkie" for over 200 inmates in November and December of 1992.

The word began to spread, and in 1991 we received requests for theater workshops at the Cotton Correctional Facility in Jackson, the Western Wayne Correctional Facility in Plymouth, and from lifers at the Egeler Correctional Facility in Jackson. In winter term 1992 English 319 student teams led theater workshops in the three facilities, while two other teams worked with high school students from Willow Run and Ypsilanti, preparing forum theater pieces for performance in high school classrooms. Now English 319 students would collaborate with community members to produce significant plays for those communities, performing themselves only if other participants invited them to do so. In April inmates performed plays or collections of monologues and scenes for either inmate or outside audiences in all three facilities. At prisoner request, we continue as volunteers to conduct workshops at Florence Crane, Cotton, Egeler, Western Wayne, and a new workshop at the Scott Correctional Facility in Plymouth. The Cotton troupe performed in March, and the other three will perform in April and May. Maxey Boys Training School, a detention facility for youth offenders, has requested a workshop, which English 319 will provide in January 1994.[2,3]

Why Students?

Why do I work with my students rather than on my own, as do many other socially engaged faculty? I do so out of respect for my students, for their sense of decency and for their ability to act upon what they believe. I assume that at some level almost all of them do not want an unjust world. And so the material I place before them in my more conventional courses—Simon Wiesenthal's *The Sunflower*, Elie Wiesel's *Legends of our Time*, J.M. Coetzee's *Waiting for the Barbarians*, Alice Walker's *Meridian*, Stanley Milgram's *Obedience to Authority*, Jonathan Kozol's *The Night is Dark and I am Far from Home*, Susan Brownmiller's *Against Our Will*, films like *Interviews with My Lai Veterans, Breaker Morant, Memories of Underdevelopment*, and *The Official Story*—provides them the opportunity to respond as they wish to hunger, disease, incarceration, homelessness, torture, and the complicity of consent, and to decide where these matters fit with their world view, their career aspirations, and, if they wish, their personal commitments.

Some of these students and some others then come to English 310 and 319. Those who come are aware that they need to know about those places in this country to which their own privileges have denied them access. Or they know such places and know they need to learn how to work there. Or they are already working there and seek new opportunities and methods. Or they have come from such places and wish to return to be of service in their own neighborhoods. 310 and 319 offer them some background and training and bring them into the presence of inspiring human beings surviving and resisting against painful odds. And 310 and 319 offer them a supportive space in which to discover their own capacities for such work and to begin to know the degree of their own commitment.

Course Admission

English 310 and 319 attract students from a wide range of backgrounds and disciplines, including many students not otherwise drawn to English courses. Those who locate the courses, often through word of mouth, learn that they must interview with me for admission. During the 310 interviews, I and sometimes a veteran student from the course ask candidates for their background and the causes for their interest. We also thoroughly describe the methods, goals, and demands of the project. If they still wish to join, they then submit a written statement of one to two pages. We also invite them to accompany one of the teams to the Dewey Center and to join one of our class meetings in Ann Arbor. With 319 I ask candidates to clarify their interest in the course and their backgrounds in theater and social change, if any, and I tell them of the opportunities and stresses of forming and facilitating theater workshops in the community. I take a maximum of fourteen students in 310, around 25 for 319. 319 is more likely than 310 to have a waiting list.

Why "permission of instructor?" Why not open the courses to the first to enroll, as do other community outreach courses? Because I do not wish to send into communities at risk the curiosity-seeker or casual student who thinks "hey, this might be interesting." The University of Michigan is an elite institution, in good part composed of students from mainly white suburbs and small towns.

Median parental income is approximately $70,000. The Dewey children come from a variety of economic backgrounds and some are relatively affluent, although they are 99% African-American. Many are from locations with every known symptom of urban decay, and some are even homeless. Inmates in the state correctional facilities are overwhelmingly from lower income backgrounds, many have been abused as children and young adults, and a disproportionate number are African-American. None of these community populations need to further experience either arrogance or neglect. Too much is at stake. I seek students who realize that they have more to learn from children, prisoners, and other community members than they have to teach them, who are humble and dedicated.

This does not mean I reject many candidates. The Course Guide and student word of mouth make plain the purposes and demands of 310 and 319, and only a small percentage of students are attracted. It also requires extra thought and effort to risk an interview with a professor; the students who take this step are usually very motivated. Furthermore, the interview reveals to some students the course was not what they imagined, and they decide not to apply. So of the students I interview, I turn down very few. It is not an elite course, but a course that seeks to find students who are prepared and appropriate for the work.

The Courses

English 310: The Dewey Center Project

In our first two class meetings, usually both before our first working session at the school, we share at length our backgrounds and motivations for the project, and I and continuing students describe our past experience at the school. We discuss such logistical matters as transportation and budget and we choose our two-three-person teams, according to interest in drama, photography, or video, in some cases according to a sense of mutual compatibility.[4]

In subsequent weeks we meet Thursdays at the rotating cube behind the Literature, Science and the Arts Building, scramble into three or four cars of varying reputation, and head for the northeast corner of MLK Drive and Lodge Freeway in Detroit, arriving close to 1:15, for the special-interest "club" period held that day.[5] At 1:30 either the children appear or we call them out of their classrooms, devoting a quarter to half an hour to focusing their lively, scattered energy on the task at hand. The school day ends at 3:00. From the very first moments of the term, the video and photography teams place our equipment in the children's hands, letting them know immediately that the work will be theirs. With some elementary instruction, they are all over the school, interviewing teachers, schoolmates, and each other, and recording classroom and playground activity. In the following weeks, gradually or suddenly a topic will emerge—a girl will announce that her grandmother has a restaurant over on Woodward and that her mother baked the cake for Rosa Parks' 70th birthday, or children will express their outrage at the bad rap Detroit and the Cass Corridor receive from outside—and the group will have a project. Eventually they will come up to Ann Arbor on a weekend to edit their tape or develop their photos. The drama club begins with games, including games the children invent, variations on sound and motion, reidentification of objects ("This is not a bottle, it is a....," and the others guess from the way the object is shown), and improvisations (a creature from outer space arrives at the Dewey Center and the actors take on various characters to show it what the school is like). Again gradually or suddenly a theme will emerge—a school election, resistance to isolation and humiliation by peers—or the children will turn up with a script, as three girls did in January 1992 with the first two scenes of what became a six scene play about relationships in a beauty parlor. Over the remaining weeks the groups will work towards performances to be held at the Dewey Center and the University of Michigan. At 3:00 the University teams find each other in the pot-holed parking lot behind the school, across an alley from the Rescue Mission and across the playground from Detroit's Wigle Recreation Center where the homeless slept during the winter's most frigid nights. We drop into our cars, elated or discouraged, and are back in Ann Arbor in time for 4:00 classes.

At 7:00 that night we meet in a student apartment for two hours. If someone remembers, we have munchies, a quart or two of soft drink. We share our experiences of the afternoon and our concerns about individual children, we voice our doubts about our working methods or the topics the children have generated, we rethink our relations with the school, we try to understand an incident in the hall, and we seek ideas and assistance from the others. We also work out logistics, e.g. whose turn is it to drive the following Thursday? who will write up the permission slips so the children can leave the school grounds two weeks from now? how can we make up for the session lost to a school holiday or half day? who will drive, host, and cook when the children come to Ann Arbor? what does our liaison need to communicate to our teacher liaison at the school? [6]

In these sessions we also discuss our readings: Ken Goodman's *What's Whole in Whole Language?* enables us to understand the Dewey Center philosophy, Herbert Kohl's *36 Children* tells us of the overwhelming impediments and rich possibilities of teaching in an economically deprived inner city, Clyde Taylor's *Dangerous Society* gives us a picture of some of the grimmer options facing Detroit youth, while Paulo Freire's *Pedagogy of the Oppressed* and Myles Horton's *The Long Haul* evoke larger dimensions of the pedagogy that inspires our work. We raise our own questions: what is at stake for us, what is at stake for the children in our work? where does this work fit our individual notions of political activism, of social change? what are the challenges of working within a governmental institution, within the Dewey Center, within the University of Michigan? what, really, does our short time with the children accomplish, if anything? At the end of the term, each student writes a ten-fifteen page paper from whatever angle they choose, usually addressing one of those questions and reflecting on their work at the school in the light of the readings and our discussions.

Between this evening session and the next trip to Detroit, each team meets with me for at least an hour, usually over coffee or a sandwich. In these casual but focused gatherings, we review the previous week's work, we calculate the children's progress toward a production, and we analyze group problems, including team problems in working with the children and with each other. We may carry further an earlier evening session discussion. And we plan for Detroit:

who will pick up the equipment, who will phone the children and their parents to remind them about permission slips or about the script they promised to write? what strategies should we adopt during the club session? do we need to ride in the same car to discuss last minute arrangements?

The children's trips to the University of Michigan campus, to perform, to edit tapes, to work in the lab, to see a play, are a particularly important and particularly arduous part of our project. We put in many extra, demanding hours. We describe the excursion in letters to the principal, teachers, and parents, we send permission slips home and make follow-up calls, and we mobilize sufficient vehicles and enough drivers to pair up late at night if we are driving into tricky territory. Since the children come from all over Detroit, those of us who know the city arrange car assignments that will get them home efficiently. Some of us cook or—if our budget allows—take the children to a fast food restaurant, or we might have pizza delivered for a picnic in Burns Park. Some of us host the children overnight in our homes when they come for an entire weekend of editing, lab work, or rehearsal and performance. Others plan and lead visits to dorms, the swimming pool and basketball courts, the radio station, the zoological museum, and the Baker Mandela Center or Black Student Union, whose representatives introduce them to the history and struggle of African-Americans on campus and help them know the University of Michigan as one of their own options.

English 319: Theater and Social Change

We spend our first Saturday at Canterbury House in a large sprawling living room. We wander the space to feel it out and play a quick introduction game. Someone apologizes for having brought only a bag of chips or a quart of Squirt for lunch. Another student had an asthma attack during the night and can't join us until later. We start in, one at a time, answering in our own way—with deadly seriousness, with wit, with a boast here and there, laughter, stories of growing up, of a relative serving a prison sentence, of an encounter in the street that turned us around—the question "what is it in my life that has brought me at this point to a class on theater and social change?" Early on someone takes a risk, and we begin to venture more. We respond to each other with questions, quick anecdotes. Around midday a faculty member from the School of Social work joins us to emphasize the responsibilities of working in the community and to respond to apprehensions. After lunch a student collaborates with me in leading a game of "To Get to the Other Side of the Mountain, I must Have...," then we return to the introductions. Late in the day I lay out field assignments and students make their decisions: Brandon, Julia and Sebastian will go to the Egeler Correctional Facility, Jenny and Shannon to the Cotton Correctional Facility, Blake, Michael, and Valerie to the Western Wayne Correctional Facility; Maria and Stephanie will attempt to form a workshop at Prospect Place, a model shelter in Ypsilanti; David, Derek, Julie, Lori, and Terrence will work with high school students; and Sarah, Chelli, and Steve will prepare a Columbus quincentennial guerrilla theater piece. They then go out into the dark January evening knowing what they normally have little opportunity to know about their classmates: that they are deeply interesting people with poignant and provocative personal histories, people loaded with questions, doubts, anger, compassion, high spirits, and intense desires to cross boundaries. They leave with good will and an initial willingness to risk with each other. This alone does not mean we will work well, but it gives us a chance. We try to keep this spirit alive by pairing and tripling off each week over coffee or soup, sharing journal writings and experiences in the field.

We meet Tuesday afternoons from 2:00 to 4:00 for theater games, exercises, and improvisations useful for our work outside class. In one exercise students pair off into prisoners and visitors. In quick dialogues they decide their characters: a father visits his nineteen-year-old daughter, a woman her lover and dealer. They then blindfold themselves and are led one at a time by guards into a visiting room with two long rows of facing chairs. They are forbidden to touch each other and may not leave their spot without terminating the visit, policies enforced by the role-playing guards. In a ten minute dialogue they explore their relationship. The prisoner then speaks a five-minute interior monologue which the visitor hears, but cannot allude, because in actuality one cannot hear an interior monologue. The visitor then takes their turn. Ten more minutes of dialogue deepen the relationship, and then a final twist is added: the visitor is given three minutes to explain it is their final visit. The dramatization completed, prisoner and visitor write each other poems and read them aloud. And we know some of the little we can know about prison life from outside the prison. In other exercises students learn to sculpt each other into scenes of conflict, then alter the sculpture or animated versions of it, to explore the possibilities of their material. In still another exercise students scattered throughout the room simultaneously converse aloud with an absent person with whom they need to talk, imagining all the while the other's response. Those who wish to do so then share these conversations with the group. One of them volunteers to direct two other students acting out her or his dialogue: as the scene progresses, we substitute actors and add characters to investigate further the situation.[7] Thus we begin to see how community participants might discover dramatic material in their own experience. These exercises and improvisations continue throughout the term, with students bringing their own ideas and actual struggles to be tested out, e.g. a correctional facility recreation director is taking over two students' work, and the class improvises the meeting the two students and I will have with her the next day, strengthening our position. A few Tuesdays we view videotapes of Nicaraguan or South African or previous English 319 performances and discuss them immediately afterwards or later, in team meetings. Now and then during classtime or over a potluck dinner we share with each other our work in the field.

Each team meets with me another hour or more each week. I spend the first three meetings of the term helping them anticipate their workshop. I share my own experience, I arrange a prison orientation, I ask them to share stereotypes, apprehensions, goals, and reactions to the orientation (why is there such insistence on the manipulative strategies of prisoners, why must we keep such distance from them?), and I help them plot out introductory exercises and discussion. After they begin their workshop, in the fourth week, we concentrate on problems and progress and on bureaucratic obstacles, and I share further exercises and improvisations that seem appropriate. The workshops differ: male lifers have different needs than female short-timers, and both have issues at variance with high school students rehearsing a forum theater piece on parent/adolescent alienation or on the closing of the General Motors Plant in Willow Run. But all workshops share the goal of a performance by the end of April.

More than I like, discussion of our texts goes by the way (see syllabus Appendix I). We begin with readings and videotapes exemplifying community-based theater, then move through other non-mainstream political drama toward more classical plays—we might read Sophocles, Shakespeare, or Ibsen—and let our own practice and Boal's *Theater of the Oppressed* aid us in questioning the underlying politics of such rich art. However, we occupy most class time creating dramatic material, and the weekly workshops, which require travel, several hours on site, and extensive planning take the rest of student energy and focus. And while we give fragments of our group and team meetings to the readings and I ask students to respond to them in their weekly journals, I mainly hope it will inspire ideas for their own productions.

Journal entries must be four pages each and must address experiences and issues that intrigue the student. My weekly responses strive to challenge them further along the lines they have chosen. Some terms students choose to exchange journals and have me review them every three or four weeks, but because inevitably a few students become lax and let the others down, I find this less satisfactory. Some terms, instead of a journal, I assign three short papers on what we see as key subjects, a practice that fuels conversations during our weekly pairing and tripling. In their final analytic papers, students think through their field experiences, putting them in relation to such larger issues as social change, group process, alternative aesthetics, and their own career goals.

Creating Space[8]

In both classes, our teams do not lecture. We do not envision ourselves as teachers come to teach city children or state prisoners what we know. Instead we create spaces within the institution where children and prisoners can bring into play their own ideas, energy, and creativity, tapping personal and community resources and voices. And we enter those spaces with them, bringing equipment and technique, totally open to what they and we make of the possibilities. We enter humbly, with full respect for their experience, power, and needs, eager for what they will teach us and what we will learn together. We have relative autonomy: the space is physically within the institution but to some extent liberated, and we work nearly always without the presence of teachers or guards, while respecting policies of the institution. Thus when a dispute or a long digression on crack house administration or a moment of chaos wells up among us, we can allow these to feed the imagination and lead to material for a play or video tape. The work is shared, collective: the children run the cameras, decide on topics, conduct interviews, edit the final tape, invent, alter, and co-direct the plays; Marty at the Egeler Correctional Facility imagines and then directs a cafeteria confrontation in the play about a prisoner's self-rehabilitation, and Marc and Larry, in the lead roles, improvise from their own experience; Smitty at the Cotton Correctional Facility becomes the key motivator and most energetic co-director, while the others create a rap piece and improvise a humorous, poignant funeral scene; the men at the Western Wayne Correctional Facility plan a play for incarcerated youth; and the Sisters

Within decide to create a play in my absence. We help make connections, ask questions, provide focus, run interference with the administration, type up scripts, handle logistics, bring in ideas and resources, take our turns exploring characters and scenes.

My students, like me, have been drawn to these courses because of inquietudes of their own, because they need information and new risks, because they need to develop skills and talents and need useful channels for their anger, compassion, indignation, and love. While I bring texts, exercises, knowledge, and some sense of direction to class, I see my significant work here too as the creation of a space in which each student is accorded complete respect, a space in which their individual and collective aspirations, instincts, anxieties, and ideas lead them where they need to go.

Making Contact, Staying in Contact

To initiate contact with a prison or school, I begin with friends in the field, with prisoners, educators, social workers, and colleagues, asking them with whom I should talk. Then I phone those people, meet them, explain the project, learn the institutional possibilities, and ask them to help pave the way. It is essential that I make clear my respect for administrators and staff and my desire to work towards their best ideals, while I seek from them the maximum autonomy possible, the most uncensored space they can provide within the institutional framework. Generally this gives us freedom and a wide latitude. Without these, we cannot work, and if they are denied, we leave.

Every institution has some staff who welcome lively, creative outsiders and the opportunities they bring, and also some staff who are suspicious of outsiders and hostile to innovations or disruptions of well-established order, whose pedagogy or penology is repressive rather than liberatory.[9] Friends, of course, can be helpful, and foes need not remain foes. Ongoing contact and sincere and respectful collaboration with key staff and administrators are essential. Even under duress, we must take the time and energy to make an extra phone call, to stop by an office, to ask advice, to keep allies and critics alike apprised of our work. As an example, eight months of rehearsals at the Florence Crane Facility brought us to our performance date, a Saturday evening in November. Expectations were high throughout the Main Building. And then, when a lead actress was not ready on time to be brought from the Annex to the Main, the shift commander decided she could not come at all. We called out to all five of the warden's phone numbers, including her beeper, and at the last moment she called in to give the shift commander a direct order to bring our actress over. The show went on because the warden is a strong supporter of the Sisters Within, and I had called to update her at least once every two or three weeks over the past months. On the other hand it is perhaps in part because I failed to do this at the Dewey Center, relying only on supportive teachers and failing to establish a working relation with the new principal, that she found it easy to restrict our role in a way that made it impossible for us to continue there.

Costs

Transportation and materials, how do we pay for them? English 319 has no budget. Now and then the respective prison's Inmates Benefit Fund is a resource. Otherwise we share gas costs and come up with our own dollars for props or for the official workshop certificates the inmates sometimes request for their files. If we have permission to videotape a performance, either the Facility provides equipment and personnel, or we bring them in from outside. English 310, with its video and photography clubs, its excursions and meals, has more need of funding, and we have been fortunate enough to find university support. When we lack funding, we each contribute $30 and survive on the budget that allows. We cut costs by limiting excursions, by cooking instead of ordering pizza, and by sharing gas expenses rather than paying each driver $5 from our account. Up until this point letters of inquiry to outside foundations have been discouraging.

Grades

Because students interview for the course, I assume they are highly motivated and will work well. I also understand us to be colleagues working collectively in the field, trying our best to facilitate discovery in the spaces we create. Accordingly—and I make this clear at the outset—I do not make comparative quality judgments on their community work, and only quantitative failures—absence from class and workshop, brevity and tardiness with journals, non-participation in discussion—lower the grade from an A. I do judge quality of writing and of critical thinking on term papers, making extensive comments and meeting with individual students about their work. I also make it clear that blatant neglect or abuse of children or prisoners, who for economic and social reasons are all too likely already to have experienced such treatment, also lowers a grade. The final grades are usually A's, with some exceptions.

Difficulties

The Dewey Center

Although the clubs meet during class time, they are not normal classes led by teachers, persons of authority and status. We appear once a week at best, we lack full power, we are younger than the teachers, and we represent a break from the tighter classroom. The children, testing us out in many ways, spring loose their pent-up energy. They also bring into the club space their enmities and jealousies, their boy/girl rivalries, and other disruptive influences from home, the neighborhood, school. We are also deprived of a continuous presence at the school by both scheduled and unexpected school half days for teacher conferences and parent consultations. And so we expend extra energy, attempting to focus the children, seeking and integrating new members, and making up for any lost time. Our process and our idea of the play, video, or photographs are constantly under challenge.

The Correctional Facilities

Prisoners come to the workshops from an environment of frequent humiliation and ongoing punishment, an environment with its own pecking order and rivalries, where at any time they might be confined to their cell or dormitory or to the "hole", or to their bed with an inadequately treated illness, an environment that separates them from their children, siblings, and parents, an environment of alienation and much loneliness. They bring this environment with them, or sometimes because of it they are unable, or too depressed, to come. Their attendance at the workshop is volunteer activity, perhaps giving them credit towards good time, and its exercises and games seem frivolous at first, indicative that nothing worthwhile will emerge. We struggle with attitudes and with pain and give much time to necessary talk. And here too we lose a week now and then, because of a snowstorm or lock down, because unfriendly staff stall us at the gate, because a supervisor who insists on being on the premises whenever we are there is absent.

And so the work at all of our community sites requires immense patience and acceptance, an ability to roll with the punches. We acknowledge these obstacles as part of the work, and we move together toward our photograph book, video tape, or play with whatever sporadic rhythms we are granted and with guarded optimism.

The University of Michigan

We too come into our spaces from an alienated environment, with its own rivalries, competition for grades, stress on individual performance, and social pressures, and we bring this with us, bring our tensions, evasions, bad vibes, and struggles. We do not always treat each other well, nor do we always bring our best selves to the children or prisoners. And while it may be good that our discussions are collective, that our principal work is away from campus, and that we share journals and have no exams, the demanding reading, quizzes, mid-terms, finals, and competitive grading policies of other courses attenuate our time and emotional commitment to 310 and 319. If we are not watchful, a few of us become lax and renege on our responsibility, experiencing guilt as well as causing resentment among those who are giving full energy.

Outcomes

Workshop and club participants profit to one degree or another from a rich process. They move about freely, laugh together, share leadership, create images and stories, and struggle as a group towards presentation of their work to others.[10] In some cases their increased ability to express themselves and to work cooperatively with others is dramatically evident. In addition, they have personal and sometimes physical proof of their creative ability, for always in the school and whenever possible in the prisons, we make copies of the original videotapes, of the videotaped plays, and of the photograph books and make them available to the facility and to each child.

Beyond this it is less easy to be confident of outcomes. For "The Show" at Florence Crane, one inmate created a stunning opening telephone monologue about a rape, followed later with a comic tour de force about losing her tooth in a bowling alley, and finished the night with her poem, "I'm a Proud Black Woman." Shortly thereafter, she left prison, returned home, and was back in time to take a lead role in "Junkie." Others have left and returned: our recidivism rate is probably no different than that for prisoners in general. And family, school, and neighborhood circumstances are much more powerful than our one or two semester intervention with the Dewey school children. Yet we know of their joy in the work they produce and their pleasure with our presence in the school, and prisoners testify to their pride in performing sometimes deeply personal material to the applause of their peers. They take pride, too, in having been our teachers. Perhaps these achievements become a small piece of their potential, stored where it might accumulate with other positive resources to take them someday where they need to go.

And my students? In addition to the usual sharpening of reading and writing skills and in addition to making acquaintance with authors who deepen their knowledge in the relevant educational and cultural fields, they gain photography, theater, and video skills and new aesthetic perspectives: raw, honest performances by children or prisoners challenge elite, polished performances by highly trained actors for sophisticated audiences. They develop facilitating, collaborative, shaping, directing, and performing skills. Most of them radically expand the range of their societal acquaintance and knowledge. Working with prisoners and a range of inner city children, they gain a deeper sense of how our society works, or doesn't work, for so many of its citizens. They gain access to and stand in awe of the strength, creativity, and wisdom of people they had earlier been at least a little prone to stereotype and simply write off. And most of them initiate or deepen a commitment to make social service or community organizing the center or at least a significant part of their careers.

NOTES

1. In the following text I describe only the Dewey Center work, because we have only just begun at Henry Ford and because my sabbatical prevents me from being present there with my students.

2. The high school performances took place as well. For efficiency's sake, in what follows I will elaborate only on the prison work.

3. In winter term 1991 I initiated another new course, under English 317 (Literature and Culture), subtitled "Drug and Prison Cultures." In this permission of instructor course of around 23 students, each student is placed in a correctional facility, a rehabilitation center, or some other relevant site. Class visits and group phone conversations with prisoners, ex-prisoners, prison guards, recovering addicts, and social workers, plus these site placements, underlie our discussions of texts and issues. I taught the course a second time in the fall of 1991.

4. Each team works with only six or seven children. This enables us to focus the children's energy and help them to the success of completing a project. When, as in the fall of 1992, we are assigned to work under a teacher in a much larger drama or video class, discipline and focus become more difficult, and we achieve a project only by negotiating a smaller unit or units within that class.

5. Sometimes, because of our own schedules, we have had to come in on a non-club day and take students from their regular classes, with consent of the teachers. The school has seen our presence as very supportive of the children, as providing them with community and communications skills, as fitting the Dewey Center's own whole language pedagogy, a pedagogy that begins where the children are, in their lives, interests, needs, and energies.

6. This communication is very important, to keep the school informed of our activities and to avoid misunderstanding. We wish we could meet more frequently with the teachers. Their time is at a premium: they have full and fatiguing duties the entire school day, with usually

only a quick half hour free during their lunch break or after school, when a long, hard day has left them eager to get home to family and other commitments. During the summer of 1991 we invited incoming 310 students to meals with three teachers, who shared school history and their own teaching experience and philosophy and explained the Dewey Center's whole language pedagogy. This was a valuable beginning, which we unfortunately neglected to repeat in 1992.

7. The prison exercise is based on an improvisation involving a visit to an institution for the blind that I learned from Robert Alexander, Director of the Living Stage Theatre Company, during a workshop he led in Detroit. The sculpting exercises are derived from Augusto Boal, Brazilian theater activist and author of *Theater of the Oppressed*. And I learned the conversation exercise from John Malpede, director of The Los Angeles Poverty Department theater troupe.

8. Here and throughout this essay it should be clear that I am profoundly influenced by the pedagogies of Paulo Freire and Myles Horton and the Highlander Research and Education Center. The largely institution-bound nature of what we do places limits on the resemblance of our work to theirs, which is firmly focused on community organizing and structural social change.

9. There is reason for suspicion: in many instances the University of Michigan has earned its reputation as an elite university that ignores, looks down upon, or uses others for its own ends. If it is not clear from the outset that our behavior and goals are different, we are in trouble.

10. Because this success is so important, we are careful to set viable goals with each group. A prison play might be an hour and one half performance of a complete work, or it might be a short performance of monologues and scenes. A Dewey Center video tape might be a fifteen minute exploration of a local soul food kitchen or a three minute edited series of interviews.

Appendix

English 319   THEATRE AND SOCIAL CHANGE

Texts:

Amiri Baraka, *Dutchman & The Slave.*
Agusto Boal, *Theater of the Oppressed.*
Bertold Brecht, *The Jewish Wife & Other Short Plays.*
Dario Fo and Franca Rame, *Woman Alone & Other Plays.*
Henrik Ibsen, *Four Great Plays.*
Larry Kramer, *The Normal Heart.*
Ntozake Shange, *For Colored Girls who have Considered Suicide When The Rainbow is Enuf.*

Course Pack:

Ross Kidd, "Popular Theatre and Popular Struggle in Kenya: The Story of the Kamariithu Community Cultural Centre," *Theaterwork Magazine*, September/October, 1982, 47-59.

Ross Kidd, "From Outside in to Inside Out; The Benue Workshop on Theatre for Development," *Theaterwork Magazine*, May/June, 1982, 44-48, 50-53.

Ross Kidd, "From Outside in to Inside Out (Part II); "People's Theatre and Landless Organizing in Bangladesh," *Theaterwork Magazine*, January/February, 1983, 29-39.

Madeleine R. Grumet, "In Search of Theatre: Ritual, Confrontation and the Suspense of Form," *Journal of Education*, Winter, 1980, 93-110.

Keith Johnstone, "Masks and Trance," in his *Impro*, pp. 143-205.

Jorge Huerta, short selection on Teatro Campesino in Chicano Theatre.

Teatro Campesino, "Las Dos Caras del Patroncito," "La Quinta Temporada."

Deborah Levenson, "The Murder of an Actor and a Theater," NACLA Report on the Americas, Sept. 1989, pp. 4-5.

Sanjoy Hazarika, "Street Dramatist in India Slain Over Play," *NY Times*, Jan. 4, 1989.

"Testimony from Nicaragua: An Interview with Nidia Bustos," *Theaterwork Magazine*, September/October, 1982, 32-40.

Maxine Klein, "Guerrilla Theatre," from *Theatre for the 98%.*

"Four Guerrilla Theatre Pieces," *The Drama Review*, Summer, 1969, 72-77.

Richard Schechner, "Guerrilla Theater: May 1970," *The Drama Review*, 1970, 163-167.

"An account of the ideas and planning behind the performance events held in Washington, D.C., July 27, 1982, in protest of U.S. military aid to El Salvador."

Bertold Brecht, "Theatre for Pleasure or Theatre for Instruction," "The Street Scene; A Basic Model for an Epic Theatre," "A Short Organum for the Theatre," from *Brecht on Theatre*.

Amiri Baraka, "Slave Ship; A Historical Pageant".

Films:
"El Teatro Campesino."
"The AIDS Show."
"MECATE: A New Song."
"Junkie."
Videos of past plays by English 319 groups.
Catalyst Theaters' forum theater play (for the group doing forum theater in the high schools and anyone else).
We may also have an evening together to screen plays like "Woza Albert" and "The Brig."

Schedule:
January 11	Retreat, 9:00-5:30
January 14-30	Meet as a full class on Tuesdays, meet in groups in place of Thursday class.
By January 21	read three Ross Kidd essays in coursepack.
By January 28	read Grumet (course pack). During this period also read Johnstone (course pack).
February 4-6	Huerta and Teatro Campesino plays and Levenson and Hazarika (course pack). Film: "El Teatro Campesino."
February 11-13	The Normal Heart. Film: "The AIDS Show."
February 18-20	Nidia Bustos reading (course pack). Film: "MECATE: A New Song."
March 3-5	For Colored Girls... Film: "Junkie."
March 10-12	Klein; Four Guerrilla Theatre Pieces; Schechner; "An Account of the ideas and planning behind the performance events held in Washington, D.C." (all in course pack) Films: A video or two of plays by past groups in English 319.
March 17-19	Theater of the Oppressed (except last section).
March 24-26	Ibsen, Enemy of the People.
March 31 -April 2	The Jewish Wife & Other Short Plays and Brecht selections from course pack.

April 7-9 .... Woman Alone & Other Plays.

April 14-16 .... Dutchman & The Slave plus "Slave Ship: A Historical Pageant" (course pack).

April 21 .... Wrap-up.

Assignments:

The main assignment, of course, is your group project. Each of you will be in a group with other 319 students and some of you with others from outside the class: you will either be co-facilitating a prison theater workshop, co-facilitating a theater workshop with formerly homeless people in Ypsilanti, creating (possibly with high school students) a forum theater piece for performance in area high schools, creating a play about Columbus, or creating guerrilla theater pieces for performance in the university and larger community. We will form the groups during the retreat. Out of this group project will come from each of you a final, informal (like a journal entry) but serious written assessment of the theatre work you and your group do. We will discuss the nature of this assessment, but at the least it should analyze the process from the very beginning, how the group worked together, the purpose of the piece performed, the audience and staging choices, the response, its relative success as a social change piece. This written assessment should run at least ten typed pages.

In addition you will do some shorter writing assignments during the course of the term. We will discuss what these should be during the first session or two of the class: perhaps three five-page papers on subjects we choose as a group or that you choose individually; perhaps some kind of shared journal.

Chapter 5

INTEGRATING SERVICE-LEARNING INTO A COURSE IN CONTEMPORARY POLITICAL ISSUES

Gregory B. Markus

I have learned three main things from my experience with service-learning in my course on "Contemporary Political Issues." First, it is absolutely practicable to integrate community service successfully into a large undergraduate course in political science—although it does require a non-trivial investment of time and effort to do so. Second, the pay-off to students can be substantial: as compared with classroom instruction alone, service-learning significantly heightens students' tolerance and respect for others and their sense of social responsibility; perhaps more surprisingly, I have found that incorporating service-learning into my course has resulted in higher class attendance rates and increased knowledge of course material, as measured by performance on examinations and writing assignments. Third, if service-learning is to help prepare students as public-minded and effective citizens, the instructor must counteract a tendency for students, campus volunteer centers, and community agencies to perceive community service as person-to-person "helping" behavior that is largely devoid of, or even antagonistic to, overt political considerations.

The Course

"Contemporary Political Issues" attracts a broad audience of undergraduates, predominantly sophomores and juniors, from all areas of academic concentration at the University of Michigan. The course focuses upon the place of citizens in the politics of the United States and upon important policy controversies of the day, such as the federal budget deficit, welfare reform, racism, and the environment (see Appendix I). The class meets twice weekly as a group in 50-minute lecture sessions. Students also meet twice weekly (50-minutes per session) in smaller discussion sections of fewer than 25 students each. The discussion sections are led by political science doctoral graduate students.

Why Service-Learning?

I decided to incorporate service-learning into my course for two reasons, one which pertains to the pedagogical goals of any academic course and another which is of special relevance to teaching and learning *about politics*.

The first reason was that service-learning held promise of increasing the breadth and depth of what my students learned. From a pedagogical perspective, service-learning is one form of experiential learning, in contrast to the "information-assimilation model" that typifies classroom instruction (Dewey, 1938; Coleman, 1977). The information-assimilation model emphasizes a "top-down" approach to learning: principles and facts are presented symbolically (e.g., through books, lectures, or videotapes), and specific applications of principles are learned primarily through deductive reasoning or "thought experiments." The method's advantages are its efficiency in terms of conveying large amounts of information and its emphasis on the logical, coherent cognitive organization of that information. Its weakness is that students' actual acquisition and long-term retention of information are problematical—that is, students may not truly *learn* very much. Experiential learning is more of a "bottom-up" method, in which general lessons and principles are drawn inductively from direct personal experiences and observations. This approach is less efficient than readings and lectures in transmitting information, and general principles can be slow to emerge. On the other hand, experiential learning counters the abstractness of much classroom instruction and motivates lasting learning by providing concrete examples of facts and theories, thereby "providing connections between academic content and the problems of real life" (Conrad & Hedin 1991, p. 745). *Thus, when community service is combined with classroom instruction, the pedagogical advantages of each compensates for the shortcomings of the other.*

The more specific reason I decided to incorporate service-learning into my course stemmed from the fact that it was a course about politics, and in particular about public policy and citizenship. In his influential report to the Carnegie Foundation in 1985, Frank Newman wrote: "If there is a crisis in education in the United States today, it is less that test scores have declined than it is that we have failed to provide the education for citizenship that is still the most important responsibility of the nation's schools and colleges" (p. 31). Among the various approaches that have been advocated for addressing this failure, perhaps none has received as much attention as the proposal that high school and college students should engage in community service as part of their formal education (see, e.g., Barber, 1992; Evers, 1990; Moskos, 1988).

Unfortunately, although well-intentioned service-learning programs often invoke hortatory references to enhancing students' understanding of their "civic obligations" and the "responsibilities of citizenship," it is not uncommon for such programs to be apolitical or even anti-political in actual practice. For example, Serow (1991) found in his study of four public universities that the norms surrounding community service encourage students "to become directly engaged with the problems of vulnerable individuals rather than viewing them in terms of broader, abstract social or political phenomena" (p. 553). He concluded (pp. 555-556):

> "Applied specifically to community service, the message from the campuses is that students can combat their own alienation by bypassing official channels and finding one person or program that needs their help. Thus in the words of a national volunteer organizer, students "would rather

teach English in a Spanish speaking neighborhood than work
for a political action group. They would rather visit a senior
citizen than get involved in city politics."

Harry Boyte of the University of Minnesota's Humphrey Institute of Public
Affairs concurs. Boyte (1991a, p. 766) has found that students in community
service programs "usually disavow concern with larger policy questions, seeing
service as an *alternative* to politics." In a related article (Boyte, 1991b, p. 627)
he argued:

> "Most service programs include little learning or discus-
> sion about the policy dimensions of the "issues" (such as
> poverty, homelessness, drug use, illiteracy) that students
> wrestle with through person-to-person effort. Volunteers—
> usually middle-class and generally white—rarely have occa-
> sion to reflect on the complex dynamics of power, race and
> class that are created when young people go out to "serve" in
> low-income areas."

It is doubtful that such programs do much to advance students' understanding of, experience in, and commitment to participation in the political work of
citizens. There is no good reason why community service programs must
inevitably be apolitical or anti-political in practice, however. Boyte's pilot
program, called Public Achievement, is one successful example of teaching
young adults about politics through practical experience. The new Civic
Education and Community Service Program at Rutgers University is another
(Barber, 1992). Because mine is a course in politics, my graduate assistants and
I try self-consciously to prepare and encourage students to reflect upon and
draw lessons from the *political* aspects of what they observe and experience
in their service activities rather than get caught up entirely in the "person to
person" aspects of their work.

For example, when college students work at a homeless shelter, they
provide valuable service for the shelter and its clients, and the students typically
feel a great sense of personal satisfaction from helping others. But students may
not consider the broader social and political dimensions of the issue of
homelessness unless they are provided regularly with the time and space within
a classroom setting to discuss those dimensions: Why do substantial numbers
of Americans go without adequate food and shelter within the world's richest
nation? Is this matter a proper responsibility of government, or is it better left
to charities, religious institutions, and private individuals? Why? How are such
questions decided in the United States? Where do citizens fit in? Where do you
fit in?

An Experiment in Service-Learning

The first time that I used service-learning as part of "Contemporary Political
Issues" (Winter 1992) was within the framework of an experiment on the impact
of community service experience upon student learning (see Markus, Howard
& King, 1993). Prior to class registration (and unknown to students registering

for the course), I randomly designated two of eight discussion sections as "service-learning" sections, in which students would be assigned to engage in 20 hours of service over the course of the 13-week semester with their choice of one of a number of designated community agencies. The remaining six "control group" sections used a traditional format, in which section meetings were devoted largely to discussions of course readings and lectures. Students in the control sections were required to write term papers based upon library research intended to take an amount of time and effort equivalent to that expended by students in the service sections. Regardless of assignment to treatment or control sections, all students attended the same lectures, were assigned the same course readings, and took the same mid-term and final examinations, graded according to a common set of standards.

At the first lecture meeting of the course, students were informed in general terms that we would be experimenting with different types of teaching methods in the course and about the differing requirements associated with the two kinds of discussion sections. They were also informed that in order to prevent possible biases in the study, transfers between community service and traditional sections were not permitted. A total of 52 students were enrolled in discussion sections using the traditional format, and 37 students were in the service sections. There were no significant differences between treatment and control groups in terms of demographic factors (sex, race, and year in school), nor did the two groups differ in terms of student responses to a questionnaire about personal attitudes and values that was distributed early in the semester.

During the first two weeks of the term, the University's Office of Community Service Learning assisted in placing the designated students with local agencies and organizations that were selected from a larger list of ones with which the Office had worked previously. The service opportunities included working at a homeless shelter, a women's crisis center, or the Ecology Center, or tutoring at-risk primary or high school students. The particular agencies were selected because the focus of their activities meshed with the subject matter of the course and because the agencies reported that they could put students to work in meaningful and educationally worthwhile jobs immediately and without extensive training required on the part of the students. The graduate teaching assistant who led the service-learning discussion groups visited each agency at least once during the semester and contacted the agencies periodically to ensure that students were fulfilling their time commitments and that the tasks to which students were assigned were consistent with the goals of the course. A small grant from Michigan Campus Compact provided a salary increment for the service-learning sections' graduate assistant and covered miscellaneous costs, such as transportation and materials.

Over the course of the semester, a few students worked individually on their service assignments; the vast majority worked in teams of three to eight students each. Section meetings for the experimental group were devoted to discussions about the service in which students were engaged and how their experiences related to course readings and lectures. Students were encouraged to link abstract ideas and theories (for example, the dilemma of collective action) to their particular experiences (the agency I work with is chronically under-funded). Near the end of the semester, students in the service sections also wrote short papers and presented brief oral reports based on their experiences. The oral presentations were made during a three-hour evening session attended by all students in the service-learning sections, their graduate assistant, and the course instructor. Soft drinks and snacks were provided.

Effects of service-learning versus traditional instruction were assessed in a variety of ways, via pre- and post-semester questionnaires, course grades, and data on class attendance. Students in the community service sections differed markedly from their counterparts in the traditional sections on many measures of course impact. For example, students in the service-learning sections displayed significant increases in their ratings of the personal importance they attached to "working toward equal opportunity for all U.S. citizens," "volunteering my time helping people in need," and "finding a career that provides the opportunity to be helpful to others or useful to society." As compared with their counterparts in the traditional sections, students in the service-learning sections also provided higher mean ratings of the degree to which they thought that participation in the course had increased or strengthened their: "intention to serve others in need," "intention to give to charities," "orientation toward others and away from yourself," "belief that helping those in need is one's social responsibility," "belief that one can make a difference in the world," and "tolerance and appreciation for others."

Students' *academic* learning was also significantly enhanced by their participation in course-relevant community service: as compared with students taught by traditional methods, students in service-learning sections were more emphatic in their judgments that they were performing up to their potential in the course, were more likely to affirm that they had "learned to apply principles from this course to new situations" and had "developed a set of overall values in this field," to mention some illustrative findings. Students in the service-learning sections also had higher attendance rates for both lecture and section meetings and attained significantly higher course grades on average.

Students' anonymous written comments in their course evaluations speak to the value of service-learning:

> *The community service project was the most valuable part of the course. It made the issues discussed in class so much more real to me. It made me realize that there are social problems— but that they are not unsolvable.*

> *The community service gave me first-hand knowledge of the issues discussed in class. I also think my experience will make me a better citizen.*

> *The community service project was a very good idea. I'm even working there again this week (at the shelter association). It provided me with a better understanding of the homeless problem.*
> *I really enjoyed the community service aspect of this course, even though I didn't expect to like it. I actually saw the concepts we had discussed in lecture come to life. I think it should be continued.*

Expanding the Service-Learning Component Course-wide

In light of the positive results achieved in the pilot experiment, the service-learning component of Political Science 300 was expanded the following semester (Fall 1992). As in the previous term, the service commitment was for 20 hours over the course of the semester. This time, however, all 150 enrolled students were assigned to work with an off-campus agency or organization in the public sector. Another important change in the course was that the range of service-learning options was expanded to include assignments of an explicit political nature, including work with local party organizations, voter registration drives, and issue advocacy groups (e.g., abortion rights) during the fall election campaigns. Approximately half the class selected one of these new options, while the other half chose from among the service agencies that had been utilized the previous semester. Students generally preferred to work in small teams of approximately three to eight individuals per team, a practice which worked well both logistically and educationally (see Barber, 1992, pp. 253-261).

Some might question whether work on behalf of a political party, candidate, or issue is "service." I submit that such an opinion is indicative of the sorry state in which American politics finds itself today. Historically, democratic politics is the work of the citizen. Today, however, most Americans see politics as a spectator sport—and a not particularly popular, reputable, or meaningful one at that. In place of a politics in which citizens have an active role and a personal stake, we have a government that provides us with services in return for payment of taxes. To say that American politics is in trouble is not to presume that there once existed a golden age in which most citizens most of the time were informed, active, and empowered participants. The assertion is that however imperfectly the political system used to operate, it functions dramatically less satisfactorily today. William Greider's book *Who Will Tell the People* provides ample evidence to support this contention, as does E. J. Dionne's recent best-seller *Why Americans Hate Politics* (both of which were read by students in Political Science 300). It follows from this argument that when students work in political party organizations and issue advocacy groups they are indeed performing worthwhile public-oriented "service," an appellation that should not be bestowed solely upon work with "needy" groups.

The University's Office of Community Service Learning once again assisted in placing students with local agencies other than political organizations. A graduate assistant contacted the latter organizations directly and arranged for student placements. The graduate teaching assistants also maintained communication with the community groups over the course of the semester to monitor the nature of the work students were performing and to ensure that students were fulfilling their commitments. Our experience was that, with only one or two exceptions, community agencies and political organizations were quite happy to make use of student volunteers.

As in the previous semester, section meetings were regularly devoted to discussions linking students' experiences outside of the classroom to the subject matter of course readings and lectures. The graduate teaching assistants and I met weekly to share information about what students were accomplishing in the community, how well the service experiences were meshing with other aspects of the course, and any other ideas we had or problems we were facing. One side-benefit of integrating service-learning into the course was that the graduate assistants found the discussion sections more interesting to lead, and they gained experience with new approaches to teaching.

As for the students, their assessments of the course via the post-course evaluation questionnaire, their written and oral comments about their experiences in the community, and, especially, their performance in the classroom and on examinations all indicated that, even on this fairly large scale, classroom instruction and service-learning can be combined synergistically to enhance academic learning. For example, in their responses to the evaluation questionnaire, 45% of the students "strongly agreed" with the statement "Overall, this is an excellent course," and another 45% "agreed." Fully 51% strongly agreed with the statement "I learned a great deal from this course," and another 40% agreed with the statement.

Conclusions

Community service has many laudable purposes and outcomes—fulfilling civic responsibilities to one's community, helping persons in need, gaining an insight into one's values and prejudices, developing career interests and job skills, and so on, all of which are important. The primary focus of my experiences with Political Science 300 has been a less well-understood aspect of service: its *academic* value. The academic benefits of having students engage in community service are substantial when that service activity is integrated with traditional classroom instruction. The key word here is *integrated*. Time in class meetings should be set aside consistently for students to reflect upon and discuss what they are learning in their service activity and how it illustrates, affirms, extends, or contradicts points made in readings and lectures. These recommendations are consistent with those of others who have studied service-learning (see, e.g., Barber 1992; Hedin, 1989; Stanton 1990).

Integrating service-learning into a traditional classroom-oriented course requires an investment of time and resources, especially the first time around. If one's institution has an Office of Service Learning, Office of Volunteer Services, or similar entity that is experienced in placing students with service agencies in the community, using it can reduce the start-up costs considerably. It is also important to reach agreements with local service agencies in advance of the beginning of the course regarding the kinds of duties students will be expected to perform, how students will receive any necessary training, how many volunteers and how many hours of service should be anticipated, and so on. Finally, the instructor (or a course assistant) should monitor the agencies and students over the course of the term to ascertain that both are fulfilling their mutual obligations.

Appendix

Political Science 300
Contemporary Issues in American Politics

Course Description

This is a serious course for serious students who are genuinely interested in learning more about critical political issues and choices confronting the United States. The course is aimed at undergraduates generally and not at political science concentrators alone (although the latter are certainly welcome) Curiosity, skepticism, and energy are the essential prerequisites. You will read, listen, discuss, write, and do a lot in this course, consistent with its four credit-hour value. (Translation: If you're looking for an easy, undemanding course, look elsewhere.) In return, my goal is to make this the most rewarding, valuable course you will take as an undergraduate.

This course has two main objectives. The first is to help you develop a framework within which to think about politics. That framework will include some ideas about what the legitimate purposes of government are and where you fit in. Voting and elections constitute a natural topic in this regard. The other objective of this course is to examine some specific political issues that are the focus of contemporary political debate in the United States, such as the politics of race, taxes and the budget deficit, the place of the U.S. within a global economy, and national and global ecology.

Political Science 300 stresses the utility of scholarly knowledge as a means to understand current events—especially those events related to campaigns and elections. To that end, scholarly readings are intermixed with articles about current issues, and our discussions often move freely from assigned readings to the latest news.

Grading is on a no-curve 100-point system. The mid-term and final examinations are each worth one-third of your grade. The remaining third of your grade is based by what you do in your discussion section. As part of section responsibilities, you will be required to engage in 20 hours of learning activities that are carried out in the community, such as working with a local service agency or with a group working on behalf of a political party, candidate, or issue. You will write at least one term paper in your discussion section.

Required Materials

Coursepack

Dionne, E. J. (1991) *Why Americans Hate Politics* (New York: Simon & Schuster).
Edsall, Thomas B. and Mary D. Edsall (1991) *Chain Reaction: The Impact of Race, Rights, and Taxes on American Politics* (New York: Norton).
Gant, Michael and Norman Luttbeg (1991) *American Electoral Behavior* (Itasca, IL: Peacock).
Greider, William (1992) *Who Will Tell the People* (New York: Simon & Schuster).
Jacobson, Gary C. (1992) *The Politics of Congressional Elections,* 3rd ed. (New York: HarperCollins).
Kettl, Donald F. (1992) *Deficit Politics* (New York: Macmillan).
Reich, Robert B. (1991) *The Work of Nations* (New York: Vintage).

Course Outline

I. Voters and Elections in American Politics
A. How voters decide
Gant, Michael and Norman Luttbeg (1991) *American Electoral Behavior*, ch. 1, 2.

B. Turnout
Gant & Luttbeg (1991) *American Electoral Behavior,* ch. 3, 4.
Powell, G. B. (1986) "American Voter Turnout in Comparative Perspective," *APSR*, 80: 17-43.

C. The paradox of mass politics
Converse, P. E. (1990) "Popular Representation and the Distribution of Information." In Ferejohn,
    J. A. and J. H. Kuklinski, eds. *Information and Democratic Processes.*

II. Why Americans Hate Politics
Greider, William (1992) *Who Will Tell the People* , Introduction, ch. 1, 4, 5, 8-12.
Lapham, L. H. (1990) "Democracy in America?" *Harper's* (November), pp. 47-56.
Dionne, E. J. (1991) *Why Americans Hate Politics*, Introduction, ch. 3-6, 9-13.

III. Media and Politics
Kinder, D. R. and D. O. Sears (1985) "Public Opinion and Political Action." In G. Lindzey and
    E. Aronson (eds.), *Handbook of Social Psychology,* 3rd ed., pp. 705-714.
Arterton, F. C. with R. A. Fein (1984) "Reporting the Campaign: The Journalist's Perspective." In
    F. C. Arterton, ed. *Media Politics.*
Lichter, S. R. (1988) "How the Press Covered the Primaries," *Public Opinion* (July/Aug.), pp. 45-
    49.
Lichter, S. R., D. Amundson, and R. E. Noyes (1989) "Media Coverage," *Public Opinion* (Jan./
    Feb.), pp. 18-19, 52.
Adatto, K. (1990) "The Incredible Shrinking Sound Bite," *The New Republic*, May 28.

IV. The Politics of Congressional Elections
Gant & Luttbeg (1991) *American Electoral Behavior,* ch. 5.
Jacobson, Gary C. (1992) *The Politics of Congressional Elections* (entire, but skim pp. 172-200).

V. Race, Class, and Politics
Edsall, Thomas B. and Mary D. Edsall (1991) *Chain Reaction,* ch. 1, 6-12.

VI. The Federal Budget: "Watch what we do, not what we say."
Kettl, Donald F. (1992) *Deficit Politics*, ch. 1-3, 7.
Howe, Neil and Phillip Longman (1992) "The Next New Deal," *The Atlantic Monthly* (April).

VII. The Politics of the Global Economy
Reich, Robert B. (1991) *The Work of Nations*, Introduction, ch. 6, 10, 12-14, 16, 17, 20-25.
Greider, William (1992) *Who Will Tell the People*, ch. 17.

VIII. Politics, Values, and Ecology
Brown, Lester R. (1991) "The New World Order." In L. R. Brown et al., *The State of the World 1991*
    (New York: Norton).
Ophuls, William (1977) "Towards a Politics of the Steady State." From Ophuls, *Ecology and the*
    Politics of Scarcity (San Francisco: Freeman).
Schumacher, E. F. (1973) *Small is Beautiful* (New York: Harper & Row), ch. 2, 4, Epilogue.

IX.   Self-Interest and the Liberal Tradition in American Politics: Who Gets What?
Federalist Papers 10, 51.
Greenberg, Edward (1986) *The American Political System*, ch. 3.

X.   Liberalism and the Tragedy of the Commons: Conservative and
     Communitarian Alternatives
Schwartz, Barry (1986) *The Battle for Human Nature* (New York: Norton), ch. 9.
Will, George (1983), *Statecraft as Soulcraft* (New York: Simon & Schuster), ch. 2, 4.
Sandel, Michael (1988) "Democrats and Community," *The New Republic* (Feb. 22).

Chapter 6

DETROIT SUMMER: A MODEL FOR SERVICE-LEARNING[1]

Bunyan Bryant

> "The purpose is not only to rebuild the city, but to rebuild a sense of community as well...We built parks and a baseball diamond. We renovated an elderly woman's house, painted a mural and worked on anti-gang activities...The most important work, however, was the decreased sense of racial and age polarization between all involved as well as new feeling of hope. Hope that as we continue to reform our city, we also could reform bonds among all people."

As we move towards the 21st century we need a philosophical change in our approach to education that will enable us to redefine our relationships with each other, with our communities, and with Nature. Much of our education today is based upon the Cartesian view of the duality between mind and body, between the knower and the known. According to this philosophy, Nature is like a giant machine to be understood mathematically. Any phenomena that cannot be quantified are not worth knowing. Today this philosophic dualism is embodied not only in our research paradigms (subject/object, detached/involved, spiritual/material, culture/nature) but also in our teaching.

When market forces were joined to this philosophical approach, it became possible to exploit Nature beyond our wildest imagination. Nature, regarded as savage, inferior, and needing to be tamed, was to be exploited, shaped, changed, molded—all in the name of progress. Likewise with people of color and women. Over the last two hundred years this approach has brought rapid industrialization and material improvement for many in the Western world. But, it has also legitimized racism and sexism, destroyed the basic metabolism between human beings and the earth, and created a split between spirit and matter. Work was transformed into a commodity—labor—to be bought and sold, and the earth was transformed into land or property. Mechanized farming forced people off the land and into cities to work at repetitive, alienating work on factory assembly lines. Four-fifths of the world was turned into a supplier of raw materials for the industrialized countries, resulting in soil degradation, deforestation, drought, aridisation and mineral depletion in the so-called developing countries. Now the industrialized countries are threatened by toxic waste, pollution, garbage disposal and sewage problems, and our whole planet faces environmental catastrophe from global warming.

Today millions of Americans are caught up in the work ethic of making a living. To make a living requires us to be specialists or generalists, preoccupied with survival, creature comfort, or greed. It requires us to hire out our labor in exchange for remunerative rewards. It fosters a primary allegiance to the paycheck. Making a living often either detaches us from, or puts us in an antagonistic relationship with, other people and/or Nature. This is particularly true in a market system that depends upon growth and development for its very survival.

Focusing on making a living has led us to become oblivious to what has happened to our families, communities, and our planet. Our situation continues to get more bleak as opportunities for making a living in factories and offices are being foreclosed by the introduction of high-tech and the exporting of jobs overseas. In addition, there is a growing recognition of the damage that we have been doing to ourselves and our planet by the way we have been making a living. As a result, an increasing number of people are beginning to ask such questions as: How can we create work that will meet our material needs and at the same time rekindle our spirituality, build family and community, and re-establish our connectedness with one another and with nature? How can we make our living in ways that empower us to make a difference in the world in which we live? How can "making a life" be equal partners with "making a living?"[2]

Making a life is more than survival, creature comforts, and a paycheck. It is a commitment to work and family, community and Nature. It is a process by which we rekindle our spirituality by establishing our connectedness with one another and with Nature. It has to do with a spirituality of a larger self and a spirituality that becomes the basis for our political action of saving each other and the planet. In making a life, work takes on a different meaning of teaching, learning, creating, and healing the earth (Ellis, 1993). From making a life comes the feeling of empowerment that one can make a difference in the world in which one lives.

Unfortunately our educational system has been geared to primarily prepare students to make a living. Therefore, we must begin to refurbish education in a way that prepares students to also make a life. If we are to do this, we must enable them to engage in real life experiences in the community, along with people who are wrestling with this duality. We need to provide young people with opportunities that enable them to see that their own quality of life is intricately connected to both the quality of life of others as well as to our treatment of Nature. Beyond this, we must help them to understand that the quality of one's life is enhanced by extending one's self to the larger self or community.

Seventy-five years ago progressive educators, like John Dewey, advocated for an emphasis on the *process* of learning rather than the *outcomes* of learning, learning how to learn rather than learning facts and theories. To properly prepare students for a future commitment to people, community, and the planet requires us to change education from outcomes-based to process-based.

To make this change will require new role definitions for teachers and students. Teachers will have to be less dependent upon lecturing accumulated material and less detached from students. Students will have to be involved as active participants in the teaching and learning process in order to become more self-reliant and to take the initiative for their own learning. Teachers will have to affirm students' own experiences and knowledge as important and worthy of sharing with their peers. This shift will require that students cease perceiving teachers as the only source of worthwhile knowledge, and begin to see themselves as sources of important information; at the same time it will require that teachers cease seeing themselves as experts and authorities of accumulated knowledge, and begin to see themselves as facilitators and enablers of others' learning.

These role shifts are difficult. Students have been relegated to passivity for so long that education has become a spectator sport, leaving students unprepared for active learner roles. Similarly, many teachers would be uncomfortable or threatened by the view of students as resources actively engaged in their own learning. Yet, it is critical that both students and teachers be intricately engaged in the teaching and learning process if we are to move toward a process-based education.

Only so much learning can take place in the classroom, which detaches students from real life experiences. Whereas in the 19th century it was possible to learn considerably more within the classroom than outside of them, today the classroom, though sufficient for the dissemination of facts, is wanting in the process of learning how to learn. And, as we move further into an information age and as more and more information becomes accessible through media technology, both teachers and educational institutions will continue to lose their prior monopoly over the learning enterprise. This, too, will undoubtedly demand a change in the role of the teacher and the teaching process. All this begs the question, How can we move education toward a process-based orientation that shifts roles, broadens the concept of "classroom," and encourages connectedness with others and with Nature?

Detroit Summer: A Model for Service-Learning

In Detroit, as in other large cities, the decline in the value of labor, along with runaway shops and corporations that are insensitive to the consequences of their decisions on the city and her residents, have all contributed to high unemployment, underemployment, a life of serious crime and family discord, a lower tax base, a decaying infrastructure, and environmental degradation. In this context, Detroiters can no longer afford to wait for others to make things right for them; they will have to be both creative and self-reliant in order to rebuild and recivilize their communities.

Detroit Summer was the outgrowth of these concerns and realizations, along with the idea that young people could play an important role in the building of a social movement to change the face of the city. This program began for the first time during the summer of 1992. In the spirit that students left institutions of higher learning to work in the Civil Rights Movement in the 1960s, students were asked to come to Detroit to help rebuild the city. Approximately 50 community organizations in Detroit put out this call and approximately 100 students responded, with about half of them coming from outside the city. Detroit Summer is a community laboratory for service-learning that enables students to extend themselves to a larger self (the community). But it is more than just an effort to refurbish homes and offer a hands-on learning experience; it is a social movement that fills the void of powerlessness (expressed in terms of alienation, crime, hate, and anger) with meaningful work and cultural and intellectual activities. It is a grass roots movement to rebuild our community from the ground up, to rekindle the spirit of togetherness, and to foster caring and meaningful relations. It is a movement that supports small businesses, urban gardens, urban greenhouses (including fish farming) and neighborhood day care centers in order to provide mothers and fathers with opportunities to work. It is a movement that supports solar technology, energy conservation, more efficient mass transit systems, urban parks, and official bicycle and pedestrian circulation systems in order to be more kind to the environment. In essence, this is a movement to build *community*, where people can interact with others and with their environment, confident that they are safe, nurturing, and sustainable. In the process, student participants are transformed.

There are several important ingredients to building this social movement. First, it requires an understanding of the strengths and weaknesses of various past movements so that we can learn from those who have gone before us. Second, it calls for understanding and celebrating our diverse cultures, as reflected in music, painting, art, poetry, and eco-raps, so that we can become strong and firmly grounded to the past. Third, it requires that we write stories and create images of the future so we know the path to follow. And fourth, through the struggle to create a movement we will have to build our own culture to provide the nourishment and the fiber to propel our collective action into the future.

Therefore by helping students work effectively in multicultural work teams focused on rebuilding, recycling, and recivilizing our city, Detroit Summer contributes to the following three goals:

- To enable students to make a difference by unselfishly giving of themselves to the broader self so that they will become a part of a transforming process.

- To help students understand other students and the community people with whom they work who are from different social, economic, cultural, and generational backgrounds.

- To offer up a new model of education in which students empower themselves by being active participants in their own learning of how to make a life.

Students of Detroit Summer '92 were engaged in such community projects as: turning vacant lots into parks, painting and repairing homes, cleaning and painting up alleys, helping to develop urban gardens, and informing fisherpersons regarding toxicity in fish.

But beyond community improvement projects, they were involved in activities intended to integrate them into the community. Activities included intergenerational dialogues held once a week for students to converse with longtime community activists; weekly cease-fire vigils that were a part of anti-handgun demonstrations organized by Save our Sons and Daughters (SOSAD) and the Anti-Handgun Association; and an eco-tour of the city in which they explored the topics of food, water, transportation, and refuse. They went on downtown walking tours to observe architectural, ethnic, historical, and artistic treasures, and participated in an evening of discussion with an eco-feminist on women's spirituality and the weaving of community. They toured the Arab community and the city of Hamtramck, visited the Museum of African American History, and joined in neighborhood anti-crack demonstrations organized by We the People Reclaim Our Streets (WEPROS).

To insure a complete experience, they participated in: survival revivals dealing with methods of conflict resolution, featuring former members of the California youth gangs and local youth organizers; workshops on how to make an ideal community from an eco-perspective; international children's day workshops on how to help children express their feelings by creating hand-painted tiles (these tiles were then joined together to make a GREAT PEACE WALL); and making puppets and developing a larger than life mural with neighborhood youth.

The political, the cultural, the cognitive, and the community improvement experiences all played a critical role in the empowerment of students to make a difference. Students were necessarily an integral part of the process rather than detached and uninvolved. Neither books nor the classroom stood between them and their direct experience of people and community building. Though completing individual community projects was important, perhaps more importantly, the projects served as a medium by which students were able to learn from those different than themselves. And through the ensuing dialogue, they were able to learn about each other, their respective diverse cultures and backgrounds and kindness to the environment. Working in teams became a social system from which they learned some very important lessons.

The experience of Detroit Summer had a profound effect upon the students who participated, as evidenced by the following quotes:

> *Detroit Summer had a special way of making you forget the fact that you weren't getting paid. It filled your head with answers to questions that you'd had all your life and questions that no one can answer. It made you feel you were an important part of the changing and molding of future generations. It made you see the hole you dug, the garden you watered or the swing set you painted made a difference.*
> —Tracy Hollins, Detroit

> *Why am I in Detroit? To work in the community helping to create an ongoing reclamation of the city.*
> —Neal Vasquez, Little Rock, Arkansas

> *Young black males are in trouble. But there is hope. And the bearers of this hope are their peers. I am a peer. That's why I want to be a part of Detroit Summer.*
> —Carl Edward McGowan, Hanover, New Hampshire

> *The purpose is not only to rebuild the city, but to rebuild a sense*

*of community as well... We built parks and a baseball diamond.
We renovated an elderly woman's house, painted a mural and
worked on anti-gang activities...The most important work,
however, was the decreased sense of racial and age polarization
between all involved as well as new feeling of hope. Hope that
as we continue to reform our city, we also could reform bonds
among all people.*

—Mary Trombley, Detroit

*Forget about the politicians. Come up from underneath them,
push up from the roots. It was so great working on the park with
the kids.*

—Andrea DeFrancesco, Penobscot, Maine

Extracting Meaning from Experience

The experiences of these students will impact them for the rest of their
lives. Detroit Summer provided them with an opportunity to make a difference.
Working in multicultural teams of young men and women provided opportunities for them to learn about leadership, cooperation, cultural values, and the
giving of themselves unselfishly. Though it was not incorporated in Detroit
Summer '92, enhanced cognitive learning could have been facilitated by having
students write daily logs and meet regularly in discussion groups.

Logs would help participants to more fully understand their community
experiences. They would help students to translate their experiences into
personal and intellectual meaning as well as integrate their actions and
reflections, thoughts and feelings. As students are giving of themselves to the
larger self, they can use logs to gain personal clarity: Who am I? Where do I come
from? Where do I want to go? How do I plan to get there?

To further enhance the learning agenda of a service-learning program like
Detroit Summer, students also could meet twice a week in trios, using what they
have written in their logs for the basis of discussion. Not only would this provide
the opportunity to learn through dialogue with peers, but it would be within
the context of these discussion groups that students would come to learn to use
themselves as resources for each other in both teaching and learning. Although
each week there would be a different combination of students in the trios, these
trios would be constituted by members of the same work team so as to foster
cohesiveness and teamwork among team members.

A critical question to help students to understand themselves and how they
experience their community work would be, what difference do the following
make: your racial and/ethnic background, area where you were raised (e.g.
urban, rural, suburban), the major breadwinner in your family and the major
decision maker, assumptions about "smartness" made in your family, and your
religious background? Other important questions for student reflection and
discussion would be: What messages did you receive about your racial/ethnic
groups when you were growing up? Describe an incident when you were
mistreated because you were a member of your racial and/or ethnic group?
How did you get disconnected from your racial/ethic group? In what ways can
you get reconnected or make your ethnic or racial heritage connections

stronger?

While these questions above require students to reflect on their past, they are intended to precipitate and facilitate intra- and inter-personal understanding of and appreciation for ethnic and racial differences and similarities. By sharing the many answers to these questions, students can foster that spiritual connectedness that is necessary to build a multicultural and multi-generational movement in this country.

Questions related to this community building movement that students could answer are: Who or what relative from your ethic background or what historical event can you draw upon for building a social movement? Name a heroine or hero (alive or dead) with whom you identify. What can you learn from them, regarding leadership and building a social movement? Based upon your ethic or racial background, what are the forces that may hinder or facilitate your actions in building a movement? In what ways is it a sacrifice for you to build a movement for recivilizing our cities?

Personal development questions could include: What does this experience mean to you? What are you learning with regard to leadership and cooperation? Explain in your own words what is meant by "making a living" vs. "making a life." How does making a life contribute to building a movement? In what ways has this experience of Detroit Summer transformed you? In what ways has it failed to do so?

Once a week students could hand in their logs to the instructor for comments, and each week students could meet with their community supervisor face-to-face, either individually or in small groups. The discussions with their peers, with the community supervisor, and the written logs could serve as major vehicles for not only precipitating but also assessing student learning.

Although it would be naive to think that we can completely change the fundamental philosophy underlining American education, we can at least demand more space in the curriculum in order to bring students in direct relationship with experiences of the workplace and community. These direct learning experiences will help students affirm that they can make a difference in the world in which they live. Students, as history has shown, have the potential power to build a movement that is transforming of themselves as well as society. Through Detroit Summer and programs like it, with students working hand in hand with community groups, we can begin to transform our community and our educational system. We can help students to make a life by engaging in a social movement that is transforming and that also brings forth new and creative opportunities that will support sustainable communities that are safe, friendly, and just. Building a movement for revitalizing and recivilizing our cities and our schools is critical if we are to survive the 21st century. The time is now or it will be too late.

NOTES

1. Much of the material and suggestions for this article was supplied by Grace Boggs and the Detroit Summer '92 Project. She is one of the founders of Detroit Summer '92.
2. James Boggs speaks of the difference between "making a living" vs. "making a life." Boggs is one of the founding members of Detroit Summer '92.

Chapter 7

COMMUNITY SERVICE WRITING IN AN ADVANCED COMPOSITION CLASS

Karis Crawford

Background of Practical English

Practical English, as it was originally developed in the mid-1980s at the University of Michigan, was a workshop simulating a business or professional environment by means of extensive peer evaluation, student consensus on writing assignments, and, most prominently, a corporate project devised and executed by the class as a whole (Rabkin & Smith, 1990). Each of these elements of the course was interlocked through a complex syllabus, with direction from the instructor but with considerable input from the workshop members.

Peer evaluation was carried out primarily in four-student editing groups, assigned by the instructor at the beginning of the term with regard for balance of gender and race. Members of each group learned to edit their own writing--an ultimate goal of the course—by editing the writing of their peers, with the instructor monitoring the progressive revision of each assignment. In my management of Practical English, student editors strengthened their grammatical expertise each week from my brief interactive lectures. Material started out simple (comma rules, common pronoun errors) and gradually required more critical thought (patterns of development, sentence variety, transitions).

Writing assignments were varied to simulate the multiplicity of writing modes that students might encounter in life beyond college, and students worked on assignments of different length simultaneously. For example, I set up ideas for letters to the editor or letters to public officials by playing a videotape of a controversial segment from a recent television newsmagazine program. Students could adopt the persona of any of the people involved in the controversy or they could voice the concern of an irate citizen of their own description. We did memos, press releases, process descriptions, and prospectuses in a similar fashion, always reaching consensus in class on the purpose, audience, and length of each assignment.

A key set of four assignments centered on rotating formats: the four members of each editing group attended an event together. Then one member wrote a 250-word summary, one wrote a 60-second radio commercial, one wrote a 500-word newspaper review, and one wrote a 1000-word critical analysis. For the second event, the assignment rotated, so that after four events each member had cycled through all formats. As the instructor, I set the events (Let's Go to Dinner, Let's Go to a Movie, for example), but the students were free to pick their venue and accommodate their schedules. In peer editing this set of assignments, we often regrouped the class so that all the summary writers edited each other's summaries, all the commercial writers edited each other's commercials, and so forth (Rabkin & Smith, 1990).

The corporate project was the term-long assignment, and the tenets of the course required that it include everyone in the class, involve substantial writing and speaking, and address some social need outside the classroom. This project went beyond editing-group boundaries and was totally open to class decision; I turned over all debate to the students themselves. With varying levels of commitment and of success, sections in different terms chose a wide range of corporate projects: a booklet of interviews with senior citizens, a multicultural fair for elementary students, a newsletter for Michigan troops stationed with Operation Desert Storm, a drug-abuse education program for middle-school youth. Between the corporate project and the series of overlapping assignments throughout the term, each student produced finished prose of about 25 to 30 pages, not including mandated drafts.

I taught a number of highly successful sections of Practical English in this form between 1988 and 1992, attracting primarily seniors. These students, drawn from many departments, needed to fulfill an upper-level writing requirement and wanted to gain skills for the workplace. Clearly, Practical English, even in its original form, accomplished many of the goals of service-learning by empowering students to direct their own education and by basing that education in the world outside the university. The course was very popular and became known on campus as an excellent path to writing improvement.

Problems with Practical English

Frequently during these years of Practical English some members of each class would propose specific community service as a corporate project only to be voted down by students intent on producing an independent creation. For instance, a proposal to write a booklet on handicap accessibility needed by the campus Services for Students with Disabilities lost narrowly one term. In another term a student's idea of leading tours and writing brochures for a local museum was defeated. As successive classes of Practical English opted for innovative projects, finding a totally new one became more difficult for students.

In addition, although the course received high marks in standardized evaluations (consistently above 75th percentile), students regularly made two complaints. First, the fundraising imposed by the costs of printing and distributing written materials or producing programs was burdensome. Almost all students had participated in fundraising for extracurricular organizations on campus and wanted their advanced composition course to be directed more toward writing. Second, the inevitable haggling over the choice and execution of a project conducted by up to 40 people could get exasperating. In lively classroom interchanges, I always pointed out the utility of such group experience for the workplace. Students accepted this argument but still repeatedly found the level of uncertainty and of bickering too high.

The Role of the Office of Community Service Learning

In 1992, when I was seeking alternatives for a corporate project, the work of the Office of Community Service Learning at the University of Michigan came to my attention. Though this office knew of no individual local agency needing the writing skills of the 30 to 40 students in a section of Practical English, the staff were able to formulate a list of 12 community service agencies that had writing needs and from which small groups within a Practical English section could choose. These agencies, all near campus or on the city bus line, included the county child care network, a tutoring program, two teen crisis centers, a shelter for battered women, the state Department of Social Services, the local chapter of the American Red Cross, a network for low-income youth, a prisoner reintegration agency, an anti-racist education office, and an agency for women re-entering the job force in midlife.

The Office of Community Service Learning provided a brief description of the written work needed at each agency as well as the name and number of a person who had agreed to serve as liaison. These established agencies, it should be noted, deal with clear-cut social needs in the community and are not significantly oriented toward student internships in writing. But because students would not be doing their writing assignments at the agency sites, less agency supervision would be required than with some other forms of service-learning. The situation was nearly ideal for a first run at community service learning for an advanced writing course.

A Study of the Effects of Service-Learning

In the first term that I tried community service learning, I was teaching two sections of Practical English and decided to investigate whether writing as service-learning enhanced the level of academic engagement amongst my students. The syllabi of the two sections I studied were identical in content except that the control section did a standard self-initiated independent corporate project and the experimental section was broken up into small groups to write for nonprofit agencies. There were 32 students in the control group and 30 in the experimental group.

In *both* sections the students followed the curriculum described above. They completed the demanding series of classroom assignments, including writing memos, letters, critical analyses, reviews, summaries, press releases, and other forms commonly used in business and professional life. Also in both sections, students participated in class sessions on techniques for writing improvement and worked with four-person editing groups for intensive revision and peer evaluation.

In the *control* section I asked each student to come up with a proposal for a whole-class corporate project. Students then narrowed down proposals in their editing groups and eventually settled on one class project: a booklet on campus life targeted at first-year students. Unable to agree on one subject for this booklet, the class decided to be all-inclusive, dividing themselves up into committees by interest to research and write segments on restaurants and night spots in town, housing possibilities, computer and library resources, campus organizations, medical and dental services, and museums and theaters.

For the *experimental* section the four-person editing group also served as the community project group, and each editing group wrote a proposal bidding on the agency the members preferred. The class then decided to run a lottery to see which editing group would be assigned to which agency. There was some shifting and trading, but at the end of class each editing group had a community project from the list. The agencies required several different kinds of writing, including brochures, newsletters, grant proposals, and letters to potential donors.

The structure was well suited for outcomes comparison. Students in both sections had the same instructor, the same syllabus of assignments, and the same method of determining grades—primarily by student peer evaluation. The student demographics of the two sections were very similar. The only difference between the sections was the nature of the outside writing project.

Results of the Study

With the assistance of the University's Center for Research on Learning and Teaching and the Office of Community Service Learning, I modified the standard machine-read questionnaire used for course evaluation so that it focused more on service-learning issues. I found that student ratings of the course and of the instructor were nearly identical in the two sections (both about 90th percentile) but that, statistically, the students who did service-learning writing projects had significantly higher ratings for the following items:

- Class meetings are stimulating and informative
- I create my own learning experiences in connection with the course
- I learned to tailor my writing to demands of external groups
- I can now apply academic learning to real world situations
- Written assignments make students think
- I reconsidered many of my former attitudes
- I developed greater awareness of societal problems
- I became interested in community projects related to the course

It is noteworthy that the median scores for 18 of the 20 items favored the community service writing group.

Another measure of the effectiveness of the service-learning writing projects was the grades, which were assigned mainly on the basis of peer assessment. The average grade for the two sections was virtually the same— just below B+. Service-learning students' learning about writing did not suffer because they happened to be involved in writing for community agencies.

In written evaluations the majority of students were enthusiastic about service-learning:

> *"I was glad that Prof. Crawford saw the importance of implementing community service learning as a part of English 329. I have since become quite involved in other aspects of volunteerism at the agency."*

> *"The community project was good for leadership skills, insight*

into group process, writing skills."

"Please continue the community service projects. Some may do this after the term ends."

"Students are constantly being asked to use their minds rather than letting the professor do their thinking for them."

"The community project helped us utilize our collective writing skills and styles."

Problems with Community Service Writing

The experimental section, though generally satisfied by their service-learning, also had frustrations:

- One of the eight editing groups reported having great difficulty getting in touch with the contact persons at the community agency. A month into the term, they asked for permission to work on an alternate service-learning project: editing an endangered species update brochure that a group member knew about. The class and I approved, and this editing group's booklet of interviews with professionals around the country in natural resources was submitted to the University of Michigan's School of Natural Resources.

- A second group never was able to gather adequate material for a social service agency brochure because of the director's very busy schedule. This group finally did a mock-up based on what information they had, leaving space for the agency to add information. We discussed in class the consequences of poor communication and the lack of perfection in many work situations.

- Another editing group's contact person at a health agency gave the students instructions for writing flyers only to discover that her supervisor would not approve the format of the completed work. Two-thirds of the way through the term, this editing group had to start again, but they did rewrite the flyers to the agency supervisor's satisfaction.

- The group that worked with an anti-racist center on campus found that some of the political views expressed by the center were more radical than their own. The material they submitted was edited by staff at the center, but the final brochure was acceptable to both the center and the students. The students learned that even well-written material can be altered by the boss, and they defined the line that they would not cross in maintaining their personal beliefs.

- Two groups complained that there was unequal distribution of work. This problem, which is endemic to any multi-learner classroom project that encourages independence, was discussed in class and in my office.

I encouraged students to confront the issue squarely in their groups, and I assured them that I knew who was slacking and who was working. My undocumentable impression is that slacking occurs less in small-group community service learning than in a whole-class corporate project.

- After the term, I discovered that two groups (which had created attractive brochures for a child care network and a teen crisis center, respectively) had failed to submit their final product to the community agency, even though they had submitted copies to me for course credit. I had to do some fast phoning and delivering to ensure that future service-learners would be welcome at these sites.

Refining the Service-Learning Guidelines

I was delighted by the student response to service-learning and believed that the problems were solvable with some minor adjustments. Because I saw service-learning as a highly effective means of teaching advanced writing and of preparing students for their lifetime roles in society, I made writing for nonprofit agencies a standard feature of my Practical English course, totally replacing the corporate project model. I learned several lessons from my first try at service-learning:

1. *Flexibility in agency assignment makes everyone happier.*

Since the most successful service-learning projects that came out of the comparison term were generated by editing groups that included a student who was previously a volunteer for that agency, I now allow students to group themselves as they choose for community service writing. I set the number of students at any one agency between two and six and present the list of preapproved agencies, giving a summary of the mission and writing needs of each. I also open up discussion about other agencies for which students may already do volunteer work, and then allow some class time for small-group meetings and for organizing groups by name on the blackboard. One student last term, for instance, knew that the county Council on Aging needed resource list updates. Another student had a relative at an international relief agency that needed volunteers to write grant proposals.

This process of choosing agencies may take part of two or even three class sessions, but I find that it is worth the time. When I allow students to group themselves by interest, there is much more enthusiasm about doing a good job. I still assign students to four-person groups for editing, but the community project groups are not identical with these (though they certainly may overlap). Students have, therefore, an assigned set of peers for editing of weekly assignments plus a self-selected set of peers for the community project. They can get writing feedback from both sets, as well as from the instructor—an arrangement that simulates in many ways the diverse groupings they might encounter in the workplace.

2. *Accountability is essential.*

I now hand out the following questions (Sigmon, 1990) to fix in students' minds the responsibilities borne by each partner in community service learning:

a. Who initiates the task to be addressed?
b. Who defines the task?
c. Who approves the methods used in doing the task?
d. Who monitors the daily or weekly task activities?
e. To whom is the server responsible in the community or agency?
f. Who determines when the task is completed satisfactorily?
g. Who benefits if the task is done well?
h. Who decides that a server doing a task should be withdrawn from the work?
i. Who owns the final product of a server's work with the community or agency?

In our class there could be one of seven answers to each of these questions:

- The service-learner (student in Practical English)
- The faculty member
- Office of Community Service Learning
- Staff members at the chosen community agency
- The director of the chosen community agency
- Those served by the agency; the community
- Other

In discussing these questions and answers in class, students need to be reminded that service-learning goes two ways: the agency gets writing done and students learn how to do that writing. When students themselves in their community project groups decide on accountability, they feel more bound to complete their service. They also move away from the notion that the agency contact is supposed to guide them each step of the way.

3. *Progress reports keep students on track and keep them thinking.*

In the comparison term, the first time I used service-learning, I did require occasional oral reports in class plus a written midterm report and a final portfolio of all materials produced from both the control and the experimental sections. As many experienced service-learning educators have found, however, the reflective element is what promotes learning and, eventually, civic responsibility in service-learning programs (Newmann, 1989). Students need to talk and write about the mission of each agency and about how the student work contributes. I now require a detailed timeline for community project work as soon as each group has made an initial contact. The student groups, in consultation with the agency, determine their parameters. From seeing the timelines, I can suggest refinements in content or length of the writing proposed. We then have mandatory weekly oral reports in class, a written midterm progress report, and a final portfolio.

When I presented in class the problem of final community projects not being turned in, my students suggested that I initiate a check, and I have adopted the plan they came up with. Each group prepares a letter to its agency, giving my phone number and asking if the writing agreed upon has been completed satisfactorily and submitted; I then mail these letters to the agencies near the end of the term. Students' grade reports are withheld if I receive a call from the agency that the written work was incomplete or unsatisfactory.

An Instructor's View of Community Service Writing

Service-learning has reinvigorated my teaching of Practical English. I was convinced long ago of the value of assigning writing that replicates the writing students would have to produce in business or professional life; the previous corporate-project model accomplished this. But when students write materials that will actually be used by the agency they are working with, they are much more careful than they are with a booklet of limited distribution or a skit with a limited audience. They find themselves seriously considering issues of tone or reading level as these relate to the language chosen for a brochure or letter. They attend more to grammar and mechanics of presentation. They also have, for their job-hunting portfolios, impressive materials that are in circulation. In the Winter Term of 1993, for example, my Practical English students produced:

- A donation brochure for the local chapter of the American Red Cross
- A volunteer recruitment pamphlet for a shelter for battered women
- A series of donation letters for a crack cocaine rehabilitation center for women and their children
- A publicity campaign for a children's hospital
- A history of a center for troubled teens
- A grant proposal for a hunger relief agency
- A legislative newsletter for the county child care network
- A series of brochures on community resources for the local Council on Aging
- A volunteer recruitment pamphlet for the state Department of Social Services

Students who have been accustomed to having the rules of each term paper spelled out for them suddenly find themselves figuring out, collaboratively, how to condense seven pamphlets on different types of donations into one simple pamphlet or how to organize information on current legislation at the national, state, and local levels into a comprehensible series of articles for a newsletter. Although the previous corporate-project model for Practical English sometimes also required such initiative, service-learning projects have the added accountability factor: what the students decide must be acceptable to the agency, not just to the students themselves or to the instructor. I insist that they try a draft before coming to me for help, and, indeed, most students relish the independence and the chance to integrate skills from other courses—marketing, sociology, art, journalism, organizational behavior.

The vast computer resources of the University of Michigan allow my students to produce high-quality brochures, newsletters, and flyers that some nonprofit community agencies could never afford otherwise. Agencies are presented with camera-ready copy of such materials. In addition, data banks of prototype letters, for example, can be created on disks that an agency's computer accepts, so that the writing can be accessed long after the service-learning term ends.

Although situations have varied, most agencies have invested a minimal amount of time each term (two to five hours) explaining their needs to students and have received, I believe, a reasonable amount of writing work from students in return. As agencies build up a trust of Practical English students from several terms of service-learning contact, liaison should be easier.

Service-learning students become aware of the load that nonprofit community agencies bear. They perceive quickly that they cannot expect the agency contact to coddle them through their assignment. They sometimes get deadlines shifted from under them or requirements changed. These are the situations that students will find in the workplace. Despite the inevitable frustrations, one of my service-learning students found his experience writing letters for a women's shelter so rewarding that he now wants to start a movement on campus to make a service-learning course or project mandatory for graduation. We'll see what comes of that idea. Meanwhile, my sections of Practical English have become even more practical.

Chapter 8

FIELD RESEARCH: A COMPLEMENT FOR SERVICE-LEARNING

Kathleen Daly

For close to 10 years I have been teaching Criminology, mostly at Yale University, and now at the University of Michigan. My criminology course, sociology 468, covers criminal law, theories and research on crime, and the operations of the criminal justice system. The course aims are (1) to be aware of the political and ideological dimensions of criminology and crime control, (2) to examine crime and justice across three sites (intimate violence, street crime, white-collar crime), (3) to appreciate differences in explanations of crime and responses to crime based on crime site, and (4) to understand the organizational features of the justice system and the moral dilemmas of punishment.

There are many possible community experiences students could have in criminology courses such as visiting prisons or half-way houses, riding around in police cars, working on a rape crisis hotline, or counseling in a shelter for battered women, any of which would enhance a student's engagement with the course material. One project I've assigned over the years is to conduct systematic observations of proceedings in a criminal court. Though no direct service is provided in this community learning activity, the research methodology described in this chapter may serve as a model for those courses seeking to combine community service learning with field research.

My aims for this project are twofold. First, I want students to see first-hand what happens in a criminal court. Most have never been inside a court; their only experience has been what they have seen on television. Second, I want students to learn how to systematically observe court decision-making and to compare what they find with published research on the courts. I stress that this is not an experiential project nor is it journalism. Rather, it is research project in which students are expected to observe, collect information, reduce and tabulate that information, and relate it to relevant readings.

It is essential to guide students with a clear protocol for how they should proceed (see project assignment in Appendix I). Few have ever conducted social research before; they do not know how to frame a research question nor how to pursue it in a field study. It is essential to instruct them in methods of data reduction since most have never constructed a table. Finally, and this can be the most difficult thing to convey, students must go into the field with some expectations about what they may find. Without some expectations, derived from previous research coupled with their own interests, they do not know what to look for, what to observe, and how to interpret their findings.

The criminal court observation project combines experience with structured modes of viewing and recording social phenomenon. In the Ann Arbor court, some students complained that the cases were "boring"—"it's all traffic, and all the cases are the same." These students yearned for some excitement, some adventure, perhaps more serious cases—what they're used to seeing on television as "the criminal court." I tell them that what they are seeing is what they should investigate: the routine practices of justice, the bureaucratic methods of disposing cases, the mundane. I suggest that there is drama in what seems to them to be boring or mundane cases. Imagine, I propose, that they were the defendant or the victim or the police officer in a particular case.

Larger sized city courthouses are ideal for this sort of project because the experience is more than just observing court cases. Students become acutely aware of the class and racial divisions between those prosecuted for crime and those dispensing justice. Those divisions are reproduced for them as observers (largely white and middle-class) documenting those prosecuted (disproportionately black and poor). When I have assigned this project to Yale students in New Haven, Connecticut, they said they were nervous walking into the courthouse and going through the metal detector; they were intimidated sitting in the public spectator area. For a moment, I think, they began to appreciate what it was like to be a defendant.

Although it is important to have a structured protocol, which describes the aims of the research project and sets forth specific expectations on the numbers of cases to gather information on, the project is open to student ingenuity and creativity. Some students interview prosecutors, defense attorneys, or bailiffs. It is important for the instructor to talk with the court's presiding judge to make sure he or she knows of the intended project, to find out what days are better for observations, and to iron out any potential organizational or scheduling problems. Court officials have always been helpful to me. I alert the judges when the students are coming to the courtroom; at times, the judges will invite students into chambers during a court recess. This allows the students to ask the judge why he or she handled a case in a particular way, and more generally, it demystifies the judicial robe.

I have found several readings particularly helpful in guiding the students through the research. One is an observational study of a New Haven district-level court (Mileski 1971), which focuses on race and offense charged, race and disposition, and judicial demeanor. Another reading is useful for analyzing judges' theories of punishment (Blumberg 1979: chapter 15), and a third is Packer's (1964) discussion of the dual model of criminal process ("crime control" and "due process"). Because women are no more than 15 percent of defendants, there are not enough women to do a solid gender analysis. But one angle to take is gender differences in the types of offenses charged and judicial demeanor toward men and women.

The court observation project and related lectures span about one-quarter of the course. The lecture material focuses on six major areas. First, I describe the organizational context of criminal justice by sketching the stages of justice system processing and what occurs at each stage. The stages are arraignment, the bail decision, the pre-trial period, the sentencing decision, and conditions of incarceration or probation. Second, I present the legal context of criminal justice by describing the phenomenon termed the "due process revolution." The revolution refers to a series of Supreme Court decisions that conferred federal constitutional protections to defendants prosecuted in state criminal courts. These decisions include Mapp v. Ohio (1961, the exclusionary rule), Gideon v. Wainwright (1963, state provided counsel for indigent defendants accused of a felony), Miranda v. Arizona (1966, to be advised of one's rights at arrest), and Argersinger v. Hamlin (1972, state provided counsel for indigent defendants accused of a misdemeanor). In presenting this material, I want students to become familiar with some legal history and terminology of criminal court process.

The third area, how justice gets done, contrasts the adjudicative ideal with what actually happens to defendants after arrest. The adjudicative ideal is the presumption of a defendant's innocence, a determination at trial of a defendant's guilt or innocence, and judicial care and deliberation in fixing the "right" punishment. I present statistics on court dismissal rates, the proportion of cases likely to go to trial, the conviction rate at trial, and the types of sanctions imposed. We then get behind the statistics by addressing questions such as, why is the dismissal rate high, what are the features of "solid" and "weak" cases, and why are most cases plea bargained?

In the fourth area, we examine the major theories of punishment and how each relates to different aims of the criminal justice system: to deter others who might offend (general deterrence), to change those who have offended (rehabilitation, special deterrence, social reintegration), to remove those considered dangerous from the community (incapacitation), to restore losses (restitution), and because it's right to punish those who offend (retribution). Here I have the students consider whether different theories of punishment are likely to be used toward different types of defendants and offenses (e.g., common crime versus white collar; intimate violence versus stranger violence).

Fifth, I present data on punishment disparity, by race and gender. I show how studies of the non-capital sentencing process are likely not to find race-based differences because of "sample selection bias" or a narrowing of the variability in cases. I introduce my research on gender disparity and why statistical studies find differences favoring women.

Finally, I describe the history of punishment policy and its shifting emphases from punishment to rehabilitation, and now, in the current period, back to punishment. The students learn of the different elements associated with the "individualized" and the "just deserts" models of criminal justice. The former is based on punishing and changing the person, while the latter is focused on punishing the crime with greater emphasis on equality of punishment.

I have taken some time to review the lecture areas since each can be developed in a student's court paper or could be used as a starting point for the court observations. Over the years I have taken some classroom time, but perhaps not enough, to push the students to consider how these areas relate to what they see in court. It's almost as if the world of the classroom and its theories stay in the classroom unless the instructor is vigilant in asking students to do some integration.

I do take class time to ask the students what they are seeing and learning from their observations. At times, their replies focus on particular cases or exchanges in the courtroom that interested them. I then try to frame that experience in light of previous research or theories we have been covering, e.g., what theory of punishment was the judge using in that case, and why did it differ in the next case? A second set of observations students make are of different judicial styles in interacting with defendants and managing the courtroom. Because one of the articles they read focuses on types of judicial demeanor, they compare how the judges differently handle the cases and treat the defendants (more below on this).

As frequently, the students want to know about procedure or court routines, e.g., what is a "bench warrant," what are the consequences of pleading guilty to a "minor in possession" (of alcohol) charge when they apply for a job in the future, or what does it mean to be adjudicated a "youthful offender" or to receive "accelerated rehabilitation?" They seem less interested in relating theories and research to what they see, and more interested in practical matters of their own legal standing in court or what certain legal categories mean. I have invited judges to class so that students can ask them questions about the law and their decision-making. The questions tend to focus on legal advice and protocol, rather than on what the judge's sentencing philosophy is and what theory of punishment is preferred. I can appreciate why students are more interested to grasp the legal terminology because there is much to learn and they want to understand what is going on. For some, the court proceedings move from one instance of "legal jargon" to the next. In listening to what it is they want to know, I can appreciate just why taking the next step—from observing what they see to theorizing or explaining it—can be so difficult for many of them.

There are two areas where they get tripped up doing the court research project. First, some do not know how to translate an idea—whether in a published article or in lecture—to a research question. Second, some do not know how to organize the data they collect into tables, to present and discuss their findings, and to know how to interpret them. I discuss each area and give excerpts of some fine students' papers.

Translating Ideas to Research Questions

One of the articles the students read is of observations in the New Haven criminal courthouse (Mileski 1971). The author describes the types of charges and the outcomes, the judicial demeanor and interactions with defendants, the presence of attorneys, and the role of race in the adjudication process. There are many possible research questions or hypotheses one could generate from the Mileski study for the court observation project. However, many students have difficulty translating a scholar's ideas into a guide for their own research. They will wonder, what will happen if my results do not come out the same way as the author's, or what if my hypothesis (e.g., that non-students are treated more harshly than students in the court) does not prove to be true? I reply by saying that any research finding is a "finding," whether or not it confirms an hypothesis, or whether or not it reveals the same result as another study. Most fundamentally, the students have to be shown how to approach the research: they have to go in with an idea about what they might expect to find. When I say this, a common response is, won't that bias my results? I respond that you cannot know what you're "finding" or "seeing" unless you have some idea of what you expect to see. If your expectations are not borne out, then you have one set of results; but if they are borne out, then you have another.

Moving from Observation to Data to Analysis

For most students, this is the first time they have ever collected their own data, constructed a table, and interpreted the results. I ask them to prepare a systematic data observation sheet to aid them in collecting information, and I give them examples of how to do this. Most only have a dim idea of the logic of this part of the assignment: they are used to taking notes on lined paper and have not thought about collecting information in other ways. The next step is taking their "raw data" and reducing it into tables. One week of discussion section is devoted to the technical questions of how to construct a table, and how to organize the data. It is helpful to have teaching assistants work with students on a one-to-one basis because many have questions. Finally, on the interpretation of the data, good student questions emerge about the validity of findings or inferences that they can draw. This stage can be the most exciting because the students begin to see the fruits of their reading and observation come together. They realize that the process of doing research is not an automatic enterprise of counting things and chunking out findings, but requires using critical interpretive judgment in relating their data to an initial set of questions, a theoretical stance, and previous research.

Because there is so much new for the students to learn in this project—from being in a criminal court for the first time to conducting their own research—I try to allay student anxiety and foster learning by maintaining a file of excellent papers from previous terms. I make these available in my office so students can read and learn from them. Student need models to see how research is done in order to grasp the pleasures of the research process.

Examples of Good Papers

I have received some terrific papers over the years and want to give a flavor of some of them. The most frequent opening line is something to this effect: the criminal court is "not like what I have seen on television" or it is "not like 'Perry Mason' or 'LA Law'." Drawing from Mileski (1971) students may analyze variation in judicial demeanor by identifying whether judges are good-natured, bureaucratic, firm, or harsh. For example, one student reported that "my findings for Judge E's courtroom are very similar to Mileski's: Judge E acted good-natured in 4 percent of cases, acted bureaucratic in 74 percent of the cases, acted firmly in 19 percent, and acted harshly in 4 percent." However, this student found that in analyzing the demeanor of another judge, the distributions were different: "Judge T acted good-natured in 17 percent of the cases, acted bureaucratically in 52 percent..." (J. Carson). In exploring Mileski's thesis that judges are more apt to lecture defendants harshly when the sanction is lenient, which is termed a "situational sanction," one student reported that for Judge T this did not occur: the judge "lectured defendants when he was angry" (E. LaMarca).

Another frequent research area is the role that race plays in the courtroom. The students often find race-based differences in the types of offenses charged (whites being more likely charged with public-order and alcohol violations; blacks being more likely charged with assaults and the more serious violations). Race is also analyzed with respect to whether the defendant pled guilty or not, whether the defendant had an attorney, and the type of sentences received. Here one student made connections among race, plea, and severity of the charge. He noted that "Mileski said that black defendants pleaded not guilty more often than white people, although she could not figure out why. [My findings were the same] and I think that since the majority of the felonies in my sample were committed by blacks, and since people will be more likely to plead not guilty when the charge against them is more serious, black defendants enter more not guilty pleas because they are accused of more felonies...The real question would thus become 'why are blacks accused of more felonies'?" (F. Jubb). Another student focused on the higher likelihood that white defendants had private attorneys and tried to address the question, "why were blacks not able to hire a private attorney" and the consequences of this for the quality of justice for black defendants (A. Armbruster).

Most striking to students is the routinization of justice. Here they can draw from Mileski (1971) and Blumberg (1979) on the rapidity of case processing and its highly predictable character. One student noted, "It's amazing that judges must actually be elected to office. It seems that so much of what they do is routine and repetitive, handling cases in an assembly-line fashion. People elect them in the name of 'law and order,' thinking they'll actually make a difference...but in actuality, the judge is just another cog in the machine, helping it to run smoothly" (F. Jubb). And another noted that "Before I even read [the Mileski] article I noted in my data sheets how routine, impersonal, and rushed the cases were. In many of the cases I saw, the proceedings were over before I had even recorded what the charge was...Sometimes during my observations I felt like I was hearing the same tape recorded message being played over and over again" (A. Harfeld).

From time to time I work with students who want to take on a more extended project. One year I worked with a small group of Yale students who wanted to examine what judges said in court on the day of sentencing and to relate judicial justifications to theories of punishment. In some jurisdictions, it may be possible to focus on family violence cases if these are scheduled in a way that students can accomplish the research. And in other jurisdictions, students can observe proceedings in a federal court, perhaps comparing them with proceedings in a state court. Some University of Michigan students have complained that if they study arraignment in the Ann Arbor court (as compared to preliminary examinations or sentencing) that the assignment is tedious and uneventful. Some wish to study the felony court, thinking it will be more exciting. Unless students are ready to take on a lot of extra work by spending many more hours in the felony court to gather material, it is not possible to entertain requests like these. I ask students to focus on the gathering of a sufficient number of cases for analysis, and to see in these routines the character of mass justice delivered in U.S. criminal courts.

Because a portion of my research is on the criminal courts, I share with the students what I am learning. In 1994 my book on the New Haven felony court will appear, and I can use material in it to encourage new types of student observations. The research focuses on how gender and race structure sentencing, and several chapters examine what is said in court on the day of sentencing (Daly, forthcoming).

To sum up, the student experience in the court observation project is of two sorts. First they go to a criminal court and observe the people being handled, the nature of their offenses, and how judges and other court officials respond. They see that the daily workings of the court depart from the adjudicatory ideal and the television or film dramas with which they are familiar. Second, they approach what they see in the court as a neophyte researcher. They try to relate what they see to what other researchers have seen and recorded, and they engage in the rudimentary processes of creating knowledge through gathering and interpreting their own data. The latter experience is the harder and more trying of the two. If the character of justice is elusive, making claims about it as a social researcher proves to be even more challenging.

NOTES

I want to acknowledge these students, whose work I cited in the text: Anne Armbruster, Jonathan Carson, Amy Harfeld, Frederick R. Jubb, and Erin LaMarca (all UM students 1992-93).

Appendix I

Criminal Court Observation Project

Introduction

I want you to conduct systematic observations of cases in a criminal court and relate your findings to other research. You will observe proceedings in the Ann Arbor 15th District Court, collecting information on cases in courtrooms 1, 2, or 3, depending on how the judge and calendar are assigned in any given week. The dispositional routines in the court are detailed below. In general, judges in this courthouse handle *all* arraignments, traffic offenses, and small claims. They also preside over preliminary exams for more serious offenses to go to Circuit Court, and they sentence those convicted of (or pleading to) misdemeanors. They handle both civil and criminal matters of a "less serious" nature.

Focus of observations: options and approaches

A systematic observational study requires a minimum number of cases or observations to make it worthwhile. For purposes of your research paper, we need to balance a sound research approach with a realistic amount of time you can spend observing the court's work. I see *three* potential sites or foci of data collection and analysis:

1. **Arraignment and traffic**—Collecting information on cases arraigned or pleas to non-criminal violations (in Ann Arbor, this is speeding and illegal possession of alcohol). [Estimated number of cases you are likely to get in each arraignment period varies from 25 to 50.]
2. **Preliminary hearings (bind over)**—Collecting information on the preliminary hearings (the "exams") that are heard on Wednesday mornings. These cases will likely be bound over to the Circuit Court to be tried or disposed as felonies. [Estimated number of cases on any Wednesday may be about 25.]
3. **Sentencings**—Collecting information on sentencings, which can take place on different days, depending on the judge. [Estimated number of sentencings for each time block may be about 40 to 50. During the sentencing time, there are also reviews of those already sentenced, numbering 40 to 50.]

In light of the varied number of cases for each site or foci of data collection, there can be no hard and fast rule for how many cases you need to get information on. Instead, as a minimum, you should spend *at least 5 hours in the court collecting observational data*. That will mean at least two or three trips to the courthouse: one to reconnoiter and to establish a way to collect observational information, and another visit (or, more likely, two other visits) to collect your observational data.

Expectations for the project

Depending on your site of data collection, your research will take different emphases. But in general, you want to collect the following information for each defendant called: sex, race or ethnicity, approximate age, charges, and how the case was handled. "How the case was handled" will depend on which court activity you are studying.

- If it's arraignments/traffic/violations, your focus is on *routine* processes, what's coming through the court, and what dispositions are made (often fines for illegal possession of alcohol or for traffic, with fine amounts varying by whether the charges will be dismissed or "stay on the record.") Collect information on at least 35 cases .
- If it's preliminary hearings, your focus is on the characteristics of defendants and the content of the offenses for which they are being charged; you will also see how the judge, prosecutor, and defense attorney interact with one another (adversarial or cooperative), and how witnesses or victims are involved in constructing the "seriousness" of the case. Finally, evidentiary matters can be important because in this proceeding, the judge is to decide if there is probable cause to bind the case over to Circuit Court. Collect information on at least 25 preliminary hearings.
- If it's sentencing, your focus is on the characteristics of the defendants, the content of their offenses, their prior record, and the sentences they receive. Here you may be interested to see how defendants elect various options in serving their sentence, and what theory of punishment the judge is using. Collect information on at least 35 sentencings.

Creating a systematic observation sheet

The best way to record information on defendants and their cases is to create an observation sheet with coding categories in place (sex, race/ethnicity, type of charge, how disposed). If cases are moving quickly, an observation sheet ensures accurate and efficient recording of what took place. In addition to recording information on each defendant and how the case is disposed, observe and record other things that are going on in the courtroom.

Preparing to go to court

The categories of information in your observation sheet can be shaped from the readings, especially those by Chaudhuri and Daly (1992), Daly (1989), Cahn (1992), Blumberg (1967), Mileski (1971), and Heumann (1978). These possibilities are suggestive but not exhaustive of how you might proceed. Some approaches could be combined.

- You could study judicial styles in the courtroom, drawing from Mileski's typology of judges.
- You could focus on the prosecutor's role in court, using Heumann's article.

- You could use Blumberg's article and lecture material to characterize judicial theories of punishment in sentencing.
- You could focus on gender, race, class, age differences in the *content* of offenses, using Daly's article on white-collar crime as a point of departure.

The idea is that your research is guided by a set of questions raised in the readings, which you want to pursue in your observations.

Number of cases and data reduction

You should collect data on the number of cases suggested above, depending on the site you choose. The total information on the cases is your "raw data." To make sense of this data, you need to reduce it.

From your raw data, make tables showing the sex, race or ethnicity, age, charge, and disposition. You can get a good idea of how to prepare your tables by reading Mileski (1971). Data reduction is a key step in any research endeavor. For example, you may find interesting patterns emerging by comparing the race or ethnicity of defendants and theory of punishment used, or by gender and the type of offense charged.

Research on the arraignments will have more cases and thus more of a focus on tabular comparisons. Research on the preliminary hearings and the sentencings should have some tables, but it should also contain a bit more of the qualitative information that cannot be easily contained in coding categories.

Recapping the steps to take

Read Mileski (1971) and think about what kind of observations you want to make. Read the other articles relevant to what you think you'd like to focus on. Go to the court and get a feel for the kind of observations you'll be able to do and how best to record information. Construct an observation sheet, and then go to court for your days of observations. Assemble your data and reduce it. Relate your data to the themes in the articles and lectures. Compare your findings with those of other authors.

Assembling the paper

Your research paper should have these sections roughly in this order:

1. **Introduction**—What you plan to do and why; a brief sketch of the court's work. Give the reader a feel for the atmosphere of the court.
2. **Methods**—How you collected the information, including the observation sheet you used (describe it and put a blank copy of it in an Appendix) or other ways in which you collected data (e.g., talked with a court worker or defendant).
3. **Results and Analysis**—Summarize the cases you observed; profile the defendants and the disposition of their cases. In this section, you will refer to your tables. In analyzing your data, you should have these questions in mind: If someone were reading this paper, who had never

been in this court, what should they know? What's important? What's interesting? What's disturbing? What, in short, are the contours of "justice" in this court?

4. **Discussion**—This section will extend on your analysis, but take it a step further. You should integrate or compare your findings with those of the relevant authors or lecture material. The point is to make some summary statements and interpretations of what you saw, or to raise questions about the nature of justice.

5. **References**
6. **Tables and Appendices**

Chapter 9

WOMEN IN THE COMMUNITY: A COURSE IN SOCIAL CHANGE

Christina Jose Kampfner

Background

The Women's Studies course described below integrates service practicums in the community with a classroom experience based in social theory. "Women in the Community" focuses on gender issues in community organizing, and demands both intellectual as well as hands-on political engagement. It provides students with the opportunity to participate in community building and activism, while offering a forum through which students can process their ideas and create practical theory.

I came to academia after years of working in the community. In fact, my commitment to community work was a large part of why I chose teaching for my career. I knew that I would be able to combine the pleasure that I took in interacting with people and building communities with an explicitly political agenda. Thus, when I began teaching 14 years ago, it was natural for me to link theoretical teachings with student community learning.

When my teaching career began, I was quickly reminded that the confines of a classroom not only restricted the physical movement of my students, but also their potential to grow and learn as both thinkers and doers. As a student at the University of Michigan I had felt that my learning was constrained by the almost exclusively theoretical bent of my courses. This orientation was at odds with my own life experience working in communities in Mexico and the United States. I now know that most of my professors did not have the community involvement background necessary to value the use of a practical component in their courses. Having first hand experience in the community is necessary to competently develop and teach a course that links students' experiences and intellectual pursuits.

When students learn theory at the same time that they are applying it, the learning registers through all of their senses. The students remember the impact of their work in the community, and the personal theories that they produced as part of that work. They remember the environments which they helped to create, the look and the sound of the people that they interacted with and learned from, the way they felt about their experience. These sensory stimuli not only leave long-term imprints on the students' minds, but also give meaning to the theoretical knowledge that they are both studying in class and developing in their service experiences.

Course Structure and Process

Women's Studies 350, "Women in the Community," is a four credit course. Students spend at least eight hours a week working at their community placement and devote significant time to reading academic articles and books (see Reading List, Appendix I). Experience and theory are integrated in this course in order to create a learning environment which has real benefits both for students and for local communities.

The community internship experience provides an opportunity to: 1) explore the application of women's studies to work in the community, and examine the interplay between experience and theory, and 2) develop skills for working effectively within the community on issues and situations that concern and affect women.

These internship goals are set in the broader context of the following course goals:

- to develop an understanding of women's lives within a community: their roles, options, problems, resources, and contributions.

- to examine policies, leadership, and action strategies among women that can improve women's situations.

- to determine how organizational and community dynamics affect women's ability to participate and be effective in community organizations, work settings, and policy development.

- to identify and practice ways to apply knowledge gained in this and other Women's Studies courses within the community, work settings, and policy development settings to enhance the ability to provide leadership in these settings in the future.

- to work with other students and the instructors to create a class environment that encourages the productive exchange of ideas and experiences.

This class meets once a week for three hours. Participation in the class is emphasized, and the students are expected to talk extensively about their experiences in the field and to use course pack readings to reflect on those experiences. In addition, the students keep a journal and write three 10 page papers. They submit their journals five times during the semester and they are returned with comments and questions.

Social theory about gender, race, economic status, and power is integrated into every class discussion; in this way students learn to analyze and assess organizational behavior through these social matrices. They have an opportunity to study the impact of human difference without simply recognizing the traditional "other" as different; they think about how affluence affects upper class communities as well as how poverty affects poor communities.

Along with lectures, the classroom sessions include guest speakers. The instructor invites local community organizers, business women, community women, community advocates and others, each of whom shares her life history, her victories and defeats working in the community, and the ways in which her experience has been shaped by being a woman. These presentations bring students face to face with people who have many different perspectives on the issues addressed in the course. Students have a chance to see the ways that women activists use theory to guide their practice as well as how they produce theories from their experiences.

In the first session the students are given a list of about 25 possible placements. The instructor has previously contacted the agencies to pave the way for students to arrange their placements. The students choose 3 or 4 possible sites to contact. They then interview at each agency selected and decide their preferred placement. The agencies range from non-profit groups which work with and for women, to corporations and foundations with "service" components. Although students are encouraged to choose a non-profit agency, the final decision is between the student and the agency.

During the second week of class the students are trained for their agency interview. The students who have had any prior interview experience help teach those in the class who have never interviewed before. This exercise begins the building of a classroom-based self-help community. In the interview exercise, students begin to perceive each other as resources. As students with experience help those in need of further training, the students begin to understand the non-hierarchical and mutually supportive nature of the class.

By the third week all of the students are required to have finalized a placement. The course instructor follows up these decisions with letters to the agencies and personal phone calls to the contact persons to make sure that they understand that the students are there to both serve and learn. The course instructor explains that the students should not be typing or photocopying, but instead, learning as much as possible about the agency's organization at the same time that they are making a contribution.

In each class meeting, the first 30 minutes are dedicated to talking about placements. Students share their experiences and help each other with ideas and possible solutions to problems that come up in their field work. Problems that arise for students are usually resolved by the student on their own or with strategic assistance from their peers and the instructor. However, if a problem persists, the instructor will contact the supervisor to discuss the situation. Suggestions from classmates about how to deal with site issues and problems have proven to be of considerable importance to the success of many placements.

After the fourth week students divide into groups, and are instructed to learn about the broader community of Ann Arbor, the community *outside the University*. Interestingly, although many in the class have been living in Ann Arbor for two or three years they do not know much about the city beyond the borders of the campus. The students are asked to go to City Hall, the Public Library, to the wealthy and middle class neighborhoods, to poor neighborhoods and public housing projects. They are encouraged to walk through different areas of the city and to talk to residents whenever possible. These groups then bring back their impressions of Ann Arbor to the classroom, and the class discusses the different experiences that each group has had.

This assignment serves two purposes. First, and most apparent, students observe socioeconomic differences in Ann Arbor which were, in most cases, previously invisible to them. They see, first hand, who has power in the city, with whom one talks to get things done, and which communities are relatively enfranchised and which disenfranchised. They learn how to present issues to the City Council and who on City Council is responsive to which groups. Through these observations they gain insight into the way that power functions in this city.

Second, and less apparent, they learn first hand how individual opinions and attitudes shape and are shaped by group and community experiences. Students learn how other members of their own group impacted the ways in which they understood the city, and the ways in which their individual contribution to the group impacted the group's experience. By comparing their insights with the insights and observations of other groups of students in the class, they come to learn about influence. Students then write about this group experience.

A key aspect to this class is students' involvement in teaching their peers. Each week, a group of three students is responsible for presenting the readings to the class and facilitating discussion. Each group meets with the instructor a few days before the class for which it is responsible. Together, the instructor and students develop an outline of discussion topics for the class meeting and a process for creating a supportive atmosphere for the production and development of ideas. The class outline always allows for using race, gender and class factors to analyze classmate's experiences and the experiences of the people with whom they work.

Participation in the classroom is of paramount importance so that students can sharpen their ideas, produce new ones, and develop a supportive community of peers. It is important for the instructor to be available to students, and for her to facilitate the process of learning. For the most part, students dive into this part of the course with enthusiasm.

In addition to the paper based on their group experience in the community, a second paper facilitates their analysis of the particular organization in which they are placed (see Appendix II). It is an opportunity to bridge what they are learning about in their community placement with classroom learning. The final paper is an analytical portrait of the person they admire the most within their placement agency. It enables students to look critically at the difficulties most community workers and organizers, especially women, face in their job.

Evaluating the Student Placement Work

At the beginning of the course, each student creates a contract with her agency which outlines the expectations that they have for each other. This contract functions as a written commitment to the program for both the student and the agency at which she will work. The instructor maintains a placement file for each student which includes the student's statement of her learning goals, the student's placement contract, a mid-term evaluation done by the placement supervisor, a mid-term evaluation that the instructor and the student do together, and a final evaluation prepared by the student of the supervisor and the course instructor. 40% of the final grade is based on the student's service effort.

Impact

The students have been very successful in their placements around the city of Ann Arbor. According to agency supervisors they have contributed to the agencies in many ways. Several non-profit organizations have reported that they could not have accomplished their immediate or even long-term goals without the help of their student. Agency placement supervisors have consistently reported that their relationship with their students are both positive and constructive, and that they believe that the enthusiasm and creativity of the students seems to be greatly enhanced by the supportive environment created in the classroom.

The students' evaluations at the end of the course have been very positive. Ninety percent of the students have said that this was "the best course [they had] ever taken." Many comments speak to the depth of their new understanding about community organizations. For example, one student explained, "I learned through real experience how difficult it is to work in an organization, and how conflict resolution skills are very important for a community organizer!"

In their evaluations the students talk about having been profoundly changed by their experience. As one student explained, "My career goals have changed. Now I know what I want. Without my placement I could have not found out my real interest in life." Another student said, "This placement has opened my eyes to the needs of women, the need for organizing and the difficulties in doing so."

Furthermore, many students have said that this class changed the way that they understood and experienced the city of Ann Arbor. These students explained that they had become much more aware of the power dynamics which shape the city. One student wrote, "Ann Arbor's a rich town segregated by race and socioeconomic status."

For many of the students the service aspect of this course has a secondary benefit. Students have used their experience to find out what field they wanted to go into and to understand the difficulties of their choice. Students have obtained recommendations and connections in the community which have led to summer job offers. One student went as far as to become the director of the agency where she was placed. Although career exploration is not a course objective, it appears to be an outcome for many.

Instructor's Reflections

The students often complain at the beginning of the term that the reading assignments are very demanding. Nonetheless, over time they come to see the value of learning the theory as a framework for analyzing their placement experience. The students find their journals useful and have reported that this kind of writing helps them to sort out their ideas and feelings about their field placements.

One of the harder course tasks for students is the creation of a supportive "community" in the classroom. Students have difficulty with the compromises that are part of any community, especially ones which attempt to work together for change, as well as the role of group dynamics and individual personalities and opinions in the development of a community.

Similarly, students have consistently reported that the most difficult assignment has been the group project in the community. This is not surprising. We are all socialized with a strong dose of individualism, and this works against working in small groups toward a single goal as well as building community in the classroom. But this lesson is very important—how difficult it is to work with people with different backgrounds, in particular, different socioeconomic backgrounds, toward a common goal. In order to make the pain of this experience worthwhile, it is important for the instructor to facilitate the groups and the class with care and sensitivity, taking time to reflect with the students on the experience. If not, the result is that students may be angry with each other.

I believe that the course would be greatly improved if the students had access to transportation so that they could be placed in agencies outside of Ann Arbor. The issues surrounding working with people from different socioeconomic backgrounds and ethnicities are not found as often as I would like in many of the agencies with which students work in Ann Arbor. With transportation, students could participate in programs in other communities which are not as privileged. These wider placements would better help students to think about how gender interfaces with race and class, and how gender definitions alter in different contexts and among different communities.

Conclusion

A class which marries activism with theoretical readings and discussions brings both of them alive. Instead of feeling removed from social theories, students see theory in action as well as produce their own social theories. And, instead of feeling removed from the community, students are directly involved in community work.

Because students learn social and organizational theory in connection with their activist experiences, the theory means something much more profound to them. By participating in community work as well as reading theories about organizational practices students discover new ways of thinking about service work and of implementing social change. Their efforts to challenge their previous conceptions of power in society and to open their minds to more creative thinking about the effects of race and gender on access to community resources are inspirational to witness.

This course is extremely popular; enrollment reaches capacity within the first two days of a two week registration period. This popularity is indicative of the need for this kind of class among students. Active and politically aware students clearly lack the necessary channels through which they can integrate their community activism experiences with theories relevant to those experiences. It is my hope that some day more courses like this one can be offered, providing a variety of community and political experiences for young activists.

Appendix I

Course Syllabus

Week 1: Introduction to the Course and Each Other

Week 2: Creating a Feminist Experiential Learning Environment

Rich, Adrianne, "Taking Women Students Seriously," *On Lies, Secrets and Silences*. NY: Norton, 1979.

Fisher, Bernice, "What is Feminist Pedagogy?," *Radical Teacher*, 1-2: 22-24, 1980.

Crow, Ginny et al. "The Process/Product Debate," *Quest*, 4(4):15-36, Fall 1978.

Coover, Virginia et al. *Resource Manual for a Living Revolution*. pp. 140-143. New Society Publishers, 1981.

Avery, Michel et al, *Building United Judgment: A Handbook for Consensus Decision Making*. The Center for Conflict Resolution, 1981. pp. 61-68, 77-83.

Optional:

Bartholdi, Lizette, et al, "A Student Guide to Field Learning Experiences," *The Women's Studies Learning Handbook: From the Classroom to the Community*, Fisher & Reuben (eds), National Women's Studies Association, 1981.

Week 3: Becoming a Volunteer

Eugenie Bolger, "Take it Out of My Salary," *MS*, Feb. 1975.

Ellen Straus, "In Defense of Unpaid Labor," *MS* Feb. 1975.

Week 4: Methods of Analysis: Community and Organization

Brager G., et al, "The Community," *Community Organizing*, 2nd Edition, New York, Columbia University Press.

Riger, Stephanie, "Vehicles for Empowerment: The Case of Feminist Movement Organizations", *Prevention in Human Services*, Vol. 13, No. 2-3 pp. 99-117. 1983/84.

Pfouts and Renz, "The Future of Wife Abuse Programs," *Social Work*, 26(6):451-455, 1981.

Lauffer, Armand, "Your Agency as a Formal Organization," *Understanding Your Social Agency*, Beverly Hills: SAGE, 1984.

Alternative Institutions

Morgenbesser M., et al, "The Evolution of Three Alternative Social Service Agencies," *Catalyst*, No. 11: 71-82, 1981.

Freeman, Jo, "Crises and Conflict in Social Movement Organization," *Chrysalis*, No. 5: 43-51, 1977.

Week 5: Understanding Racism, Classism, and Heterosexism

Rushing, Donna, "The Bridge Poem," *This Bridge Called My Back*, Moraga and Anzaldua (eds), Watertown, MA: Persephone Press, 1981.

Ponce, Ellen, "Racism - A White Issue," *All the Women are White, All the Blacks are Men, But Some of Us are Brave*, Huss et al (eds), Old Westbury, NY: Feminist Press, 1982.

Cross, Tia et al., "Face-to-Face, Day-to-Day-Racism CR," *All the Women are White, All the Blacks are Men, But Some of Us are Brave*, Hull et al (eds), Old Westbury, NY: Feminist Press, 1982.

Corbett and Froschl, "Access to the Future: Serving Disabled Young Women," *The second mile:*

contemporary approaches in counseling young women, Davidson (ed), Tuscon, AZ: New Directions for Young Women, 1983.

Kanter and Stein, "The Trials of an O in a World of X's," *MS*, 9 (1), July 1980.

Rich, Adrianne, "Compulsory Heterosexuality and Lesbian Existence," *Women Identified Women*, Darty and Potter (eds), 1984.

Hood, Elizabeth, "Black Women, White Women: Separate Path to Liberation," *Feminist Frameworks*, Jaggar and Rothenberg (eds), NY: McGraw-Hill, 1984.

Witt, Shirley, "Native Women Today: Sexism and the Indian Woman," *Feminist Frameworks*, Jaggar and Rothenberg (eds), NY: McGraw-Hill, 1984.

Morrison, Toni, *"The Bluest Eye,"* 1974.

Klepfisz, Irena, "Anti-semitism in the Lesbian/Feminist Movement," *Nice Jewish Girls*, Beck (ed), Watertown, MA: Persephone Press, 1981.

Week 6: Women's Power and Status

Stamm and Ryff, "Introduction: An Interdisciplinary Perspective on Women's Power and Influence," *Social Power and Influence of Women*, Stamm and Ryff (eds), Boulder CO: Westview Press, 1984.

Johnson, Paula et al, "Women and Interpersonal Power," *Women and Sex Roles*, Frieze et al (eds), New York: WW Norton, 1978.

Bunker and Seashore, "Power, collusion, Intimacy-Sexuality, Support: Breaking Sex Role Stereotypes in Social and Organizational Settings," *Exploring Contemporary Male/Female Roles*, Carney & Mahon (eds), University Associates, 1977.

Cancian Francesca, "Gender Politics: Love and Power in the Private and Public Spheres," *Gender and the Life Course*, Rossi (ed), New York: Aldine Pub. Co., 1985.

Hagestad, Gunhild, "Women in Intergenerational Patterns of Power and Influence," *Social Power and Influence of Women*, Stamm & Ryff (eds), Boulder, CO: Westview Press, 1984.

Week 7: Relationships Among Women/Developing Support Systems

Bernikow, L., "Friends," *Among Women*, Bernikow, New York:Harmony Books, 1980.

Dill, Bonnie, "Race, Class and Gender: Prospects for an All Inclusive Sisterhood," *Feminist Studies*, 9(1): 131-150, Spring 1983.

Withorn, Ann, "For Better and For Worse: Social Relations Among Women in the Welfare State," *Radical America*, 18(4): 37-47, 1984.

Campbell, Bebe Moore, "Friendships in Black and White: Beyond the 'Some of My Best Friends Are...' Syndrome," *MS*, August 1983.

Lorde, Audre, "Scratching the Surface: some Notes on Barriers to Women and Loving," *Sister Outsider: Essays and Speeches*, Lorde, 1984.

Pescatello, Ann, *Female and Male in Latin America: Essays.*

Oshana, Maryann, "Native American Women in Westerns: Reality and Myth," *Frontiers: A Journal of Women Studies*, Fall 1981.

Week 8: Women's Roles Through The Life Course

Gilligan, Carol, *In a Different Voice.*

Rush, Florence, *The Best Kept Secret: Sexual Abuse of Children.*

Bem & Bem, "Homogenizing the American Woman: The Power of the Unconscious Ideology," *Feminist Frameworks*, Jaggar and Rothenberg (eds), New York: McGraw-Hill, 1984.

Sarri, Rosemary, "Family and Child Welfare Policy for Children of Single Parent Families: A Comparative View."

Ladner, Joyce, "Growing Up Black," *Tomorrow's Tomorrow: The Black Women*, 1972.

Lewin, Ellen, "Lesbianism and Motherhood: Implication for Child Custody," *Feminist Frameworks*,

Jaggar and Rothenberg (eds), New York: McGraw-Hill, 1984.

Hess, Beth, "Aging Policies and Old Women: The Hidden Agenda," *Gender and the Life Course*, Rossi (ed), New York: Aldine Pub. Co., 1985.

Jose-Kampfner, Christina, "Being Out of Your Existence: Women Serving Life in Prison."

Week 9: Economic Roles of Women

Kanter, Rosabeth Moss, "Work and Family in the United States," *American Families*, Douvan et al., (eds), Dubuque, IA: Kendell/Hart Publishing Co., 1980.

Ehrenreich and Stallard, "The Feminization of Poverty," *Feminist Perspectives on the Family*, 1982.

Quinney, Valerie, "Three Generations in the Mill," *Southern Exposure*.

Boston's Women's Health Collective, "Sexual Harassment," *The New Our Bodies, Our Selves*, New York: Simon & Schuster, 1984.

Stallard, K., & Ehrenreich, B., and Sklar, H. *Poverty in the American Dream: Women and Children First*. Boston: South End Press.

Week 10: Women as Leaders

Bunch, Charlotte, "Women Power: The Courage to Lead, the Strength to Follow and the Sense to Know the Difference," *MS*, 9 (1): 44-46, 95-97, July 1980.

Masterson, Lorraine, "Feminist Leaders Can't Walk on Water," *Quest*, 2 (4): 24-40, Spring 1976.

Alexander and Kerson, "Room at the Top: Women in Social Administration," *Leadership in Social Administration*, Perlmutter and Slavin (eds), Philadelphia, 1980.

Gilkes, Cheryl T., "Successful Rebellious Professionals: The Black Woman's Professional Identity and Community Commitment," *Psychology of Women Quarterly*, 6(3): 289-311, Spring 1982.

Bokemier and Tait, "Women as Power Actors: A Comparative Study of Rural Communities," *Rural Sociology*, 45(2): 238-255, 1980.

Bers and Mezey, "Support for Feminist Goals among Leaders of Women's Community Groups," *Signs*, 6(3): 737-748, Summer 1981.

Week 11: Activist and Community Roles

Hyde, Cheryl, "Voices of Women Activists," Manuscript, University of Michigan, April 1985.

Gittel and Naples, "Activist Women: Conflicting Ideologies," *Social Policy*, Summer 1982.

Gregory, Carole E., "Black Activists," *Heresies*, 3 (1): 14-17, 1980.

Combahee River Collective, "A Black feminist Statement," *Feminist Frameworks*, New York: McGraw-Hill, 1984.

Hollister et al., "On Organizing: A Simple Recipe for Social Change," *Michigan House of Representatives*, Spring 1979.

Hixson, Allie Corbin, "Organizing Rural Women," *Quest*, 4 (4): 64-72, Fall 1978.

Brightman, Carol, "The Women of Williamsburg," *Working Papers*, 6(1): 50-57, Jan/Feb 1979.

Fraser, Arvonne, "Insiders and Outsiders" Women in the Political Arena," *Women in Washington: Advocates for Public Policy*, Tinker (ed), Beverly Hills: SAGE, 1983

Bengamin, *Don't Be Afraid, Gringo: A Honduran Woman Speaks from the Heart*.

Week 12: Future Agendas for Women in the Community

Eichler, Margrit et al., "Strategies for the Eighties," *Perspectives on Women in the 1980's*, Turner and Emery (eds), University of Manitoba Press.

Boneparth, Ellen, "Strategies for the Eighties," *Women, Power and Policy*, Boneparth (ed), Pergamon Press, 1984.

Blakely, Mary Kay, "Are my Students Ready for Life?," *MS*, October 1983.

Gordon, Suzanne, "The Feminist Mystique," *Working Papers*, 8 (4): 61-64, 1981.

Searles and Follansbee, "Self-Defense for Women: Translating Theory into Practice," *Frontiers*, 8(1): 65-70, 1984.

Berkley Men's Center Manifesto

English, Deirdre, "The War Against Choice," *Mother Jones*, Feb/Mar 1981.

Erenreich, Barbara, "The Women's Movements: Feminist and Antifeminist," *Radical America*, 15(1-2): 93-101, Spring 1981.

Sanborn and Bird, "The Big Giveaway: What Volunteer Work is Worth," *MS*, Feb 1975.

Kaminer, Wendy, "Volunteers Who Know What's In It For Them," *MS*, Dec 1984.

Appendix II

Paper Assignment: Analyzing Your Organization[1]

Goals

1. To learn how to describe and analyze a "social system" by investigating your internship setting
2. To understand how your internship setting operates—its particular strengths and problems
3. To understand the presence and consequences of gender, race, class, age, sexual orientation, and disability within a social system
4. To integrate feminist and gender-sensitive concepts into a social system analysis

Task

In this assignment you will accomplish these goals by responding to the statements and questions in the following outline and then synthesizing that information into a 10 page paper.

Analysis Outline

I. Internal analysis of your internship setting:
    A. Goals:
        1. What are the formal goals of your organization? How did you find out about these formal goals?
        2. What are the informal goals of your organization? How did you find out about these informal goals?
        3. Do any of these goals potentially or actually conflict with each other? How do they conflict? What are the consequences of these conflicts?
        4. To what degree do these goals reflect feminist and "ism" sensitive concerns? To what degree do they conflict with these concerns of different oppressed groups (e.g. women, the disabled, older people, racial and ethnic minorities, gay men and lesbians)?
    B. Formal and informal structure:
        1. Formal Structure:
            a. Create a map of your organization which depicts the formal structure. The Lauffer reading may be helpful; however if your setting does not fit a hierarchical model you will need to be creative. Include any policy boards or committees that exist.
            b. Briefly describe the purposes of the positions (e.g. director, counselor, attorney, secretary) which exist in the organization.
            c. Identify which positions have authority, and the types of authority, within the setting according to the diagram.

2. Informal Structure:
   a. Depict the informal structure and influence system. You may use a diagram to indicate key groups and linkages.
   b. Who has the most influence in the informal structure? What accounts for their influence?
3. Interaction of the structures:
   a. To what extent is the informal structure and influence system compatible with the formal structure and authority positions?
   b. To what extent do the formal and informal structures reflect the formal and informal goals of the setting?
   c. To what extent do both the formal structure and authority positions and the informal structure and influence systems reflect the status of different oppressed groups?

C. Decision-making:
   1. What are the various kinds of decisions which are made in the organization? Who is responsible for making the decisions in these different areas?
   2. Select a particularly important decision in your setting. Describe how the decision was made (e.g. who initiated the process, who was involved, how much input was solicited, how was a final decision made, how was the final decision communicated to others).
      a. How were process and product issues addressed in this decision?
      b. How did this process affect and reflect the status of women and other oppressed groups differently? How did status affect the process used?

D. Rules:
   1. Give some examples of formal rules in your setting and what areas of behavior they address.
   2. Give some examples of informal rules. How are they conveyed to others?
   3. How would you place your organization on a continuum from very formal (lots of written rules) to very informal (no official rules)?
   4. What do the pattern of these types of rules suggest about issues and areas that are important or problematic in your setting? How is this related to the gender composition of the organization?
   5. To what extent do the pattern of rules reflect feminist and other concerns relating to class,race, and social status?

II. External analysis of your organization:
   A. Constituencies and beneficiaries:
      1. Who are the identified constituencies of your organization?
      2. Who actually benefits from its work?
      3. To what extent do constituencies and beneficiaries overlap or conflict with each other?

4. Selecting one group of beneficiaries or constituents, where and how do staff interact with them? How is this group served? To what extent is this group involved in the functioning of your organization?

5. To what extent are specific oppressed groups represented as beneficiaries or constituents? Are specific groups overrepresented or underrepresented? What groups are left out all together? Why might this be?

B. Resource acquisition:

1. Identify all of the external resources sought by your organization. Why are they needed and what functions do they serve?

2. Select one type of resource and describe the process used to identify, secure, and use the resource. Identify all positions and individuals involved. Discuss the costs and benefits of the resource, including any requirements placed by the contributor.

3. How does the acquisition of resources reflect the situation and status of different oppressed groups within Ann Arbor?

C. Environmental networks:

1. Draw a diagram indicating the key components of the environment for your organization. The Lauffer article provides an example of a diagram you can use. In the diagram indicate the nature of environmental exchanges. They can be represented by the following symbols: < - or- > indicate conflict; and -/ /- could indicate a terminated exchange. Be sure to include a key which explains your symbols.

2. What positions are responsible for managing each of these exchanges?

3. How do the nature of these exchanges differ for different oppressed groups in Ann Arbor? How is this a reflection of different status, types of contact between groups, and discrimination?

D. Alliances and Competitors:

1. Identify the groups, agencies, and organizations with which your setting cooperates. Select one of these settings and describe the nature of the relationship. What are the reasons for the cooperation? What are the outcomes or consequences? What are the costs and benefits? What position in your organization "manages" this relationship?

2. Identify the groups, agencies, and organizations with which your organization competes. Select one of these competitive settings and describe the nature of the relationship. What are the reasons for the competition? What are the outcomes or consequences? What are the costs and benefits?

3. How do these competitive and cooperative relationships affect the members of oppressed groups? How do they affect members of other groups?

    E.   Regulators and Legitimators:
1. List the various legal requirements which your setting must satisfy in order to operate.
2. Choose one of these requirements. What position is responsible for making sure that it is met? What community agent mandates this requirement? What purpose does it serve? What happens if it is not met?
3. To what extent do these requirements further or interfere with the interests of the oppressed groups in our community?

Paper Assignment Instructions

Based on your answers to the questions above, write a 10-page paper incorporating the following:

I.   Briefly describe, in 1 to 2 pages, your organization: its goals, formal and informal structure, rules, constituencies and beneficiaries, resources, networks, alliances/competitors, and legitimators.

II.   How have external relationships influenced the internal activities or structure of your organization?

III. What different formal and informal roles do members of oppressed groups play in your organization?

IV. What do you now see as the major strengths and weaknesses of your organization? What does it do well? What could be improved?

V.   Select a few of the weaknesses you identify. What recommendations would you make to increase effectiveness, and decrease problems in your organization?

VI. To what extent do the internal and external environments of your organization help or hinder the interests and needs of different groups in the community? What are the costs and benefits of addressing the needs and issues of some groups while ignoring the needs of others?

VII. What are the key things you learned in this exercise?

NOTE

1. This paper assignment has been developed and revised over the years by a number of instructors of this course.

Chapter 10

TAKING OVER THE REINS: SERVICE PROJECTS IN ENVIRONMENTAL STUDIES

Lisa Bardwell and Shannon Sullivan

Introduction

> The secret message communicated to young people today by society is that they are not needed, that the society will run itself quite nicely until they—at some distant point in the future take over the reins. Yet, the fact remains that the society is not running itself nicely, and indeed there may be little of value left for them to take over in the future, unless we reconceptualize the role of youth in the social order...the rest of us need all the energy, brains, imagination and talent that young people can bring to bear on our difficulties. For the society to attempt to solve its desperate problems without the full participation of even very young people is imbecile.
>
> Alvin Toffler, *Future Shock*

> Every now and then, I get so frustrated and feel nothing can be done. I might as well swig a Budweiser...and join the rest of society to hasten our demise.
>
> Student, Environmental Studies, 1990

Toffler's statement is particularly relevant to the problems we face with the environment. Many of these problems call out for the attention and concern of us all. Ironically, the typical approach to environmental issues in the classroom focuses so much on the enormity of the problems that students often see them as beyond repair. We lose "the energy, brains, imagination and talent that young people can bring to bear" to the anger and hoplessness reflected in the student's quote above.

We have had first hand exposure to these student feelings while coordinating a large lecture course on environmental issues.[1] Consequently, we incorporated a community-based project into the course as a way to counteract that discouragement and to provide students with the opportunity to begin to "take over the reins."

The Original Course Design

Environmental Studies 320 is a survey course providing an overview of environmental issues with an emphasis on their human dimension. The primary objective is to help students become more ecologically literate: to be able to think critically, to know how to find and evaluate information, and to understand the historical, social, and political dimensions of environmental issues. While the class addresses some scientific aspects of the environment, it focuses on how history, literature, and the social sciences contribute to our understanding of environmental concerns.

Traditionally, the course has included weekly lectures and small group discussion sections. Each lecture is presented by a guest speaker—perhaps a representative from a car company, a nuclear engineer, a forester, a poet, or an anthropologist—each of whom brings his/her expertise to some aspect of the environment (see Appendix I). During the lecture period, students have ample time to engage the presenters, actively exploring and challenging the assumptions of the speakers, themselves and their peers.

During the weekly discussion sections, which are designed and run by one of three teaching assistants (TA's), students have an additional chance to react to and discuss the lectures and related issues. Often, the students themselves are responsible for bringing in materials and facilitating the class discussion. Although the TA's share assignments and meet regularly to discuss ideas for class, each section bears the mark of the individual teacher.

One of the underlying objectives of the course assignments is to encourage students to take responsibility for their own learning. Not only does this approach reflect our educational philosophy, it also implicitly communicates our goal for having students "take over the reins." Therefore, the primary assignment has been written critiques of each lecture and of a related article that students find on their own in the library. In addition, we have encouraged involvement outside of class, e.g., to attend related lectures on campus and in the community, to join student environmental groups, to initiate their own environmental effort, and/to continue in their environmental studies.

Shortcomings of the Course:
The Birth of the Community Project

Every year, after a few lectures, students begin to realize the complexity of environmental issues. They discover that there are few "right" answers or shared and certain "facts," and recognize that many decisions reflect social and political values and priorities more than scientific objectivity. When we first taught the class, we expected students to be somewhat frustrated, but took faith in the educational value of their struggles.

Nevertheless, the depth of the students' discontent was troubling for the instructors. We were struck by how depressing the class mood seemed, and at the emotional intensity of the students' voices. In their journals, they wrote of the anger, helplessness and despair brought on by their new knowledge of environmental issues. In the face of enormous and seemingly intractable global problems, this response was difficult to lay aside.

Much of the helplessness people feel about environmental problems comes from the perception that these problems are both huge and distant. These perceptions make it difficult to identify a means of having an impact. Without feeling one can make a difference, concern is translated into despair. In learning about *global* environmental issues, many students fail to see the impact they might have on a smaller scale.

Realizing this, we looked to community-based environmental projects as a way to channel students' energy from interest to action. The projects serve two purposes: first, they encourage students to think about environmental problems on a local scale, and second, they provide a concrete outlet for resolving student frustrations, changing *knowing about* environmental issues to *knowing how* to respond to them in a way that matters.

The Community Projects

The first effort at community projects in Environmental Studies was a mid-course alteration. As the term progressed in Fall 1991, student frustration in the class was high. In response to requests for ways they could "do something," we piloted a community project assignment. Students were asked to work in small groups to address an environmental issue on which they thought they could have an impact.

Although the assignment was somewhat ad hoc and constituted a small part of the course, the response was astounding. Students put in time and energy far beyond that required by the instructors. They produced recycling brochures for their dorms and fraternities; they developed environmental education programs for elementary schools; they made a video infomercial about endangered species. Even students who previously had shown little investment in the class came through with surprisingly good efforts.

The following year, using action-research and Bill Stapp's community problem-solving model as frameworks[2], we developed a format for systematically integrating projects into the course. We were hopeful that community projects would make the class less frustrating and more meaningful. More importantly, we wanted the students to use their knowledge and develop their skills to address an issue that mattered to them.

In designing the project assignment, we provided some structure, but encouraged students to generate their own ideas—from topic to strategy to evaluation. In discussion sections, brainstormed project ideas were listed on the board. The students then milled about, congregating around ideas on which, and people with whom, they would be interested in working. While these sessions were a bit chaotic, they encouraged the sharing of ideas and enabled students to feel that they had freely crafted both their project idea and group membership.

The instructor-imposed criteria were that the projects be relevant to the course, feasible within the time frame (five weeks), and that they not be recycling projects (which had been the default option the year before and of lower quality than other projects). During the next five weeks, students worked together, met with their TAs as needed, and often used part of discussion section to share their progress with other students. In the last lecture session, a number of the teams gave brief presentations of their projects.

Structuring the Community Projects

By the time in the term that we started projects, students were already familiar with approaches to "fact-finding." We provided class time and materials to help them focus on some skills related to problem-solving, action-taking and team-building that we felt would contribute to successful team efforts. The following is an outline of our educational objectives for the projects, and some of the means by which we helped students achieve successful environmental projects:

1. **Problem-solving:** When faced with a problem, most students (indeed most people!) tend to latch onto a solution and start strategizing how to implement it. Much more is involved in good problem-solving. We provided structure to the project planning so that students would:
   —identify the problem or issue they wanted to address
   —articulate their goals, what they wanted to achieve and why
   —look at alternative approaches and the potential implications of those strategies
   —identify the assumptions underlying their choice
   —evaluate their efforts as they went along

2. **Action-taking:** We asked the groups to provide:
   —a rationale for the problem they selected
   —reasonable expectations of what they could accomplish given the constraints
   —a description of how this approach built on the strengths of the group
   —some thoughts on where they would find the additional resources they needed

   In discussing action-taking, we paid particular attention to:

   Time constraints and measures of "success." While we encouraged students to work through most of the kinks themselves, we tried to focus their efforts on something that was challenging but achievable. The aspirations of many far outshined what could happen in five weeks. We wanted students to realize that problems are ongoing, that change does not happen overnight, and that success is not defined only as "solving" the problem.

   Imagery. In discussion sections, the TAs offered information and worked with the entire class to generate a range of ideas.

   Political implications. We emphasized that taking action is political, and that the projects the teams chose had political implications. Students were encouraged to consider the assumptions about people and the political process that underpinned their choices, and to reflect on how their projects fit with their personal perspectives about social change.

3. **Team-building:** We discouraged individual projects, so that students would gain experience in a group effort. The assignment provided some guidance on role definition, and had students reflect on how well the team functioned and on how teamwork can impact an effort. The written component of the project was intended to encourage them to

practice and think about these skills.

Harvesting the Learning

At the beginning of the five weeks, students were given a project packet which contained a description of the assignment, a timeline for completing the assignment parts and worksheets to use during the various stages (see Appendix II). The packet allowed students to anticipate the scope of the project and plan ahead. It also facilitated monitoring and evaluation of the projects by the instructors. The students turned in:

A work plan. As a group, the students identified the problem they wanted to work on, their goals, their strategies and how they were going to accomplish them, the resources they needed and skills they had as a group, and their personal expectations of the project.

A progress report. Two and a half weeks into the project, the teams submitted a report to their TA on what was going well, what was going poorly, and how the team planned to proceed given the situation.

A final project wrap-up. This assignment included a brief description of the project and how the group approached it as well as any materials the group developed. The teams were to describe what they accomplished or found out; how they had tried to disseminate their results; what they would do differently next time; and what else could happen given more time, resources and/or effort.

An individual evaluation of the project team. Here, students had an opportunity to confidentially evaluate the team experience itself—how well the group worked together, how well each individual functioned in the group, and what each individual could see him/herself doing differently next time. The students assigned a letter grade to themselves and to each other person in the group.

Assessment: How It Worked Out for the Students

The students pursued community efforts that ranged in focus and level of activism. One team researched the University's use of herbicides and pesticides on the University grounds and their findings were published in the University's weekly newspaper. Another group tried to motivate coffeehouse managers to offer price reductions for customers bringing in their own mugs. Others prepared and conducted an activity on local endangered species for elementary school children. While some of their write-ups lacked the level of analysis and self-reflection we would have liked, student responses and evaluations indicated significant learning and enthusiasm.

Students felt they learned more than from lectures and readings alone. Many students echoed one's report, "By being able to decide for ourselves what the topic of our project would be, we were doing something that we really wanted to do and our interest was piqued. We learned by doing not by hearing. [This was] much better than just writing a paper and reading magazine articles. I learned a lot from this project and it wasn't boring at all."

They learned the value of perseverance, problem solving and flexibility.

Students' thinking had a real world check. The intensity of emotion generated by many environmental issues drives students to want to change everything NOW. Many of the projects ran into delays due to administrative redtape, telephone tag, and information snags. As one student so aptly put it, "Change takes time." The teaching assistants worked closely with the groups, problem solving around the roadblocks, helping students think of alternative strategies.

One team, for example, was sure they were going to expose the University as wasteful and negligent in its management of its buses. They found, to their surprise, that the University is conscientious about recycling oil and tires, and meticulously maintains its vehicles. They changed their project in midstream, choosing instead to do an analysis of the benefits and costs of re-routing the campus buses for a bridge repair. Rather than muckraking, they ended up providing the university's transportation department with valuable information.

They began to understand the complexity of social issues and the dynamics of social change. In some of the most striking evaluations, students reflected on having learned to recognize alternate views and to respect that people have different interests and causes. Rather than ranting and raving, the projects moved them to determine what it was that they really believed, and to act accordingly. They had to wrestle with their lack of expertise and, sometimes, a lack of credibility in the eyes of those they approached. Finally, they came to recognize the importance of plans and strategy as one moves towards action. One student wrote: "It gives me a lot of respect for those active in the community and the world."

If feedback from the last two years is any indication, the experience of taking part in projects has been educational and enjoyable, helping students to find both their own personal understanding of environmental issues as well as a multitude of ways to address environmental problems. The students had first-hand exposure to the frustrations, challenges and rewards of working for change. The additional work required for the projects was actually welcomed by the students, helping bring cohesion and meaning to their class experience by allowing them to apply what they had learned in class and in the readings to a real-world effort.

Assessment: How It Worked Out for the Instructors

While the projects presented both opportunities and constraints for the instructors, on the whole they were a positive experience. Just as the students learned and enjoyed from the projects, so did we.

The energy and enthusiasm of the students toward the projects generalized to the course and was contagious for the instructors. The projects infused energy into the entire course. Discussion sections were livelier, as students were able to connect lecture topics to their experiences with the projects (Anyone who has facilitated a discussion section recognizes the value of this!). Student excitement invigorated the instuctors, and contributed greatly to our enjoyment of the class.

The projects complemented our role as facilitators, allowing for creative interaction, ongoing feedback and mutual learning. The projects provided an opportunity to interact with students in small groups. These interactions were creative, with the emphasis on helping students use their strengths to shape their own endeavors. The students often brought rich and insightful contributions to the issues on which they worked. Their fresh perspectives made reading the final projects, as well as the informal sharing of ideas, real learning experiences for us.

Time constraints

One of the biggest challenges in doing projects with such a large course was having enough time—time not only to achieve classroom objectives, but also to allow students to engage fully in a project and to provide adequate interaction and feedback between and amongst students and instructors. The projects are very labor-intensive for the instructors, requiring shepherding of the groups, both administratively and educationally, as students move through the sequence of the project components.

The challenge of "grading"

A second concern revolves around evaluation. Validating and assessing these projects within the framework of a grading system is difficult. What is it that we are to evaluate? The topic? The realized or potential impact of the project? The team's effort to function as a group? Their perseverance and creativity? Further, how do we gather reliable data on these assessment measures? A five page final report can hardly capture five weeks of intensive work. We suspect some students managed to put together a "project" in a night, and know that there were others who invested enormous amounts of time in projects that did not quite work. Other students had a head-start, building on activities they already were doing outside of class. The instructors had a sense of how much work went into a project, but, ultimately, much of this was invisible.

In an effort at fairness, projects were evaluated on the process more than the outcomes. To encourage students to try a range of efforts, and not exaggerate their accomplishments, we made it very clear from the start that success was not judged by whether or not the students "solved the problem." Evaluations were based on 1) how creatively and thoroughly the teams analyzed the issue and developed strategies to address it, 2) how well they assessed their efforts in mid-stream and overcame roadblocks, 3) how much of an effort they made to disseminate their important results to the community, and 4) the quality of the final report.

The students' confidential evaluations of themselves and their group members were also enormously helpful in assigning grades. The self-assigned grades guided the instructors and were generally very close to grades the latter had in mind. In fact, students tended to be more critical of their efforts than were the instructors. These evaluations made it possible to assign specific grades to each group member and provided the students with an outlet for expressing disappointment toward members who had not pulled their weight on the projects. While each member within a group received the same grade for their community project, individual members' participation (10% of the project grade) was evaluated separately and primarily on the basis of the peer evaluations.

Conclusion

Incorporating community-based projects into Environmental Studies 320 enriched the class immeasurably. The projects helped validate much of what students had heard in class by providing real life examples of how complex environmental problems can be. The students saw first hand how seemingly simple problems have unanticipated twists and turns. They came face to face with the inertia of the behaviors and systems they so emphatically want to change. Many discovered that just educating people on an issue is not enough to change their behavior.

One of the hardest things about teaching is finding ways to bring the enthusiasm and energy of the learner to the subject matter. In our course, the community-based projects accomplished this. For most students the projects inspired a high level of initiative, creativity and interest. The projects challenged students to be more than passive learners, forcing them to grapple with information, choices and decisions that went beyond any textbook. They had to deal with real people, make decisions with real implications, and develop skills and knowledge they hopefully did not leave behind at the end of the term.

NOTES

1. "We" refers to the two authors and TA's Jennifer Barker, Deveaux Gauger, and Eileen Ho, who have worked closely with the authors in designing and conducting this class.
2. See Stapp, W., et. al (1988) *Education in action: Community problem solving for schools.* Thomson-Shore: Dexter, MI.

Appendix I

Weekly Topics and Guest Presenters

INTRODUCTION (Instructors)

The Environment in Print (Environmental Reporter)

AIR POLLUTION AND YOU: Multiple Perspectives

National Issues Forum: Air Pollution (In-class issues exploration)
Industrial Perspectives (Automotive Industry Representative)
The Clean Air Act and Beyond (Environmental Advocate)

GLOBAL ISSUES

Natural Law, Constructed Meaning and Humanity's Ecological Dilemma
(Anthropology Professor)
Human Dimension in Global Change: Population (Sociology Professor)
The Next Generation: Reflections on Brazil (Student Activist)
Global Climate Change (Geology Department)
International Responses to Global Warming (Political Science Professor)

ENERGY

Fossil Fuels: Are They Worth It? (Instructors)
Nuclear Energy (Nuclear Engineer)
Hydrogen: An Alternative Energy Scenario (Physicist)
Renewable Energy and Conservation (Urban Planner)

WASTE

A Case Study Scenario (Natural Resources Scientist)
The Lifecycle of a Product (Engineer)
NIMBY and Beyond: Hazardous Waste in the 1990's (Political Science
Professor)

CARING FOR AND ABOUT THE EARTH: Some perspectives

Earth Warriors: Radical Action & Biocentric Vision (Author)
The Amish (Anthropologist)
The Horse and the Tractor: Farming in the 90's (Natural Resources
Scientist)
Think Locally, Act Locally (English Instructor)
Nature and the Wilderness (English Professor)

ENVIRONMENTAL ISSUES AT THE CROSSROADS

Of Health and Public Policy (Public Health Professor)

The Sustainable Corporation: Oxymoron or Necessity? (Business Professor)

PROJECT PRESENTATIONS (Class Members)

CONCLUSION (Instructors)

Appendix II

Community Project Assignments

Part A: Project Work Plan
Part B: Midway Progress Evaluation
Part C: Project Write-up
Part D: Individual Evaluation

NOTE:
Parts A-C: turn in one paper per *group*
Part D: turn in one paper per *person*

A. Project Work Plan

1. Needs Assessment
    Identify the problem and explain why there is a need to address it. In other words, what is the problem and why is it important to work toward its resolution?
2. Project Goals
    Describe the goals of the project. What are your priorities?
3. Procedures
    Describe the project work plans and strategies. Include major tasks that need to be accomplished and who will be responsible for accomplishing them and when.
4. Skills and Resources
    Identify all group members' skills and resources pertinent to the project. Identify organizations with whom the group may need to work. How does your project fit the organization's goals? What resources can they offer your group?
5. Personal Goals/Expectations
    List the personal expectations of each group member.

B. Midway Progress Evaluation

List how things are going in the group (specific tasks or goals, group dynamics, resources, etc.) using the categories below:

Positives =	what's going well, working according to plans, on schedule	
Negatives =	what's not going smoothly, not working as planned, behind schedule	
Changes =	how to remedy negatives, what to do differently, what new approaches/actions need to be done	

C. Project Write-up

The final write-up is a 5 page, typed report which should include:

1. Statement of purpose
    Briefly state the purpose of the project: what problem you identified, the goals you strived for, and why the project was important.
2. Strategy followed
    Explain the steps you developed and undertook and why: people or organizations contacted, specific tasks completed, etc.
3. Results and findings
    Describe and discuss the findings of the group and what you feel you accomplished. What did you learn as a result of this project? Who were you able to educate about your results? Was the project successful or worthwhile or valuable for the group in terms of both the goals set and the experience gained in the process?
4. Suggestions
    Discuss how the project could have been improved in terms of what you did or how you did it AND propose what more could be done with additional time, effort and/or resources. What are you interested in doing or planning for next as a result of this project?

D. Individual Evaluation of Project Group

This evaluation is confidential. In evaluating your participation in the group project as well as the participation of your colleagues, please be honest, constructive and concise. Answer the questions below.

1. How well did you work as a group (consider communication, balance of participation, follow through, meeting of deadlines, quality of work and anything else you think appropriate)?
2. How well did you meet your obligations as a member of the group?
3. Given this experience, what, if anything, will you do differently next time you work in a group (be constructive)?
4. Based on what you accomplished, what you learned, your personal growth, your approach to the problem, the group process and other criteria you deem valuable, what "grade" would you give your group?
5. What grade would you give yourself and each member of your group?

Chapter 11

PSYCHOLOGY IN THE COMMUNITY

Jerry Miller

Introduction

Project Outreach/Psychology 211 is a large and comprehensive service learning course within the Department of Psychology at the University of Michigan. Each semester the course places between 400 and 600 students into as many as fifty different service sites. The goals for the course are to:

- provide a complementary field-based educational experience to that which students receive in the classroom
- inform students about the broad scope of psychological issues in the community and the ways in which a wide variety of workers address these
- enable students to explore possible career interests with particular problems and populations and
- encourage longer term patterns of community involvement.

History of the Course

Project Outreach was begun in 1966, in the societal context of teach-ins and consciousness raising and an active counter-culture movement, "to heighten personal relevance and offer diverse experiences" to students simultaneously enrolled in the Psychology Department's very large Introductory Psychology course. Early documents concerning the course heavily utilized the words "relevant" and "meaningful" in describing it. The emphasis, from the beginning, was on educational experimentation and experiential learning. As described in a presentation at the American Psychological Association's meeting that year it was hoped that the new course offerings would help students to:

> "...live richer lives as they can see and enjoy more levels of meaning which add richness to life, continue to learn and grow toward maturity when they leave the course, empathize with diverse sorts of people, and act effectively in the world."

During the 1967 academic year over 2000 students were able to choose to work in traditional community placements, such as hospitals and training schools, or elect to participate in a very wide variety of other experiential mini-classes ranging from T-groups and Black Consciousness sessions, to ones on Psychology and Television or Values in American Cinema. Not surprisingly the course, in those early days, had to defend itself against charges of being too radically "anti-intellectual" or "anti-classroom."

The course became free-standing by 1969 out of an appreciation both for the level of administration and coordination required to operate the program, as well as the belief that students participating in the course would be more highly motivated if they could voluntarily elect it.

One of the important issues course founders struggled with was grading. On the one hand, there were serious concerns about how to assign a traditional letter grade to students in experiential activities, and the worry that student concerns about grades could distort their experience. At the same time, there was the hope that if grades could be eliminated it might further ensure the enrollment of more self-motivated students. By 1974, with the Department's consent, the course changed to being offered on a credit-no credit basis.

One of the inadvertent effects of the changes to free-standing status and the elimination of course grades (as well, perhaps, by a decline in the level of student activism), was a gradual reduction in enrollments through the 1970's. In order to re-emphasize the Psychology Department's commitment to field-based experiences, and to bolster course enrollments, the Department, in 1981, agreed to count placements in two different sections of Outreach as the equivalent of one of the two advanced labs required of all Psychology majors.

Outreach Today

Presently, the Outreach program is staffed by a half-time Faculty Coordinator, a part-time Administrative Assistant, part-time transportation coordinator, and a part-time graduate student teaching assistant for each of its sections. Group and/or individual planning and supervision meetings between these people occur each week.

Each graduate student, in running a section, is assisted by a number of advanced undergraduates, in a position called Group Leader. The Group Leaders, who have already taken the course and demonstrated an enthusiastic commitment to its goals, receive training and supervision from the graduate students, directly coordinate the activities of students in the field, and run weekly small group discussions with their students. Students may elect to be Group Leaders for no more than two semesters, a policy that was initiated to ensure that this special educational experience would be open to a large group of students. Group Leaders receive special training in such topics as group facilitation, section stereotypes, teaching in a multi-cultural classroom, and sensitizing students to their impact on the people with whom they will be working, as well as in the basic content areas of the section in which they will be working. Graduate students meet with their Group Leaders, for ongoing administrative and educational supervision, each week during the semester.

The current organizational chart for Project Outreach appears like this:

Faculty Coordinator
— Administrative Assistant

Transportation Coordinator

Section Graduate Students

Group Leaders

Outreach Students

All of the course policies, requirements and forms are now contained in a fifty page handbook that is distributed to all new graduate teaching assistants. In keeping with the experiential nature of the course, there are no exams. The basic requirements for students to complete in order to receive two hours of course credit are:

1. 35 to 45 hour community placement commitment, in addition to any other special training time required by specific agencies.

2. Weekly two hour lecture/small group discussion sections, with no more than two unexcused absences. All absences, regardless of the reason, must be made up by submitting a short make-up assignment which is typically a reaction paper to an assigned reading. (Details concerning the lectures and small group discussions are reviewed below.)

3. 1-1/2 to 2 page journal entry during each week of placement. The journals should contain student reflections on their placement experiences of that week, and attempt to integrate field experiences with academic concepts.

4. 3 to 5 page double-spaced mid-term project. The project may be a more thoughtful look at the student's experience related to a particular concept, or be a special project planned for the student's placement.

5. 5 to 7 page double-spaced final project. Like the mid-term project, the final project may be more conceptual or experiential. In a childcare setting, for example, the final project may be a paper, with references, reflecting on the meaning of any observed gender differences in children, or may consist of the planning and implementation of a special group activity with the children.

6. Lab Fee Payment, currently set at $20 (up somewhat from the initial $2 fee assessed in 1967). The majority of the money received from the lab fees goes toward transportation expenses (leasing several cars, purchas-

ing bus passes, and renting vans and buses, sometimes with drivers, to transport students to placement), with a small amount going for other program expenses (copying, special supplies, etc.).

Placements

There is never a shortage of excellent placement sites in a service-based course. The Outreach office receives a steady stream of requests for student volunteers. In a typical experience, a short time ago, when a special school decided, at the last minute, that they would not be able to accept the five volunteers for which they had planned, a single call to a local special education office resulted in almost immediate offers from six new sites that were able to accommodate over twenty students. The sites to which students could not be placed were added to a long list of potential placements for the future.

A bigger issue with regard to placement sites is how to choose from among the many valuable offers and requests that are received by the program. Placement settings for Outreach are selected on the basis of several criteria. The most important of these is that the placement program can offer a positive, constructive and reliable experience to the students. In general, programs looking for clerical help or babysitting are not acceptable. Programs offering potentially very worthwhile experiences but which are too disorganized to do this on a regular basis are likewise rejected. Placements must also provide safe environments for students, and be within relatively close proximity to the University (primarily to keep transportation costs down, but also to minimize student travel time). Finally, only non-profit programs are generally considered, and priority is given to settings that can accommodate groups of students. The latter criterion again helps with transportation logistics and costs, but also allows students in the same setting to share their experiences. Once selected, placement sites are regularly evaluated by the Group Leaders and graduate students to ensure that they continue to meet program criteria.

Placements are currently organized into seven sections, basically by population served. Each section offers both direct placements, where students work face-to-face with a particular population, and indirect placements, where students work with organizations trying to reduce the incidence of problems faced by this population or are trying to increase resources and/or programming for them. Outreach students register for a specific section, and are then matched into a particular placement site based on their preferences and number of available openings. The current Outreach sections are:

Preschool Children—provides placements into preschool settings for children who are at-risk of developing intellectual, emotional and/or behavioral problems, or with organizations trying to reduce the number of children facing these situations.

Big Sibs-Community and Opportunity—provides an individual Big Sib experience with a child in need of companionship of a consistent caring adult, or places students with organizations trying to address the social factors that impact on these children.

Juvenile Justice and Education—provides placements in which students can establish relationships with disadvantaged students in after-school tutoring or social-recreational programs, or with youth who have become involved with the juvenile justice system, including those currently in restricted settings. In addition, students may work with community groups working to increase educational opportunity and juvenile justice.

Social Justice—provides placements in a wide variety of settings dealing with persons who have been affected by racism, sexism, domestic violence and/or homophobia, and with programs attempting to combat these forces in society.

Interventions for Mental Health—provides placements in both community and institutional settings which serve children and adults with mental illnesses or developmental disabilities, as well as with organizations advocating for improved services for these people.

Health, Illness and Society—provides placements with children and adults in both inpatient and community health care facilities, as well as with programs working for health promotion and/or advocating for improved health care for particular populations.

Exploring Careers—in coordination with the University's Career Planning and Placement Office, this section allows students, in an experiential setting, to explore their personal career interests, investigate the realities of particular career paths, and increase their awareness of how societal issues affect people's career decisions and work lives.

Linking Concepts and Experiences

Service-learning courses are deliberately designed to provide complementary forms of learning to that which is available in traditional in-class courses. Providing field-based experiences alone in no way guarantees this complementarity. A critical part of running such a course is designing and implementing those educational elements that can help students to maximize the learning which can occur in the field, and to help them to integrate concepts and theory with their experiences. In Outreach, several different mechanisms have been developed to help assure the success of these efforts.

Students are, first of all, prepared for their field experiences by three or four weeks of orientation lectures, readings and activities. The focus of all of these is to review basic concepts in the selected field, challenge common stereotypes and myths concerning persons with whom the students will be working, increase student comfort, provide practical beginning skills for interaction with persons in the field, help students to begin to explore the personal aspects of their work in the selected area, and begin to raise questions that they should try to answer in the field. Using the *Interventions for Mental Health* section as an example, students are urged to utilize their upcoming experiences to think about such questions as:

- What kinds of persons are served in the public mental health system and why?
- How well do existing diagnostic categories fit with the persons with whom they are interacting?
- What are the most important social forces that impact on persons with mental illnesses or developmental disabilities, and how are they helped or hurt by these?
- What are the strengths and weaknesses of current mental health services and why do these exist?

During this pre-placement period, small group discussions, which are led by the Group Leaders, focus on exploring the student's personal reasons for, and anxieties about, the choice to work with a particular population, and what they hope to gain from their experiences. Role-plays may be used to prepare the students for situations they can encounter. In large group meetings, previous service consumers may come to discuss their experience of participation with the Outreach program students.

Once the students begin their field experiences, they continue to have weekly lectures, readings and small group discussions, as well as maintain weekly journals, but the orientation of each of these is changed from that of the pre-placement period. Whereas the early lectures, for example, are provided by course faculty, the latter ones are provided primarily by a diverse group of professional and non-professional workers in the field, who speak both about their contribution to the total service picture as well as to the personal aspects of their roles. Again using *Interventions for Mental Health* as an example (see Appendix I), a typical lecture series might include a psychologist speaking about behavioral treatment of emotionally disturbed children, a staff of a group home or hospital about work in these facilities, a social worker about the concept and realities of Community Mental Health programs, a person with mental illness about their experience of this and the services they receive, a psychiatrist about psychotropic medication, a worker at a community recreational center about community activities for persons with mental illness and developmental disabilities, an attorney about processes and issues in civil commitment and guardianship, and an advocate for persons with developmental disabilities about perceived deficiencies in existing services and how students can help to remedy these. Small group discussions at this point are directed not only at helping students to integrate their experiences in a personal way, but to introduce concepts related to what they are observing, and to have students evaluate the apparent validity or usefulness of these concepts. The journals which students write following each placement experience also have the dual purpose of providing a regular format for recording reflections about the personal impact of their experiences, as well as critical thoughts about the relationship between field concepts and research and their own observations. To help ensure the latter goal, students are required, on a regular basis, to include in their journals a discussion concerning the relationship between a specific lecture topic and their placement experience that week.

The final way that Outreach attempts to assure an integration of concepts and experience is through the mid-term and final projects. In these the student is required to integrate previous lectures and readings with their own experiences in a lengthier and more thoughtful project than is available in their weekly journals (see Appendix II).

Things We Have Learned in Running a Field-Based Learning Course

In over a quarter century of running a large experiential learning course, we have learned a number of important lessons related to ensuring the course's success and the sanity of all the people associated with it.

1. **Service-based learning courses need an investment of resources**. Staffing levels in Outreach have, through its history, varied enormously. There are an endless number of details in running such courses and in assuring that every student has close to an optimal experience. The investment of adequate resources in these programs is essential for their success. Inadequate staffing, in particular, can quickly lead to chaos and a much lower level of quality of student experience.

2. **Keep the course academically respectable**. The early fears and charges, by the larger faculty, that an experiential course is anti-intellectual and not a serious educational endeavor never really fully go away and need to be addressed continuously. These charges are best answered by being sure that the course is genuinely conceptualized, and operates, as a serious educational enterprise in which theoretical concepts and research findings are fully integrated. Such courses need to be considerably more than just community service experiences for students. It is most important that written course requirements are established and implemented so that the course does not get an indefensible reputation as a "blow-off" course with an "automatic A."

3. **Don't fight student interests**. As faculty of service-based courses there are many experiences that we feel are valuable for students. Likewise, as citizens in our communities, there are causes that we deem in serious need of volunteer support. Course offerings, however, need to be responsive to ever changing student interests. Years ago, the Outreach section placing students with persons with mental illnesses or mental retardation was very popular. It was, in addition, seen as a section that fit solidly within a Psychology course. Student interest in this population, however, especially the mentally retarded, has waned a great deal over the years. Our response has been to redistribute the level of graduate student support from that section into others that students currently find more appealing.

4. **Keep transportation simple**. Of all the issues in running field-based courses, transportation can be one of the most frustrating. In addition to providing van or bus transportation to more distant sites, Outreach maintains a fleet of four cars that are available for student use. Almost every semester brings a series of problems, such as late returns or short-

term disappearances of vehicles, and minor accidents. Each of these adds much aggravation to affected students and the transportation coordinator, and frequently costs the program significant amounts of money. If at all possible, transportation should be minimized either through the selection of sites within walking distance of campus or are on a bus line.

5. **Get a good administrative assistant (or two)**. While sending students into the community enriches their learning immensely, it also creates a very large number of new details to monitor and problems to resolve. These range from the trivial, such as students losing lab fee payment slips or running out of gas on the road, to the moderately serious, such as students not going to placement or placements cancelling out during the semester, to the genuinely very serious, such as car accidents or student/client injuries. In a large program, some of these occur each day (although it must quickly be noted that for all the worries about sending hundreds of students to dozens of diverse off-campus settings, the number of genuinely serious problems is remarkably rare). Having a capable and patient administrative assistant who is very knowledgeable about the program, the placement sites and university policies, can make all the difference in the smooth running of these programs. (Project Outreach has been extraordinarily fortunate to have had such a person for almost twenty-five years.)

6. **Keep priorities straight**. As the coordinator of a service-based course, there are numerous decisions that have to be made concerning placements to be added or deleted, the number of students to send to various placements, and student course requirements. Once the program is established and known, countless community agencies call upon the program to help provide needed volunteer resources. It is very helpful in making decisions regarding all of these matters to have clear guiding course priorities. While providing meaningful services to the community is an important activity, and essential to the service-based enterprise, the first priority of such courses has to be to ensuring that students have the richest educational experience possible. Thus, some very worthwhile placement requests are denied because the nature of their settings cannot ensure a positive and constructive experience for an entire semester.

7. **Encourage innovation**. Project Outreach was founded to encourage innovative experimentation in psychology education. While the course is not as free in this regard as it once was, innovation continues to be encouraged at all levels. Through the years many of the very best new additions to the course have been independently started and nurtured by students. As part of a hospital visiting program, for example, students began a highly successful clowning project in which, each week, they would dress up as clowns and enhance the lives of children in the hospital. Last year several students applied for, and received, a grant to help start an innovative evening program to recognize adults with

mental illnesses that were employed in the community. Graduate students have always been encouraged, within course guidelines, to take real ownership of their sections: changing the placement mix to fit the interests of themselves and their students, inviting the kinds of speakers that they feel would be most valuable, and putting the kind of educational slant on their section with which they are most comfortable.

8. **Don't pay guest speakers**. In a typical semester, Outreach invites about fifty persons to be guest speakers for one of its sections. Some of these are university faculty with special knowledge about a particular topic. Most, however, are community workers who share their personal expertise and experiences with the class. If speakers were paid even a nominal $25 honorarium for their appearance, the costs would quickly accumulate. It is course policy, therefore, that no speakers are paid for their visits. All guest speakers, instead, receive a letter, on university stationery, thanking them for their contribution to the course. The only exceptions to this policy have been occasional payments for childcare or parking for indigent service consumers who are sharing their experiences with the students, or the payment of very low fees to persons who provide a critical and specialized training experience that is not available in any other way.

9. **Have well-defined policies and procedures**. Until fairly recently, most of Project Outreach's policies and procedures were part of its vast oral traditions, known most broadly only to the course's long-tenured administrative assistant. Three years ago it was decided that every time a policy or procedure question arose it would be discussed with the graduate student group and administrative assistant, and then recorded and disseminated. It is not surprising, in a course as complicated as Outreach, that more than fifty formal policies and procedures were eventually codified in this fashion. These include such things as standardized course requirements for students and Group Leaders in any section, requirements for lab fee payments and automobile trainings, establishing the approximate ratio of Group Leaders to students (at about 1:6), limiting the number of terms a student can be a Group Leader, and specifying the documentation that must be submitted in order to deny credit to a student (in that students increasingly appeal such denials sometimes several semesters after they were in the course).

Concluding Thoughts

Coordinating a large service-based learning course, for the person who is genuinely committed to this type of educational format, is immensely rewarding. The course can provide an unusually rich and educationally sound set of unique student experiences. It is not at all unusual to hear from students (or occasionally even from their parents), that the course was the best and most relevant one they took during four years at the university, and that it has profoundly affected their views of the world, themselves and their career choices. At the same time, there is great satisfaction in knowing that one is playing a part in helping students to provide dearly needed services for real problems in the world around them. Running such a course, in short, is a most gratifying experience.

Appendix I

**Interventions for Mental Health
Project Outreach**

Weekly Topics

Introduction, presentation of syllabus and settings.

Film: "Any Place But Here"

M. Mendel, Ph.D.: "Treatment of Severely Disturbed Children"

H. Miller, Ph.D.: "Forensic Psychology"

Benjoya, M.S.W.: "Community Mental Health"

G. Miller, M.D.: "Psychotropic Medications"

A. Berman, J.D.: "Civil Commitment"

JV, B.A., founder of Schizophrenics Anonymous: "Hope of Recovery and Self-Help for Recovery"

Group presentations and discussion of the settings

R. Freidmann, M.A.: "Art and Music Therapy"

C. Fielder, Ph.D.: "Psychosocial Rehabilitation of Persons with Mental Illness"

T. Goldberg, R.T.: "Recreational Therapy"

K. Dann, R.N.: "Social Injustice and the Mentally Ill"

Appendix II

Paper Assignments (All Sections)

Mid-term Paper

Some of you are volunteering in institutional settings; others of you work in the community. The purpose of this 3 to 5 page paper is to discuss institutions and deinstitutionalization. You should discuss your thoughts and ideas about mental health care in and out of institutions: what are the advantages and disadvantages, in your opinion, of each approach? Should some people who are institutionalized not be? Should some people who live in the community be in institutions? How could institutions be improved? How could the community mental health system be improved?

Final Paper

The purpose of this paper is to allow each of you to reflect honestly and meaningfully upon your personal experience with people you will have met this term at your setting. Papers should be 5 to 7 pages.

Below are some guidelines to help you organize your paper. These are only suggestions; feel free to structure your paper in whatever way you feel will be most helpful to you in your exploration of what the Outreach experience has meant for you.

Your role: In which part of your facility did you work? What were your duties? What types of things did you do?

Your experience: How did the setting compare with your initial expectations? What were your most positive experiences? Most negative? What is life like for the clients and/or patients at the setting where you worked? Is the setting helping these people? How do the clients/patients experience themselves and their illness? How did you feel while interacting with these people? What did you think of the professional staff who worked at your setting?

Your education: What did you learn about mental illness and mental health? What did you learn about yourself? What advice would you give future Outreach students at your setting? How did your experience add to your undergraduate education?

Required Book Reading

You are required to read a book that pertains to issues of mental illness. Possibilities include Kessey's *One Flew Over the Cuckoo's Nest*, Greenberg/Green's, *I Never Promised You A Rose Garden*, Sheehan's *Is There Anyplace on Earth for Me?*, Vonnegut's *The Eden Express*, Plath's *The Bell Jar*, Szasz' *The Myth of Mental Illness*, Goffman's *Asylums*, or Torrey's *Surviving Schizophrenia*. You are by no means limited to these books. If you would like to read a different book, please just discuss it with the section instructor first.

There is no written assignment related to the book you read unless you have to write a make-up assignment. However, these are truly classics in the area of severe mental illness and its treatment. You will be doing yourself a disservice if you do not take the time to read one of these books.

Chapter 12

ADAPTING DRAMA ACTIVITIES FOR INDIVIDUALS WITH DISABILITIES

Hilary U. Cohen

The service-learning course that I taught, "Adapting Drama Activities for Individuals with Disabilities," was offered in the Theater Department as a non-degree required elective. It combined the study of improvisational acting skills with an innovative application in the community with disabled children and adolescents. Course members both developed their own acting techniques and used what they had learned in this course and other university courses (theater, education, and psychology) to make drama accessible to underserved populations and to develop it as a learning tool. In the experiential part of the course, students assisted in leading eight-week drama workshops with groups of disabled participants.

Reasons for Developing Course

Theatre and Drama 437 was developed as part of a broader set of activities and enquiries in which I have been engaged for ten years. One of my main areas of research has revolved around how to make theater accessible to disabled audience members and disabled participants as well as what affect accessibility measures have on the nature of theater and performance. I have written a number of papers based on my own work and my observation of other performance companies and activities. For example, in The *Children's Theater Review*, I explored a program in Stockholm, Sweden that makes drama workshops available to all the disabled children of the city at forty different sites in order to raise self-esteem and develop communication skills. I have also written extensively about a variety of theater companies made up of deaf individuals in the United States and abroad. In my own work as Artistic Director of Wild Swan Theater, I have been engaged in a number of practical applications ranging from innovations in audience accessibility to a variety of workshops for disabled participants.

Course Goals

Most students who take acting classes at the university do so either because they are interested in developing their skills as performers or because acting exercises help to polish their public presentation of themselves. Acting can build self-confidence, self-awareness, and improve communication skills. By its very nature, the study of acting usually has participants focusing intensely on themselves.

Drama also, however, may be used as a tool with therapeutic and educational purposes. The goal of this University class was to explore these other applications, widening the students' understanding of acting activities, providing them with opportunities to see numerous applications of the skills they were acquiring, and encouraging them to think broadly and inventively about how they might use the study of theater in their futures.

Course Description

The course involved classroom and community components. In the classroom students studied and refined acting techniques such as improvisation, role-playing, and theater games. They participated in the activities themselves as well as observed the skill development of their peers. The students then moved out into the community, for an eight-week period, working in school and institutional settings with a targeted disabled population.

The workshops for each of the community populations met once a week for about one hour and were led by the course instructor with three to five class members. As the workshops proceeded, the University students took on more and more of a leadership role. In preparation for the workshops, guest special education teachers and therapists gave background presentations. In advance of the workshops, students also spent at least one hour observing the group with which they were to work. Each workshop session also included preparation, evaluation and assessment, and a report back to the assembled class which continued to meet once a week as a whole. Three or four distinct workshops, each at a different site, were run during each course.

The sites for the workshops were varied:

High Point—school for mentally retarded children and adolescents
Kellogg Eye Center—visually impaired adolescents
New Horizons—elementary school for mobility impaired children
Adolescent Psychiatric Hospital Day Treatment Program

Community Component Goals

The goals for the community component of the course included the following:

- Adapt and develop drama activities that will be accessible to a specific disabled population
- Develop activities that will provide an appropriate creative experience for the workshop participants
- In collaboration with classroom teachers and therapists, present age and ability appropriate activities that further the educational goals of the classroom teacher

The workshops were process rather than product oriented. The focus was on the development of the participants rather than on the creation of a culminating production.

Examples of Sample Workshops

1. High Point Program for Developmentally Disabled Children

Five course members worked with a class of 12 developmentally disabled first graders. Working with the classroom teacher, a physical therapist, and the course instructor, they presented drama exercises that presented the concepts "stop" and "go" and "over" and "under." They also presented activities that helped the children distinguish between leading and following and encouraged group collaboration. For example, in one group collaboration game, the children built a human sculpture of which they were all a part. This game incorporated several levels of participation, including the decision to take part, observing the beginnings of the statue and deciding how to add on to it, actually shaping their bodies into the ever-growing statue, and working creatively and cooperatively in a group.

2. Kellogg Eye Center

Four course members worked with 8 visually impaired adolescents, one of whom was also autistic. The course members developed physical exercises that helped participants develop greater physical awareness. They also worked on interpersonal communication skills through drama activities that promoted give and take. They developed side coaching techniques that permitted the blind children access to the nonverbal components of other participants' performances.

3. Adolescent Psychiatric Hospital Day Treatment Program

This workshop was held with emotionally disturbed adolescents who were attending school through the Day Treatment Program of the UM Adolescent Psychiatric Hospital. The six teen-agers we worked with ranged in age from thirteen to sixteen. Although they had all graduated from in-patient to out-patient status, they still had a number of serious problems. They were abusive and hostile to each other and their teachers, lethargic and resistant to most activities, unable to sustain interaction with other people, and very tense and afraid of taking personal risks.

The first several sessions were spent in gaining the group's trust and overcoming their resistance. From comments and actions, we knew they were intrigued with drama and very positive about working with UM students even as eliciting participation was difficult. In this group, we had to be very sensitive to the students' sense of vulnerability and fear of losing face. Thus, many of the standard warm-ups and ice-breakers were not available to us. We began each session with a simple warm-up, even though not everyone participated at first, and then worked on environment improvisations and content-less scenes. A breakthrough occurred in this group when pairs of UM students did improvisations for the whole group with the "audience" allowed to coach. The combination of empowerment and the fun of rapid transformations caused a dramatic change, with students not only becoming willing to participate and take initiative but also beginning to work with excitement and creativity.

Course Membership and Evaluation

The course attracted a mixture of theater, psychology, and education students. For the most part, they were predisposed to want to work in the community. This made for an extremely supportive group, as students shared their expertise with each other and worked constructively in developing the workshops. The students tended to be extremely enthusiastic about the course and rated it as one of the most meaningful they had taken at the University. They almost all reported some trepidation about whether they would be successful in the workshops and whether they would know what to do with disabled youth.

Part of the value of the course was the students' sense of personal growth, of taking something they could do themselves and transforming it into something that would create a meaningful and creative experience for someone else. They also reported an enthusiasm for drama as a tool in their future work as doctors, teachers, social workers, and actors. They liked the format of working in small groups in the community but having a weekly opportunity to talk with the group as a whole. Those later sessions were extremely valuable for sharing successes and mistakes and for talking over problems with each other. They wished that they had had the opportunity to participate or at least observe more than one community group, something not possible because of scheduling difficulties. Some also chafed slightly at the increased responsibility the course required in terms of attendance and promptness.

Instructor Assessment

While this is a course that is particular to my own individual interests, it points to a format that might be adapted by teachers from a variety of disciplines. There is great value in some of the features that the course's organization encourages:

- understanding something well enough to be able to teach it to someone else
- coming to see broader applications of ideas and activities
- encountering a more diverse population than a university typically provides

Moreover, such a course fosters critical thinking and the ability to connect theory and practice while also encouraging community service. Students have the opportunity to test ideas, examine them from several perspectives, and assess their value.

One drawback of the course is that it is labor intensive for the instructor. While students participated in one on-going workshop, or possibly two, I was present at all of them. Perhaps a different format could be devised that permitted the instructor to be more in the position of observer than as necessary participant. That might work for students with some experience, although probably not for novices. Another drawback is that the coordination of schedules is time consuming and cumbersome. These two problems, however, seem vastly outweighed by the value to the students, the community, and to myself.

Chapter 13

ENVIRONMENTAL ACTION PROJECTS AS COMMUNITY SERVICE LEARNING

Peter B. Kaufman and Mari Ziegler

The goal of this paper is to convey how we have involved undergraduate students at the University of Michigan in community service learning through the vehicle of environmental action projects (EAP's) in our course, Biology 106: Plants, People, and Environment.

Course Goals

Biology 106 was developed by Peter Kaufman while on Sabbatical leave at the University of Colorado in 1973 at the height of the environmental movement. His own motivation for this initiative was to make biology, and especially plant biology, more relevant and exciting to undergraduate students who had to meet a science distribution requirement.

The purposes of the course continue to be as they were then:

- to help learn about major environmental problems that confront each of us today both locally and globally
- to learn about practical solutions to our major environmental problems
- to become an active participant in solving environmental problems to learn the practical ways in which plants can be used to solve environmental problems
- to develop a "green thumb" in growing plants
- to develop a lifestyle that is environmentally oriented

Students, from the beginning and up through 1985, were asked to write term papers on environmental problems and solutions to these problems. We called such projects "environmental alerts." This passive activity involved over 125 students each time this course was offered. The course instructors not only found reading this plethora of papers extraordinarily time-consuming, but more important, wondered what students learned from such an endeavor except maybe to learn to write better. What did it accomplish for the environment? So, we abandoned the environmental alert term paper project, and in its place, started a new adventure for our students in Bio. 106—one that would get them involved in community service by carrying out "environmental action projects" (EAP's) that utilized their skills and talents individually, in groups, and as a class. It was a concept that was hands-on in nature, and would trigger the students to accomplish, through their own efforts, something beneficial and positive for Planet Earth. The greater community—local, national, and at times, international—became the focus of our efforts.

Our goals for the community component are to take the same goals we established for the course and translate them into hands-on environmental action projects in the community—the local schools, local businesses, local residences for students (homes, apartments, dormitories, sororities, fraternities), family homes and properties, public parks and natural areas, recycling centers, food distribution centers, local farms, local or distant industries that have not yet become green, and government agencies at all levels. Oral reports on these community service projects are made to the entire class. These reports are each 15 minutes in duration and are reinforced with student-produced video tapes, dramas, music, poetry, stories, slides, and posters. Opportunity is given for student- and instructor-generated questions and discussion of different points of view related to each project.

Course Organization

Biology 106 is organized into three modules. Module I deals with "Plants, Their Way of Life, and Uses by people." Module II addresses the questions, "What Is Happening to Our Environment and What Can We Do About It?" Module III focuses on "Constructive Ways to Improve Our Environment". The topics we cover under each module are spelled out in Appendix I.

Service and Learning

In what ways did the community serve a learning function? Basically, these included on-site interviews with community individuals (e.g., teachers, Ecology Center personnel, Project Grow personnel, business managers, Recycling Center personnel, food store managers, government officials), library searches, making arrangements with Ecology Center individuals for service at the Recycling Center and with teachers in local schools for hands-on environmental education projects with children in the classroom, writing to key environmental organizations for information on action projects, and working with conservation organizations to help carry out environmental action projects, such as "adopting an endangered animal species", adopt a river or roadside for cleanup, and soliciting funds to buy land with Nature Conservancy to save a bit of tropical rain forest (we bought 2 acres in Costa Rica last year).

Service Opportunities

We made arrangements for student service projects through direct contacts, letter-writing, or telephone calls. For example, because of their receptivity to volunteers, we sent students directly to the Ecology Center in Ann Arbor for work at the Recycling Center. In some cases, students contacted teachers in the Ann Arbor elementary schools and did EAP's in conjunction with their practice teaching. And still another avenue was through having a personal contact within an agency, company, or organization (e.g., the University of

Michigan Matthaei Botanical Gardens, Willow Run Farms, U. S. Army Corps of Engineers, Michigan Department of Natural Resources, Project Grow, Leslie Science Center, local food coops). At the beginning of the term we provide students with a list of possible projects for their consideration (see Appendix II).

Student Accomplishments

We have watched great transformations in students' attitudes toward community responsibility. Students turn from disillusionment with problems they have inherited to belief in what one person can do to change things. The following are two examples of student EAP's:

Emily B., now a U-M junior, targeted the polluted Potomac River for her class project. Living on the Army post at Fort Belvoir, VA., she contacted the base commander and proposed a cleanup of a portion of the waterway that flows behind Belvoir. The general supplied a group of soldiers to work with her and a class of fifth-graders. In one day, she remembers cleansing one-third of a mile of shoreline.

Patrick S. planted trees in the inner city of Detroit and supervised the planting of a community garden.

Student Outcomes

- Students learned to work together in teams to carry out most of the EAP projects. Those who chose to work individually due to the nature of their project or by choice learned that even one individual can make a difference in improving our environment.
- They learned how to present their EAP project results before their peers using the spoken word, drama, music, overheads, slides, posters, and video tapes. They also received evaluations from the other students in the course and from the instructors via questions after their presentations and written critiques (see Appendix III A and B—"Environmental Action Project Presentation Form" and "Feedback on Your Oral Report and Project").
- By accomplishing so much in a single term, they were left with a drive to do more for the environment after graduation. In addition, many students provided means by which their project could be carried out by others (e.g., recycling programs in sororities, fraternities, and dormitories).
- Many changed their majors as a result of Bio. 106—e.g. from Irish studies to environmental studies, from regular law to environmental law, and from mainstream poetry to nature/environmental poetry.

Course Evaluation

We have achieved the course objectives beyond our wildest dreams. We owe this to the amazing talents, diversity of backgrounds and experiences, and motivation of our students. Alumni from Biology 106 come back every year to tell the students how they have applied what they learned in our course in their own careers out in the real world.

We are going to implement two basic changes in order to eliminate students who are only "out to get an A." These changes include: opening the course only to 1st and 2nd year students, and giving a rigorous assignment early (e.g., an outline of intended EAP projects) to eliminate uncommitted students.

Appendix I

Course Topics

Module I—Plants, Their Way of Life, and Uses By People

Getting Acquainted With Plants & Their Economic Uses:
Part 1. Blue-green algae, bacteria, viruses, and fungi
Getting Acquainted With Plants & Their Economic Uses:
Part 2. Other types of algae, mosses & liverworts, clubmosses, scouring rushes, ferns, cycads, conifers, and flowering plants.
Medicinal, Poisonous, and Psychoactive Plants
Basic Steps in Making Wine, Mead, and Beer
Uses of Medicinal, Culinary, and Fragrance Herbs
"Barking Up the Right Trees": Human Uses of Wood & Wood Products
Plants Used for Crafts and Dyeing Fibers

Module II—What Is Happening To Our Environment and What Can We Do About It?

Atmospheric Ecology and Air Pollution
How Can We Prevent Air Pollution & Obtain Clean Air?
Aquatic Ecology, Wetlands at Risk, and Our Polluted Water Systems.
How Can We Prevent Water Pollution & Clean Up Our Aquatic Ecosystems Including Wetlands?
Ecology of Temperate Ecosystems. How Are They Being Destroyed, and How Can We Prevent Their Destruction?
Ecology of Tropical Ecosystems. Why Are They At Risk, How Can We Prevent Their Destruction?
Agricultural Ecology: Pros & Cons of the Green Revolution.
Agricultural Ecology: Organic Gardening and Farming As An Alternative To Chemical Agribusiness Farming and Gardening.
Our Changing Urban Environment
Urban Restoration at Work

Module III—Constructive Ways To Improve Our Environment

Foraging for Edible Wild Plants
Wild and Tasty
Edible Wild and Natural Foods
Oral Reports on Environmental Action Projects (EAP's)
Oral Reports on EAP's
Using Plants to Improve the Indoor Landscape
Using Plants to Improve Urban and Home Outdoor Landscapes
Oral Reports on EAP's
Endangered Plant & Animal Species & the Importance of Saving Natural & Wilderness Areas.
Oral Reports on EAP's
Nature Interpretation: Concepts and Ways to Get it Across To People of All Ages
Recycling at Work With Plants, Garbage, Paper, Metals, Glass, Rubber, and Plastics
Oral Reports on EAP's
Oral Reports on EAP's
Putting Alternative Energy Sources to Work & Energy Conservation Strategies
Hydroponic Gardening With Herbs
Oral Reports on EAP's
Oral Reports on EAP's

Appendix II

List of Environmental Action Projects

This is by no means meant to be a list from which you must choose, but rather is meant to be a grouping of possibilities in order to prompt your creativity. But, if you see something you like, feel free to choose it, whether it's in your field or not. Work in teams, if your project is conducive to doing so.

- Anthropology/Ethnobotany: genocide of indigenous peoples in rainforest habitats; native lifestyles in harmony with environment; native uses of medicinal and food plants.
- Art: graphic art as a medium for education/influence/protest; design environmental poster; attend and report on National Workshop on the Arts in Environmental Education, sponsored by Roger Tory Peterson; design T-shirt for class; wildlife painting.
- Biology/Botany: naturalists do an observation journal on a wilderness area with descriptions and sketches; do a presentation on the wild-community activities in a natural area with slides etc.; do personal observation of local threatened environment (how does habitat change composition of inhabitants?); volunteer for Michigan Nature Conservancy (pull up buckthorn and loosestrife—aggressive non-native invaders); report and petition on extinction of plants: death of fir trees in Smokies, American Chestnut, medicinal plants in S. American rainforests, do a flora/fauna taxonomy on a wild-area.
- Economic/Business: studies on how the new "green consumer" has affected the economy and how businesses are changing to meet the new informed consumer.
- Education: do a demo/guest presentation for local elementary science class (influence the future—influence the minds of the children); produce an education information brochure about how to live an ecological lifestyle.
- Engineering: demonstrate models for alternative energy, i.e., solar panels, wind generated power etc., methane generators, solar powered cars, electric cars.
- Journalism: investigate local environmental problem/interview local activist and offer to U of M or AA or Ypsi paper for publication (do an article for Mich. Daily on the activities of this class).
- Law: investigate/interview latest environmental lawsuits with National Wildlife Federation/Audubon and violators (spotted owl/Pacific Northwest).
- Media: Educational video of instruction in ecological lifestyles, or environmental problem, or children's natural science program etc.
- Medical: Report on toxics; local cases of Minamata's disease from mercury in Great Lakes, Detroit River, River Rouge; alternative therapies; medicinal plants.
- Music/Dance: songs for the environment; choreograph the plight of an endangered species; also, take to elementary schools (polish piece and donate time for next Rainforest Action Movement benefit, Blue bird

festival, Earth Day).

- Poetry: medium of protest/awareness, read to class, send to nature magazines for publishing; collect anthology of environmental poetry.
- Politics: information campaign—canvas neighborhood with info on latest environmental legislation; petition/find out the latest wildlands (e.g. forests, wetlands, dunes) to fall under the developers destruction; lobby to renovate inner urban areas rather than spread outward; present speech at next city-hall meeting; letter writing campaigns; canvas your local neighborhood with copies of how to separate household wastes with a map to local recyclers (stick in door-not mailbox)
- Research: paper on environmental issue not commonly covered; essay or opinion paper on effects of factory on workers/neighborhood.
- Theater: children's theater; present at a local elementary school; adult theater; street theater; describe an environmental problem using theater as the educator/communicator; Earth Day presentation.
- Urban Planning: a report and slide show on alternative energy uses in area, (how is the community using alternative energy successfully? How could they improve?) report on mass transit, bicycle paths, walking trails; report on vest-pocket parks, tree planting along streets.
- Waste Management: most Ann Arbor private residences, dorms, coops and Greek houses already recycle, does your home-community? (reduce-reuse-recycle should become an international slogan, what can you do to help?); canvas your home neighborhood with copies of how to separate household wastes with a map to local recyclers (stick in door); implement recycling in your community.

Appendix IIIA

Environmental Action Project Presentation Form

Environmental Action Project Topic:

Participants:

Date of Oral Presentation:

Brief Summary of your project: state its purpose, the process used to carry it out, the results you obtained, and where it can and should go from here.

Before you make your presentation, please turn in this form.

Appendix IIIB

Feedback on Your Oral Report and Project

Grade will be from 0-50, based on the following format: 1) State the objectives of the project. 2) Tell why it is important. 3) Tell how you carried it out. 4) Describe the successes and the difficulties or the pros and cons. 5) Tell what should be done next. 6) Cite at least 3 sources such as interviews, references or personal investigation. 7) Write a test question for the 3rd Exam from your EAP which is the "take home lesson" that you want us all to learn from your experience.

Effectiveness of Project:

Quality of Oral Presentation:

Evidence of Good Group Participation:

Suggestions Regarding the Project:

Suggestions Regarding the Presentation:

TOTAL GRADE:

PART THREE
Graduate Course Models

Chapter 14

CONTRADICTORY MISSIONS OF A TEMPERED RADICAL'S TEACHING

Sharon E. Sutton

Thirty years ago, much of the neighborhood where I grew up in Cincinnati, Ohio was burned to the ground during a civil rebellion as were other African-American neighborhoods in most of the country's major cities. The Kerner Commission, appointed to investigate the root causes of these rebellions, concluded that the nation was moving toward two separate and unequal societies, one white, the other black. The burning of Los Angeles in the spring of 1992 and the tension surrounding the trial there the following year are potent reminders that an unremitting journey toward separateness is still in progress.

Although demographers predict the coming of a multicultural society, the chasm between an America-of-privilege and an America-of-poverty has deepened over the last thirty years. Disparities in the quality of life for rich and poor, educated and uneducated, well-employed and underemployed have never been greater—and race is the determining factor. Despite civil rights legislation, there is a pronounced tendency among blacks toward lower incomes, lower educational achievement, higher unemployment, and higher rates of crime. The average white family has an income that is eight to ten times higher than the average African-American family because black heads-of-households still earn less for the same work and because they are still concentrated in low-paying jobs. In central cities, black men experience more than two to three times the unemployment of their white counterparts *with equal education* and, at any given time, there are almost as many black men incarcerated as there are in college. With 43% of the nation's poor currently residing in central cities, including 57% of all African Americans, it is not unusual for grossly over-crowded, segregated ghettos and barrios to be located alongside wealthy financial centers, thus mirroring the geographic patterns of the most impoverished developing countries (Goldsmith and Blakely, 1992).

I am engulfed by the reality of these sharp disjunctures not only as a black woman who was born of lower social class, but as a professor of architecture and urban planning who is responsible for enabling students to look at the physical world, understand its impact on the quality of human life, and then visualize optimal future environments. Another urban planner, Kevin Lynch (1979), and others have commented that societal values literally are mapped out on the ground so that the material world can be understood as a museum of the dominant culture's use of power and authority. As I view this museum through the lens of my own personal history, I see startling proof of an unyielding legacy of racism. I see an "American dream" that comprises single-family houses and zoning regulations to keep land sparsely developed and remarkably segregated.

I see highways that were plowed through black neighborhoods in the 1950s, including those where my grandmother, mother and father, aunts and uncles owned property, where promises of replenishing lost housing faltered and then disappeared altogether. I see urban businesses and industries that bequeathed their deteriorating buildings, contaminated sites, and high cost of redevelopment to those people (now so maligned for their dependence on welfare) who could not afford to accompany them to the suburbs. I see development policies that displace poor, minority people and destroy more and more of the natural landscape without creating sustainable communities that offer jobs and housing to a multicultural populace. As I prepare for my classes, I see a living museum of injustice etched into the landscape of this country.

Teaching some of the country's brightest young women and men in an elite university places me—an "outsider" according to bell hooks' (1984) terminology—within an inner circle in which students are socialized to reproduce this museum. As I develop curricula I ask myself whether I can use my outsider-within position to enable students to reverse the Kerner Commission's thirty-year-old indictment while, at the same time, meeting my obligations to socialize them into professions that are surely participants in the cause for the indictment. Can I use my classes as a model for elaborating a different map of a truly integrated, multicultural society while simultaneously promoting those "rules of the game" that will allow students to become mainstream practitioners? Is it possible to center a teaching agenda around the subject of equitable urban redevelopment—a subject in which I have a deep personal stake—without appearing to be too radical, too black, too feminist? These are the questions that I ask myself as I develop the class that is described in this chapter.

The Risks of Education for Social Change

Educators in the multicultural movement argue that society will become more accepting if schools and universities broaden the exposure of students. They propose to improve the diversity of faculty and students, and to make the content and methods of teaching more responsive to groups that are circumscribed by race, ethnicity, culture, gender, sexual orientation, religion, and socioeconomic class. Those minorities who are critical of multiculturalism see it as nothing more than a diversionary tactic on the part of the white establishment. According to these folk, learning about subordinate groups constitutes a means through which the dominant culture is able to "manage" the growing numbers of minorities and to thus maintain its privilege. Other critics see multiculturalism as nothing more than a shift from one group to another of the existing power-over mentality and elitism—a view that would have little effect on the economic chasm that I have described. A third attitude toward multiculturalism (the one that I embrace) imagines it as an opportunity to bring about a new social order in which power is shared equally and broadly (Schoem, Frankel, Zúñiga, and Lewis, 1993, pp. 1-8).

From this perspective, education is an opportunity to access the life, liberty, and pursuit of happiness that is envisioned in the Declaration of Independence

—to bridge the separateness of privileged persons (who are most often white and well-educated) and oppressed persons (who are most often of color and undereducated). However as David Purpel (1989) pointed out, education for social change is risky.

> *Sometimes people like Abraham Lincoln, Malcolm X, and Martin Luther King are assassinated for insisting that we reexamine our way of being...Serious education...has a way of forcing continual confrontation with our basic moral commitments and, more unnerving, with our failures to meet those commitments.* (p. 8)

Figure 1.
Contradictory Roles in My Community Development Studio

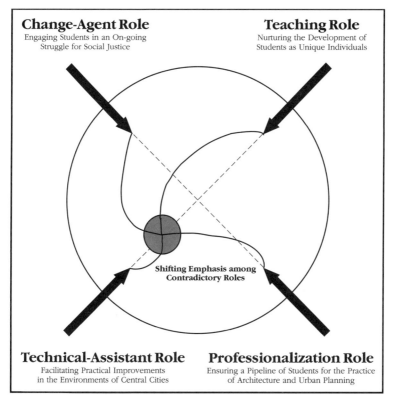

Change-Agent Role
Engaging Students in an On-going
Struggle for Social Justice

Teaching Role
Nurturing the Development of
Students as Unique Individuals

**Shifting Emphasis among
Contradictory Roles**

Technical-Assistant Role
Facilitating Practical Improvements
in the Environments of Central Cities

Professionalization Role
Ensuring a Pipeline of Students for the Practice
of Architecture and Urban Planning

In attempting to make students aware of how they can resist or join in perpetuating social inequities while pursuing their chosen careers and serving a local community, I find myself assuming roles that are not entirely complementary (Figure 1 illustrates these roles). One of these roles is as a change agent who challenges the status quo by enabling students to examine their position as privileged individuals, to understand their interdependence with those who are oppressed, and to become lifelong advocates of social justice. However since I believe that change comes from within (as those with power decide to share it), I also assume a professionalization role in which I equip students with the technical and social skills that will advance them within the professions of architecture and urban planning, especially those persons who might broaden its boundaries. My involvement as a builder of the material world defines my third role as technical assistant who seeks to find practical solutions for the enormous problems that plague central cities. My fourth role as a teacher comes from that part of myself who respects the individuality of students, and is committed to nurturing their intellectual and creative growth.

By simultaneously embracing seemingly contradictory roles, I am aligned with a group that Meyerson and Scully (1993) referred to as "tempered radicals" who precariously "maintain dual identities and commitments" (p. 11) in order to preserve their outsider-within status.

> *We both identify with our respective organizations and professions, are committed to them, and want to pursue careers and advance within them. Yet we also believe that these hierarchical institutions are patriarchies and need to change. At the same time, we believe that our profession is instrumental in perpetuating these forms and constraining change* (p. 4).

This characterization—tempered radical—has been enormously useful in helping me to understand my ambivalence in seeking to enable architecture and urban planning students to serve those persons who traditionally have not benefitted from their services. How can I nurture their individual growth while building their commitment to social justice? Given my personal experiences with the ravages of urban development, how can I help students to understand the environmental experiences of central city residents without alienating them or, even worse, making them feel guilty? Since my students have gotten into the University of Michigan by virtue of their ability to compete, how can I encourage them to share their privileges without putting them at risk of loosing their superior ranking in society's pecking order?

During the last five years, I have attempted to address these questions in a classroom setting that is called a "studio"—the term used for a six-credit-hour course in which students work hands-on with instructors to produce a range of planning and design tools (reports, maps, plans, drawings, participatory activities in the community, and so forth). Drawing from the traditional features of both architecture and urban planning studios, I have elaborated a format for involving masters students at the University of Michigan in community development projects. I will use excerpts from student evaluations of these five studios in order to illustrate the dilemmas caused by my goals of simultaneously encouraging students to change, and to get into, their professions. I will end with commentary on the conditions that are necessary to make a successful community-oriented class, regardless of the subject matter.

What is a Studio Anyway?

Design studios are the mainstay of any architectural curriculum. They not only provide a critical context for assessing a student's competence for professional practice, their output is the principle yardstick through which the national accrediting board gauges the quality of a particular program. Historically there has been a tug-of-war in architectural studios among the four dimensions of the field—esthetics, technology, human needs, and theory—that varies according to the sociopolitical mood of the country, the ideal of integrating all four rarely being attained. During the Reagan-Bush era the focus at the University of Michigan shifted from technology and humanistic concerns to esthetics and theory so that in recent years most studios (which students elect via a lottery system) center around abstract issues of form. Each studio instructor offers one or more design assignments or "problems" to a contingent of about 15 people during the course of the semester.

The style of architectural design instruction is one-on-one with public reviews (or juries) of individual student work being conducted by guest professors, local practitioners, or even nationally distinguished guests who provide an outsider's assessment of the work. In recent years, the tenor of architecture studios nationally has often been authoritarian with a heavy dose of stress and mystery. As one masters student wrote in a letter to the editor of a professional publication:

> *In my experience, many design professors seem to be cast from the same rude and irrational mold. Their egos consume them, and their intolerant vision of what constitutes "good" design typically leads to the verbal abuse and humiliation of well-intentioned and hard-working students trying to conform to unspecified standards* (Miller, 1993, p. 11).

Although architecture students have a three-year apprenticeship after graduation to hone professional skills, urban planning students rely on a single capstone studio which is taken at the end of the masters program as a gateway to the world of work. Two instructors work together to establish a one- to three-year contractual relationship with a community client; then the faculty and community client devise a list of possible projects prior to the beginning of the semester. After an orientation period of about two weeks, students form teams with each selecting a project that is usually reformulated under advisement from the team's particular constituency. Because student teams are encouraged to work independently in the field, class is scheduled for only six hours a week instead of the 12 hours that architects meet. Some of that time is used for weekly meetings with the entire group or with team captains who coordinate a public presentation in the community at the end of the semester. Above all, emphasis is placed on delivering a professional-quality product to the client which usually includes an illustrated report.

Each of these studio formats had advantages and disadvantages relative to my own instructional approach. Since the architecture studio had extended contact hours there was greater potential for accommodating both reflection and applied work, or praxis, than in urban planning where the focus was clearly on application. In its favor, the urban planning studio had both a long-term collaborative community relationship as well as an in-class team structure while the norm in the architecture studio was for individualistic enterprise hardly suited to community work. However since the outcome of the architecture studio was subject to national review, it was far riskier to deviate from the norms of the profession in that setting. On the other hand, architects elected a particular instructor and presumably were committed to the studio offering while planners were required to take a single offering. After attempting one community development studio solely in architecture, I began to find different ways for combining students from both architecture and planning, using aspects of both formats. The benefits were that an interdisciplinary group could execute more comprehensive projects; and the burden of navigating a real-life setting could be shared by the faculty .

In general, the organizational principles of the combined architecture and urban planning studio were that (1) faculty made a commitment to a given community that extended beyond any particular class of students to an ideal of three years; (2) students developed their own course "syllabus" or project requirements in consultation with the constituency for that project; (3) community clients paid out-of-pocket expenses and received a community development plan with projects ranging from short-term practical interventions to long-term visions involving structural change; (4) projects reflected the community's needs, faculty expertise, and students' interests; (5) grades were based on an assessment by one's teammates, faculty, and the community client; and (6) equal emphasis was placed on the team's working process, written or drawn final products (copies were given to the client), and a public community presentation.

In reviewing the evaluations from the last five years, what is most striking is students' varied experience of the same situation—a variation that is far more extreme than in any of the more standard courses that I have taught in the last 18 years. It seems reasonable to assume that their contradictory perceptions of the class may have been due, in part, to my ambivalent stance as a tempered radical who had to "respond to competing constituencies, project multiple purposes, and cope with multiple images" (Meyerson and Scully, p. 15). They may also be due, in part, to the two competing priorities inherent in any community-service classroom—providing a meaningful service to a disadvantaged group while, at the same time, assuring a quality learning experience for students.

The following section contains excerpts from student evaluations of the five community-development studios which illustrate the students' experience of the competing tensions that I try to balance in my class.

Multiple Readings of a Tempered Radical

The combined architecture and urban planning studio required all participants to reconsider their traditional roles. In developing the requirements for their projects, students were asked to take responsibility for setting their own standards of performance; and to weigh what they needed to learn as aspiring professionals while accepting and valuing local residents as experts on their subject matter. Their challenge was to walk a thin line between being independent, self-determining agents, being cooperative teammates, and being empathic with the "other" in the community. Additionally the architecture students had to violate the norms of their program by focusing on their clients' individual and social needs rather than on theory or esthetics, by giving over some of their individual creative time to group discussion, and by making drawings that communicated to lay persons rather than to other professionals.

For some students these new roles were at odds with their previous schooling experience in which efficiency was emphasized over democratic decision making. Those students perceived the studio as chaotic, the instructor as undirected. For other students (far fewer in number), the freedom to define one's own path was stimulating and provided an opportunity for honing leadership skills. Typical are these differing experiences of the same studio.

> *Does not lead the class enough. Lets us make up our own programs and do things at our own pace. Good idea except nothing ever gets done unless the instructor pushes you. With students taking the initiative deciding the direction of the term, the majority rules.*

> *One weakness which affected utilization of time was the freedom of the students to make democratic decisions about the direction of the studio. It was good to have some initial input, but the democratic process is frustrating and time-consuming and doesn't enhance camaraderie amongst students.*
>
> o o o o o
>
> *The independent nature of the work and responsibility to group were important aspects of the course. I developed leadership qualities because of the organizing requirements within the group. However, I learned the most from observing the professor interact with others and how she organized the class' work in a way that could be presented to an audience in a persuasive manner.*

> *The only criticism I have is that perhaps we could have been more efficient if we better defined a goal earlier on. We really were defining all the way up to the last day. Then again, isn't that reality? We may have benefitted from better organization but, conversely, we gained something from the confusion of the process.*

Being asked to evaluate one's own work within a real-life context also was read very differently by students. Some mistook the nonauthoritarian mode as an invitation for producing sloppy work when the reality was quite the opposite; others sensed the fact that while faculty had given up the protection that their superior status usually offers, they also had become more accountable for their students' behavior in the local community and for the quality of completed work for which our clients were paying out-of-pocket expenses. In a few instances students flagrantly abused the open-ended quality of the studio and failed to complete work appropriate to a masters-level course; however, even the most engaged students expressed varied understandings of the quality of work expected as the following evaluation excerpts illustrate.

> *She isn't very demanding and where having an instructor that is too demanding tends to crush morale, having an instructor that doesn't make many demands and lets the class just go along, tends to allow laziness.*

ooooo

> *TOO MUCH WORK!! ~~Demands~~ Expects (better word) perfection. If we didn't have other demands on our time that would be fine. It's obvious we're not lazy, but most of us must work in addition to being full time students. There's only 24 hours in a day.*

> *She worked as hard or even harder than the students throughout the term. She has high expectations of her students and works at helping everyone do their best.*

Although the architecture studio was more accommodating of a theoretical component, both groups of students were more comfortable with action than they were with the self reflection and theorizing that is needed to imbue action with a social change dimension. The emphasis in urban planning on a quality product increased the tension between understanding and action because the architect's drawing is more labor-intensive than the planner's writing, and thus is more compromised by large blocks of time being devoted to reading or discussion. Yet there were students in both groups who lined up on different sides of the issue of action versus reflection and theorizing. This may have been due to students placing unequal value on the *content* of the inquiry as well as having differing views of what constituted individual development. Compare for yourself the first three excerpts with the last three.

> *The most valuable aspects of the course were the readings that introduced the social problems at hand. The course could be improved with even more readings dealing with value systems within architecture and other cultural manifestations.*

> *The strengths of this course are that it gave me an opportunity to develop personal interests, to take leadership, to be experimental, to learn without being told what to think or believe...It was also important to deal with an issue that has been too long ignored by our professions.*

> *We were all made aware of the issues and the almost unfathomable depths of the problem of low-income housing and low-income community development. We all for the most part were made to be more people-oriented in our approach to architecture and this is nothing but a plus.*

○ ○ ○ ○ ○

She is a feminist extremist who is judgmental and opinionated (unreasonably).

First half of term was wasted with coursepack readings, discussions, etc. Most of it was relevant, but it was way too much for a studio.

Too much class time was given over to discussion and reading. Not enough doing. Four months of time with three months of talking about the same issues. People who want to draw should take another studio and those who want to read and talk can do such.

Lessons from the Margin

Academicians, politicians, all the people that are sup-posed to be guiding this country say you've got to be neutral. As soon as I started looking at that word 'neutral' and what it meant, it became very obvious to me there can be no such thing as neutrality. It's a code word for the existing system...Instead of saying I am with the dominant, I say that I'm neutral (Horton and Freire, 1990, pp. 102-104).

The five community development studios that I have described accorded some of my most exciting moments in eighteen years of teaching; however, I can say without reservation that they also posed my greatest challenges—and defeats. Even though I moderated my views on social justice, even though I balanced commitment to community with nurturance of students' creativity, the subject matter itself voided the long-held tradition in education for neutrality. Clearly, the studio was not in the realm of the dominant but rather took students into a world with which most of them were quite unfamiliar. Being asked to participate in setting the direction of the class and to determine the nature of their learning was annoying to many students because it seemed to detract from the technical proficiency that had been so underscored throughout their schooling.

I am acutely aware that the success of a particular studio depended on the students who elected it—their capacity for self-direction in carrying out individual as well as collective work, their level of technical skill for expressing and executing ideas, their compassion and curiosity for understanding the root causes of social injustice, their aspirations for identifying with professional norms. These four traits—capacity for self-direction, technical expertise, orientation to social justice, identification with professional norms—deter-mined how students perceived my contradictory roles as a tempered radical, thus creating extremely varied views of the same situation. For example, students with a strong social justice commitment who were critical of the mainstream attitudes of their profession valued an indepth investigation of structural inequities especially if they were skilled and disciplined enough to complete the final product with ease. Alternatively, students with a weak commitment to social justice and a strong identification with their professions felt that discussions of social issues were distracting—a perspective that was exaggerated by inadequate skills or self-direction.

You can imagine how the strengths or weaknesses that individuals brought to class impacted the degree to which I fulfilled my faculty roles as well as the students' perceptions of those roles, creating the dynamic situation that is shown in Figure 2. In this example, the students had a fairly strong social justice orientation, excellent capacity for self-direction, moderate professional identification, but weak technical skills. Thus, they were more favorably attuned to the studio's social justice and community service dimensions (which were more emphasized) and less favorably reconciled with its teaching and professionalizaton dimensions (which were less emphasized).

Figure 2.

Intersection of Student Traits and Faculty Roles as Determinants of the Studio Experience

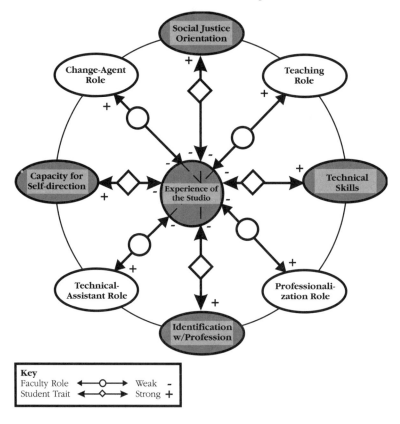

However, some general organizational principles follow that should be useful to anyone (including those who do not consider themselves to be tempered radicals) wishing to conduct a community-service class, whether in architecture, urban planning, or some other field altogether.

Negotiate a long-term mutual commitment between a community and your academic unit. Most students are painfully aware that social problems can not be addressed in a meaningful way within a fifteen-week semester. When they know that they are part of a larger on-going intervention, they may be less pressured in feeling that there is not enough time for theorizing and reflection. On the other hand, poor receptivity on the part of a community client will assuredly undermine any class. My colleagues and I have found that asking community clients to pay out-of-pocket expenses for travel and printing costs guarantees that they are interested in the work that students produce. There are probably many other ways of accomplishing the goal of mutual commitment.

Reinforce instructions regarding the mutual responsibilities of faculty and students. It is important to remember how much at odds the type of class described here is with normal classroom procedure. Therefore, faculty need to be tireless in finding multiple and creative ways for making sure that students understand what they are being asked to do (in class and in the community) as well as what roles the faculty member will assume. I have found that articles, such as this one, are enormously effective as are individual conferences and debriefing meetings, provided there are students who are willing to communicate.

Accept that there will be widely varying reactions to the class. Involving university students in disadvantaged communities assures that most of them will encounter people and circumstances that are outside of their own experience. It is unlikely that all students will be able to be empathic with this new experience, or they may be unable to act on their feelings of compassion because of an inability to work independently in a field setting, weak technical skills, or what they perceive as a conflict with professional norms. The needs, values, and abilities that students bring to a class will determine how they perceive the faculty's role which necessarily will be more complex in a community-service class than in a traditional seminar or lecture course.

If possible, offer a separate seminar to cover the theorizing and reflection components. Although this may be difficult to schedule for both students and faculty, I have experienced repeated difficulty in trying to combine action, theory, and reflection. The problem is not simply one of time for surely 12 hours a week should be sufficient for an integrative approach to praxis. Rather it seems to be one of the students needing boundaries—needing to know that one class is for hands-on activity and another is for intellectual work.

Find satisfaction in the struggle since real progress is unlikely. To avoid the sense of being overwhelmed, it is important for both students and faculty to keep in mind what Derrick Bell (1992) so eloquently stated:

> *The challenge throughout has been to tell what I view as the truth about racism without causing disabling despair...Black people will never gain full equality in this country. Even those Herculean efforts we hail as successful will produce no more than temporary "peaks of progress," short-lived victories that slide into irrelevance as racial patterns adapt in ways that maintain white dominance. This is a hard-to-accept fact that all history verifies. We must acknowledge it, not as a sign of submission, but as an act of*

ultimate defiance...We believe in fulfillment—some might call it salvation—through struggle...As a matter of faith, we believe that despite the lack of linear progress, there is satisfaction in the struggle itself.

Chapter 15

STUDENT WORKSHOPS AS COMMUNITY SERVICE LEARNING

Barry Checkoway

Student workshops are a form of community service learning in which students develop knowledge and learn lessons by serving the community. They may engage students in housing reform, health care, environmental change, neighborhood revitalization, and other fields of service. They may take the form of organizing for social action, planning programs at the local level, or developing new community-based services. They enable students to serve the community, reflect upon their experience, and learn lessons or derive principles for the future.

Student workshops can complement coursework in academic disciplines, and provide field training for public health, social work, urban planning, and other professional fields. Studies show that service-learning can develop new substantive knowledge and practical skills, and contribute to lifelong social responsibility and civic values.

Student workshops also can contribute to community problem-solving and program-planning. Studies show that they can help people to assess needs, set priorities, formulate plans, implement programs, and create change. As such, they can provide technical assistance that makes an important difference at the community level, especially in traditionally underserved areas.

This paper describes three student workshops for community service learning. They include a community planning workshop in an area of rural farmlands and small cities, a neighborhood revitalization workshop in a low-income area of a large industrial city, and a voter participation workshop which promoted the participation of traditional nonvoters in agencies and communities. They are based on my belief that students learn by serving the community, and my experience as a faculty facilitator of the process in various settings over time.

Community Planning Workshop

This workshop took place in east central Illinois, an area of agricultural farmland and several small and medium-sized cities located midway between Chicago and St. Louis. The focus of the workshop was on Champaign-Urbana, a twin city of roughly 100,000 persons and home of the University of Illinois.

The academic base for the project was the Department of Urban and Regional Planning at the University of Illinois. Urban Planning faculty rely heavily upon field courses—studios, laboratories, or workshops—to provide opportunities for students to make direct client contributions while gaining experiential knowledge and practical skills. Since workshops are a particularly intensive educational experience, students receive twice as much credit as for the typical class.

The workshop began with my search for students with commitment to community planning. I sought students who wanted to collaborate with community organizations, and required a written statement for screening them before approval for enrollment. I assume that acceptance into an undergraduate or graduate program is no assurance that a student is ready for this type of experience, and that a commitment to work with a community client obligates the instructor to find the best available students.

Students participated in an overnight orientation weekend at a retreat center before the semester. The weekend provided an opportunity to discuss content and process objectives, and develop group guidelines and operating procedures. The weekend included "community public hearings" to which local leaders were invited to identify areas of need in which we might contribute to the community. Planners, organizers, elected officials, and agency administrators identified more than 120 ideas through this procedure.

Students formed teams around two projects, for which they formulated proposals and learning contracts for the semester. Both teams agreed to meet on Tuesdays to discuss operational tasks, and Thursdays to reflect upon their experiential learning. Tuesday "staff" meetings included reports of progress and discussion of tasks for completion in the next week. Students sought feedback on their work and often asked questions for which there were no answers in the group. Thursday "reflection" sessions aimed to discuss relevant readings, relate theory to practice, and analyze the forces affecting the community. I facilitated most of these sessions and some students found them a distraction from "work."

The Urban Development team tried to determine whether local financial institutions were "redlining" or refusing to grant mortgage loans in older central neighborhoods in favor of newer outlying areas. Although the team was unable to document redlining with available data, they concluded that redlining might be taking place and that local governments should conduct hearings on lending practices, investigate the effects of newer development on older areas, and consider ways to provide new housing in the community.

Students prepared a report for presentation to the city council, and were asked to formulate an antiredlining ordinance for the community. They won widespread recognition in local media, and prepared an article for a statewide publication.

Students in the Urban Development team also formulated a "community impact fee" on behalf of a community organization which wanted local developers to pay for the public services required by private development. They prepared a memorandum on municipal regulation of subdivisions, reported on the actual costs of municipal services generated by new development, and recommended alternative approaches to growth management.

The Health Planning team studied public involvement in the subarea advisory council of the East Central Illinois Health Systems Agency formed "to provide the maximum potential involvement of the public." Among the findings were that 24 of the 30 council members were from the highest income census tract, and that no low income, minority, or rural area was actively represented. Council members' attendance at meeting was found to be so inadequate that one-half of them should have been terminated according to their own by-laws. The study concluded that there were inconsistencies between federal aims and local practices.

The students presented a report on their findings to the regional planning commissioners and to state and federal officials. They called a meeting of local consumers contacted during the study, and formed the Champaign County Health Care Consumers (CCHCC) to promote participation in health planning.

Local consumers conducted community forums, leadership training workshops, and an unprecedented campaign to take control of the advisory council. They recruited a large number of council members, enlisted candidates to run for positions, and finally won a majority of seats. In response, local medical providers struck back, mobilized massive political resources, and elected their own slate to the local council.

Local consumers developed a strong community-based organization. They formed task forces to increase access of low income people; investigated the compliance of local hospitals; established a hotline for consumer complaints; and published the area's first medical directory. Fifteen years later the consumer organization is highly influential and still directed by a community organizer who got his start as a student in the workshop.

Neighborhood Development Workshop

This workshop took place in the South Austin neighborhood of Chicago. In a single semester, ten graduate and undergraduate students provided technical assistance and produced a report which helped a neighborhood organization plan a housing project on a single demonstration block. Again the academic base for the workshop was the Department of Urban and Regional Planning at the University of Illinois at Urbana-Champaign.

The workshop began when I contacted the Metropolitan Area Housing Alliance (MAHA) for help in identifying a potential client. MAHA staff recommended South Austin Realty Association (SARA), an association of block clubs and civic groups working to maintain and improve the housing stock in the neighborhood. In an exploratory meeting, SARA leaders described the need for a study of the neighborhood as a potential reinvestment location and of housing alternatives for a single selected block. I described the workshop concept, assured that the students would be responsive to neighborhood needs, and agreed to undertake the project.

The workshop was advertised at the University, and ten graduate and undergraduate students were selected on the basis of a written paragraph and personal interview inquiring into their intentions and interests. Students wanted to participate in a nonhierarchical group process, or to be involved in the inner workings of a neighborhood organization, or to put social ideals into action through working with a community group.

A pre-semester orientation weekend was conducted to discuss the content and process of the workshop. The weekend was followed by a neighborhood tour, and a meeting in which local leaders described their expectations. The discussion was open-ended in nature, originating from the experience and research needs of the client but allowing room for negotiation and modification over time.

Students began meeting to develop a research strategy. Various group exercises helped clarify substantive and procedural issues, including brainstorming and nominal group process to generate ideas and set priorities. The students drafted a preliminary outline for review by neighborhood leaders, formed teams around major research areas, and selected assignments and a timetable for completion.

We met twice weekly in three-hour sessions to report progress and to raise questions. These meetings enabled us to exchange information, learn from each other, and build mutual support. They offered opportunities to discuss readings and consult with guest experts on housing and urban development. These sessions typically began with a presentation by a student or guest followed by interaction on its implications for the neighborhood.

SARA's staff director responded to early drafts and invited reactions from community leaders, thus increasing the possibility that the work would respond to neighborhood needs. Neighborhood leaders held "office hours" when they were available for telephone consultation. Research was subjected to tests of reality to judge its relevance.

Students traveled to the neighborhood for first-hand information, sought assistance from resource persons, and conducted special studies in the area. Some students stayed overnight in a neighborhood church rectory during a period of intense work, which was personally significant for those who had never stayed overnight in the city before.

Completion of the project proved more difficult than originally expected. Harsh winter weather caused cancellation of a few trips to the neighborhood. Twice students traveled to the neighborhood to meet with neighborhood leaders who did not appear. Student editors responsible for the first full draft found gaps in research and redundancies in writing; their requests for revisions met with reluctance due to the increasing outside pressures of a concluding semester. Although morale declined in this period, students finally completed the report and presented the information to neighborhood leaders.

The report concluded that the neighborhood was an excellent location for revitalization, and that housing rehabilitation was the recommended approach for the "demonstration" block. Soon after, neighborhood leaders used the report to develop plans for a project on the block, then used these plans in a proposal which resulted in a major contract from the federal government.

SARA's staff director wrote a long letter to the students citing "a superb job" and called for continuing neighborhood-university collaboration. He sent the report to federal officials who circulated it nationwide as a model of collaboration.

Students wrote short papers and completed questionnaires evaluating the workshop as an educational experience, and most felt that the course objectives had been accomplished. Some felt that the experience had broadened their knowledge of neighborhood and community development issues, or that they had acquired new practical skills and career credentials, or that they had learned more than in the classroom. They also evaluated (and graded) other workshop members, after which I reported their average aggregate grades (without change) to the university.

Voter Participation Workshop

Voting is the most widespread form of political participation in America, but some groups vote less than others and even struggle to exercise their rights. Indeed, some of the strongest stakeholders in public decisions—e.g., low income people and members of minority groups—do not participate actively or see themselves as a group that could create change.

With encouragement from the Dean of the School of Social Work at the University of Michigan, I developed a special one-semester workshop on voter participation. The School has a history of preparing students to work for social change at the community level by involving them in individual field placements.

Faculty and students formed a committee to promote non-partisan voter participation in social agencies where people seek services and communities where they reside. Committee members asked faculty colleagues to donate funds and, within one week, raised more than $500 for the project.

Students enrolled in the special workshop. Our initial meetings enabled us to get acquainted, discuss expectations, and develop guidelines for the semester. We agreed to meet weekly, form teams for major activities, and develop individual and group learning contracts. Each contract established a plan with the specific tasks and timetable for completion.

Weekly meetings provided opportunities to report progress and build support for implementation. We read books and articles, shared responsibility for leading discussions, and reflected upon our experience. I served as a facilitator, resource person, liaison between the university and community, and recorder of grades at the end of the semester.

Students worked with more than three hundred students, faculty members, agency staff, and community volunteers in various efforts to:

- Increase awareness of voter participation through campus and community forums. One forum featured a professor who described student efforts to register the disenfranchised nationwide.
- Conduct a statewide voter participation training workshop. Special emphasis was placed on skills to establish voting services, identify deputization and registration procedures, and coordinate community campaigns. More than 200 people from community agencies, human service organizations, labor unions, and grassroots neighborhood groups attended the workshop.
- Register low income people and traditional nonvoters. Students selected target districts, arranged with election officials to deputize registrars, and recruited volunteers for waiting rooms, unemployment offices, housing projects, health clinics, neighborhood centers, and places where low income people live or congregate.
- Educate voters in social agencies and communities. Students sent press releases, public service announcements, and letters to newspapers, radio, and television stations. They distributed flyers, posters, and other educational materials in agency intake and waiting areas. They prepared leaflets and canvassed neighborhoods in Detroit, Flint, Ypsilanti,

Toledo, and Jackson.

- Turn out the vote. As the election approached, students distributed additional materials to agencies and doorknob hangers to residences. On election eve, they organized telethons to remind registrants to vote and provide them with directions to polling places. On election day, they offered transportation to the polls.
- Prepare a training kit for planning subsequent projects. The kit provided general strategies and specific techniques for establishing voting services, and alternative approaches to voter education and turnout.

Some students applied their community education efforts to particular groups. For example, three students sought to involve low-income women who might lose their benefits with proposed cutbacks in federal food programs. They prepared posters and other educational materials for designated officers statewide and made several personal visits to talk directly with program recipients in Ypsilanti.

In Toledo, they targeted older and disabled people. They enlisted a private company to provide vans, office space, phone lines, and a dispatcher to take transportation requests; an equipment supply company to provide wheelchairs for use in vans; area businesses to give funds for newspaper advertisements; and other students to help drive people to the polls. They distributed flyers to senior citizen centers, nursing homes, and associations serving the blind and disabled. They also placed newspaper advertisements and received radio and television coverage.

The workshop provided participants with new knowledge and practical skills. Students formulated plans, designed programs, and produced results under time constraints. They served the community in ways which enhanced experiential learning.

Service-Learning Lessons

Student workshops provide students with substantive knowledge and practical skills. Unlike education in which the teacher lectures to listening students, workshops offer experiential hands-on learning situations with students as active participants in the process. Learning activities provide practical problem-solving and program planning experiences, on-the-job training, mentoring and role modeling, and other activities to develop "real world" skills for the future.

These workshops provided learning opportunities not readily available in the classroom, including: developing skills to promote participation in the planning process; analyzing the effects of investments by public agencies and private institutions on neighborhood change; working collaboratively in teams with student peers and community representatives; writing reports for community clients under time constraints; and formulating plans for community-based organizations. This type of "know how" is different from the "know about" information available in the classroom.

Student workshops can provide new life experiences for students. In their evaluations, students stressed the value of working with people of different backgrounds to solve problems; receiving immediate feedback and candid response; seeing the community through the eyes of its traditional nonparticipants; working with people who experience discrimination or oppression in society; addressing a problem whose solution is beyond reach; or organizing to have real impact on the world. Many university students come from backgrounds which do not afford exposure to such situations. Student evaluations of workshops revealed their educational benefits in terms of attitude development, values clarification, and greater awareness of problems in society.

The real world environment of the workshops was a unique experience for many students. University students often operate in an environment in which deadlines are easily met, information is readily available, and individual performance is rewarded. In contrast, these workshops operated in an environment with short deadlines, incomplete information, and shared responsibilities. They were evaluated by other students, held accountable by community clients, and responded to tests of reality uncharacteristic of university curricula.

Student workshops can provide experiential credentials for community careers. Following the workshops, some students took jobs as planners, organizers, policy analysts, and agency administrators, and as community advocates and political activists. They took positions in planning agencies, human service organizations, grassroots neighborhood groups, community development corporations, and private companies.

Student workshops can strengthen the lifelong social responsibility and civic values of young people. In contrast to students who sit silently in classrooms and accept community problems as given, workshop students raise questions about issues, identify root causes of problems, and formulate strategies for improvement. Some workshop students have experiences whose effects are lasting, like the one whose career as a community organizer got its start in a workshop, or another who went from a workshop to the advocacy staff of a leading city planning agency. My observation is that workshop students demonstrate higher levels of community participation in later life than do students who study community in the classroom.

Some students express satisfaction with the knowledge and skills gained in workshops, as in the following: "I enjoyed the opportunity to take a leadership role and to have the freedom and responsibility to come up with ideas and implement them." "This was my first attempt at a major project like this and I found that my abilities were adequate in several ways." "My involvement in the project helped me learn about advocacy, organizing, and managing groups." "The project helped me develop new skills and gain confidence in my abilities."

Student workshops can provide faculty with new life experiences and broader perspectives that stimulate the creation of knowledge and the enhancement of teaching. Many faculty have narrow academic backgrounds and would benefit from interaction with people outside their small circle. Faculty who facilitate workshops may more easily overcome disciplinary barriers, better relate theory to practice, and apply teaching skills conducive to student needs. There is no a priori contradiction among excellence in research, teaching, and community service. On the contrary, I assume that faculty who favor experiential education and service-learning also score high in research publications and student evaluations of their teaching.

However, many faculty members are trained in positivist research methods which discourage community participation in defining the problems, gathering the data, and using the research results; and in banking approaches to education which view teachers as providers of knowledge to passive student recipients. It is unrealistic to expect researchers to develop knowledge, or instructors to facilitate learning, when they have not had these experiences themselves.

Also, faculty perceive few institutional rewards and little support for community service learning. They perceive that service-learning does not weigh heavily in promotion, tenure, salary or other components of the reward structure. They may even become conditioned to regard service-learning as a waste of time, distraction from work, or threat to their careers in the university. Those faculty that do have commitment to service-learning may lack institutional resources for quality work.

Student workshops can help universities provide public service to society. Although some university officials discuss service as central to the institutional mission, there are few incentives and rewards to support this type of work. University officials tend not to articulate a mission for service-learning, or to formulate strategy for its development, or to recognize its benefits for faculty development and student learning.

This is ironic, for student workshops are strategically situated to enable the university to relate research and teaching to community concerns while also serving the core academic objectives of the university. They do not require bureaucratic structures or special staff, but instead allow the university to extend its traditional mission and institutional infrastructure to broader constituencies in ways which strengthen, rather than weaken its efforts. Student workshops could contribute to an approach to service that would broaden the scholarly responsibilities of the university and would make knowledge more accessible to society, but they are not recognized in this way in the present environment.

Student workshops can contribute to community development. These student workshops mobilized people to vote in elections, prepared plans for neighborhood revitalization, and strengthened community representation in the health planning process. They joined efforts to strengthen the supply of affordable housing, to increase access to health care, and to enable disenfranchised people to exercise their rights. They collaborated with community organizations and involved people in the institutions and decisions that affect their lives.

However, it should be emphasized that community service was not the only purpose of these workshops. Community service learning is a process of learning by serving the community. Learning and service are the dual aims, and the community is the means of the process. It would be as mistaken to assess them in terms of their potential for service alone, as it would be to ignore that there are other ways to learn about the community.

What is the appropriate pedagogy for community service learning? What are the best means for reflecting upon experience and generalizing for future action? These workshops included library research and participant observation, reading and writing, individual and group assignments, problem solving and program planning, and many, many meetings to think together and reflect upon experience.

What is the role of the student in community service learning? Is the student a research scientist, information technician, problem diagnostician, truth explorer, or organizational consultant? Or an organizer, planner, or advocate? Learning and service each has its own role expectations, and there is no single definition for all situations. Perhaps it requires a juggling of hats, a skill needed in later professional life.

What is the appropriate role of the instructor? In these workshops I was a facilitator and resource person rather than a teacher or a supervisor, and this caused concern for some students. Some students were incredulous when I joined teams as a peer, helped in routine tasks, and frankly expressed ignorance of some situations in the field.

Other students resisted when I assigned readings, expected them to integrate theory and practice, and asked them to apply academic research to community situations. I was discomfited by the dilemmas that arose from the need to strengthen service and facilitate learning; structure the situation and promote participation in the process; encourage self evaluation and report grades to the university; invest time in teaching while accountable for research products; show competence and admit ignorance; and work collectively in teams while dividing the labor among us. These dilemmas do not usually arise in the traditional classroom.

What is the appropriate role for the client? In these cases, community clients largely defined the work to be done, and participated in the phases of the workshop process. This helped assure that the product would be responsive to community needs, and that the students would adapt to the community agenda. The clients were thus given a central role in defining the problem, which differentiated the workshop from the traditional classroom, and appealed to some students for whom "practice" had more authority than "theory."

However, this raises basic questions about the pedagogy of community service learning. If students shape their work to the specific requirements of an immediate situation, do they lose the educational opportunity to thoroughly explore the issues and present more comprehensive solutions?

Community service learning can focus on technical skills and practical experience at the expense of broader analytic policy and critical thinking. In field education, students tend to exercise skills that they already have, to spend time in the routine work of gathering data, to concentrate on producing an end product rather than on comprehensive analysis or critical assessment of policy alternatives or a broader critique of society. Students may spend long hours discussing client needs and handling immediate demands of the present situation. This may provide a brief apprenticeship and an experience which makes students more immediately employable. But it also may fail to introduce more knowledge through in-depth intellectual experiences unavailable on the job. The deeper dilemma is that the university seeks to develop knowledge and strengthen learning for the long haul, and the community wants the information and results as soon as possible.

Conclusion

Student workshops are a form of community service learning which combine service and learning to the benefit of both. The workshops described here provided new knowledge for collective action in community planning, a written report for a low-income neighborhood organization, and special efforts to register disenfranchised people to vote in elections. They provided students with substantive knowledge, practical skills, life experiences, and a basis for social responsibility not usually available in the classroom.

Student workshops are not the only or necessarily the best approach to learning for practice in the community. On the contrary, workshops may be limited in opportunities for some types of knowledge development, and thus should be integrated with complementary coursework to provide an overall educational experience.

Nor are student workshops the only or necessarily the best source of assistance for the community. Other sources—for example, public agencies, private corporations, or other community organizations—may be more suitable than these. Outside assistance from any source is no substitute for community organizations to develop the capacity to solve problems and plan programs for themselves.

In the final analysis, however, student workshops remain valuable resources for combining service and learning. The challenge is to recognize their limitations, integrate them with other courses in the curriculum, and find ways to strengthen their quality.

Chapter 16

THE SOCIAL WORK PRACTICUM AS SERVICE-LEARNING

Lily Jarman-Rohde and John E. Tropman

Introduction

Service-learning is, quite simply, learning built around service to others in which students fulfill human service provider roles. As such, students engage in planned educational experiences designed to meet human needs through socially meaningful tasks. Like most internships or apprenticeships, actual field settings are used as laboratories for the educational and social development of the student. But what distinguishes service-learning from other forms of experiential education is its service dimension, conceived as a primary and powerful vehicle through which learning occurs. It assumes that both the experiential component of field work and the provision of service have educational value, and that both elements inform the structure of the experience and the nature of the learning assignments. Just as field education enhances classroom learning, service-learning expands it even further by using socially beneficial work as an educational tool. With its required practice training programs in human service settings, the professional practicum in social work education exemplifies service-learning.

The Professional Practicum

Students nationwide come to schools of social work from a variety of backgrounds, but what binds students is their concern for the well-being of others. The practicum is the direct vehicle through which students can act on that concern. As an integral part of the curriculum, the practicum provides opportunities to apply theoretical knowledge learned in the classroom to practical experience. It allows students to work on real social problems and to do so in the contexts of the family, neighborhood, community, and/or legislative arena.

Through the practicum, social work students make significant contributions in the community. For example, a blind social work student who had dual interests in theology and disability issues did field work through the social ministries, advocating for improved services for the disabled. Another student, with an interest in health care, started a hospice program in a prison to assist inmates in coping with their illnesses and in preparing for death. A third student, who was a recovering alcoholic and who had a child with mental health issues, was placed in a community mental health agency, and there spearheaded the creation of the county's first program for people who are dually diagnosed as chemically dependent and mentally ill. Still another student, with interests in both corrections and death and dying, developed a program to serve the families of homicide victims in her placement at the county prosecutor's office.

These kinds of service-based field experiences provide social work students with learning opportunities that they need for competent practice. Students are frequently changed by these service-learning experiences, but just as often a real difference is made in the lives of those served. Thus, the benefits of service-learning through social work field education are not limited to students, but are broadly experienced by the people with whom the students work.

The advantages of learning by doing are well-documented, and it is through the practicum that social work learning tends to occur most meaningfully. Indeed, field education is essential in order to practice in a profession that is both social and service-oriented by nature. It is for this reason that the practicum is a required component of social work education and usually constitutes the largest portion of the graduate and undergraduate curricula.

Practicum Purposes and goals

The purpose of the practicum is to provide students with field-based service opportunities that prepare them for competent social work practice. The generic goals of a practicum typically include:

- acquisition of proficiency in at least one practice method (e.g., community organizing or interpersonal practice)
- application of theory and knowledge in social work field settings
- utilization of social work ethics, values, and goals in day-to-day practice
- development of professional awareness, judgment, and decision-making abilities
- understanding the interdependence of the range of social work roles and skills within various settings and fields of service
- furthering the ability to engage in practice with diverse cultural and racial groups and with groups who have been consistently affected by social, economic, and/or legal bias or oppression.

Practicum Program Structure

Academic degrees in social work are earned through the completion of both classroom-based courses and field work. Graduate social work education typically comprises four terms or approximately 60 academic credits, with the practicum constituting about a quarter of the credits. Academic learning is generally organized by methods of social work practice, such as:

1. interpersonal practice
2. community organization
3. social welfare policy and planning
4. research and evaluation

5. social services administration

Each practice method represents a particular concentration that the student selects as her/his major. This, in turn, determines the nature of the student's practicum experience. The majority of social work students major in interpersonal or clinical practice—that area within the profession that focuses on service to individuals, families, and groups. Many schools also offer concentrations in administration, community organization, and social welfare policy and planning. A smaller number of schools have a research and evaluation concentration. In each case, the major largely determines the level at which service is provided in the practicum: either individual, organizational, local, state, or national.

The particular agency setting in which service is provided is determined by both the student's major and field of service interest. For example, a student majoring in interpersonal practice with an interest in gerontology could be placed to do counselling or group work in a nursing home or psychiatric setting that serves older people. Similarly, administration or policy students interested in the elderly could be placed in a state office of services for the aging to analyze policies, develop budgets, write grants, and/or evaluate programs that serve old people. Regardless of the student's major and service interest, all practicum settings involve service to, or on behalf of, people with pressing needs.

Schools of social work generally use one of two models to organize the scheduling of courses and fieldwork. In the "concurrent" model, academic courses and fieldwork occur concurrently within the same term. For example, a student in a concurrent program might be attending classes three days out of the week and at the practicum placement for the remaining two days of the week in a given term. In this model, the practicum usually extends over a period of three or four terms, and tends to be preferred by students interested in being placed in agencies that provide long-term, sustained, intensive service to clients. This model is also preferred by most schools of social work because it allows for greater integration between class and field content.

In the "block placement" model, class and field work occur in separate terms. A student in a block program might, for example, enroll in classes for the first two terms and then be in field placement for four or five days a week in the third or fourth term. While this model allows students to participate more fully in the daily operations of the agency, it also makes integrating coursework and fieldwork more difficult.

Most schools have a director of field education to oversee practicum program administration and to assist in the shaping of curriculum policy that affects the practicum. Field education faculty and staff may work together to develop agency-based service-learning opportunities, assign students to field settings, train agency staff who serve as field instructors for the students, and organize special programs for field instructors.

Supervision of the Practicum

There are a number of different approaches to supervision of the practicum service-learner. Most common is the "matrix" method, which involves the use of both a field and a faculty supervisor, both of whom shape, guide, and monitor the practicum. The day-to-day field supervisor is an agency staff member who meets the school's qualifications for field instructors and also participates in the school's training program for new field instructors.

Before field work begins, the student and field instructor together develop an extensive educational contract that outlines expectations, field assignments, and supervisory arrangements for the practicum experience. The field instructor is required to have regular, formal meetings with the practicum student to provide training, support, and supervision. At the end of each term the field instructor completes a performance evaluation for the student.

The other supervisor in the matrix plan is a member of the social work faculty, usually the student's academic advisor. The faculty supervisor reviews and approves the educational contract, monitors placement issues and student performance, ensures that the school's expectations and requirements related to field work are met, and assigns the practicum grade based on the field instructor's written assessment of the student's performance. Because the field instructor and faculty supervisor have joint responsibility for insuring a quality practicum experience for the student, they are in regular communication with one another throughout the duration of the placement.

Criteria for the Selection of Field Instructors

Because of the emphasis on the learning in the practicum, all schools of social work have selection criteria for field instructors. At the University of Michigan, field instructors are nominated by an agency and then approved by the School to provide practicum instruction to students if they can demonstrate:

- competence in the practice of social work
- concern for continuing professional development
- commitment to the teaching function of social work education
- interest in and time availability for the regular instruction of students

Typically, field instructors have a Masters in Social Work (MSW), at least two years of post-MSW human service experience, and at least one year employment in the program where students are to be placed. Students are assigned to a field instructor on the basis of the student's major practice method. Though the instruction of students can be shared by various agency personnel, the School-appointed field instructor assumes overall responsibility for field instruction and supervision.

Field Instructor Training Program Issues

The University of Michigan's School of Social Work requires a course for all new field instructors to enable them to effectively assume their educational roles. The curriculum for this course, adapted from Laurence Shulman's *Core Skills for Field Instructors*, includes the following training areas:

1. orientation and assessment of learning and teaching styles
   —dealing with student's initial anxiety about starting field work
   —helping students orient and adapt to the agency

—contracting around the student's learning style and educational goals
—discussing student's learning style in relation to field instructor's teaching style
—clarifying purpose for being in social work and at that particular agency
2. work assignment issues
—clarifying the student's role at the agency
—determining appropriate assignments and nature and frequency of supervision
—how to request and receive feedback
—determining when to have a student start agency work
—evaluation of student performance
3. field instruction issues
—helping the student make most effective use of the field instructor
—using effective teaching methods in field instruction
—dealing with authority issues
—dealing with student's defensiveness and resistance
4. student's interaction with the agency system
—how to communicate effectively with other staff
—how to constructively influence the agency's service delivery
—how to help students deal with emerging questions and concerns about agency policies and procedures, and develop informal and formal means for influencing policies and procedures
—how to assess the student's role in the agency system
—termination from the agency and from agency clientele

Criteria for the Selection of Practicum Agencies

Just as all schools of social work have criteria for selecting field instructors, they also have criteria for selecting practicum agencies. The selection of agencies is largely dependent on the agency's ability to accommodate the broad demands of a multi-faceted curriculum, the range of target populations and experiences which it can offer, and its commitment to the training of practitioners. Agencies must usually meet the following criteria:

- subscribe to progressive standards of practice
- commit to enter into a long-term relationship with the School involving the training of numerous students over time
- show stability of program and of financial support, or, alternatively, be at the cutting edge of programming or practice
- have one or more staff members who qualify as field instructors
- have available adequate facilities, including office space, work materials, equipment, and secretarial assistance for the student
- offer a favorable setting and atmosphere for learning
- allow all field instructors time for preparation for: student instruction, regular conferences with the student, consultation with School faculty, and attendance at School meetings
- allow all new field instructors time for attending the course on supervision in practice skill instruction

- have administrative policies regarding service to clients, to other agencies, and to the community that are consistent with the sound standards of practice appropriate to the particular type of agency
- reimburse students for expenses incurred while transacting agency business
- agree that no student trainees accepted by the agency will be discriminated against on the basis of race, sex, color, religion, national origin or ancestry, age, marital status, handicap, Vietnam-Era Veteran status, or sexual orientation
- preference is given to agencies that can provide stipends to financially needy students, and that are accessible to students with disabilities

At the University of Michigan the selection of practicum sites is largely guided by the "cluster concept" in which multiple numbers of students are placed in one agency or a set of agencies working together. The aims of the cluster concept are to:

- enhance the depth of the educational experience for students by allowing them to work with, and learn from, each other
- maintain quality control over placements, while allowing agencies to plan more efficiently for student participation
- strengthen working partnerships between the School and its field sites, allowing for cooperative research, consultation, and training efforts

The Integration of Class and Field Learning

If social work education in general, and service-learning in particular, are to be optimally meaningful for the student, content from class and field need to be effectively integrated. Concurrent class and field programs, for example, are widely used by schools of social work precisely because they allow for greater integration of academic and experiential content. At the University of Michigan, efforts to integrate theory and practice inform nearly every aspect of social work education.

A primary objective of field education is to allow students to apply classroom theory to practice to develop a range of competencies needed for professional practice. For example, theories reviewed in class about human behavior and family dynamics may be applied in the student's practicum experience in order to determine how to handle a case involving a dysfunctional family. But equally important, the student's practicum experience also informs the theoretical course content. Because real world activity may not conform to theory, the experiences of practicum students can demonstrate tension between theory and practice. This tension can then vitalize classroom content, sharpen the theory, and come full circle to further inform the practicum experience.

Faculty use several methods for incorporating practicum experiences into instructional programs. Most common is the case or issue discussion, in which students bring disguised case material or problems they encounter in the practicum to the classroom for group analysis and discussion. This allows for free-flowing movement between theory and experience.

An example of a case for class review can be drawn from a student who is working with a family in which there is a suspicion of child abuse. The agency at which the student is placed might be advocating for the child's removal from the home. However, the student's visits to the home lead him to believe that there are strengths in the family that could be built upon to help prevent abuse. The student brings the case into the classroom and asks the class for input on his assessment and on how to present a case to the agency advocating for keeping the child in the home. In addition, the class might then help the student identify the family's strengths as well as ways to "join" with the family to develop those strengths.

Interestingly, this kind of situation simulates a professional case conference or staff meeting in which colleagues are used as consultants in the review of, and assistance with, case work or issue resolution. The sense of teamwork and collegiality around service to the client is modeled and reinforced, as is the importance of bringing different perspectives and kinds of expertise to bear on human service issues. So the case study not only helps students to integrate academic and experiential learning, but also furthers students' skill-building around teamwork, problem-defining, and utilizing multiple perspectives to find solutions.

Faculty also ask students to augment their field case reports with material from class lectures, discussions, and readings. In this way, and those cited above, theory and practice are integrated so that the learning is greater than if either of the parts was absent.

A Mutually Beneficial Relationship

Besides the obvious human resource benefits that practicum students provide to social service agencies, rich opportunities exist for collaborative efforts between schools of social work and community agencies that serve as practicum sites. Faculty who serve as liaisons to agencies in which students are placed are often asked to respond to agencies' programmatic needs. Such needs may be addressed by developing staff training programs or agency-based research projects. In consultation with faculty, agency staff have developed innovative solutions to issues of program evaluation, cost-efficiency, service delivery, record-keeping and data collection.

Conversely, students' field instructors are resources for the social work school. They regularly serve as guest or adjunct lecturers at the school, thereby expanding the knowledge base with creative, tested, and/or state-of-the-art approaches to human service programs. In addition, many field instructors are active alumni, sitting on committees and contributing valuable in-kind and other resources to the school. Practicum supervisors often assist in recruiting new students, act as mentors, and, of course, in their capacity as field instructors, are critical in preparing students for future professional practice.

Problems and Pitfalls

The practicum is often described as the most significant and memorable aspect of the student's social work education. And yet, though its importance is reflected in both the percentage of its place in the training of social workers, as well as the increasing attention given to it in the scholarly literature, the practicum is structurally problematic because:

- it is difficult to control the quality of learning when it is away from campus and delegated to non-faculty instructors
- faculty and field instructors vary in ability and commitment to the teaching/learning process
- responsibility and control boundaries between the school and the agency are at times difficult to demarcate
- faculty vary in interest and ability to assume the liaison role, resulting in uneven performance
- attrition of agencies and field instructors—about 50% at many schools—requires on-going school resources to orient and train new field instructors
- students' prior experiences and current capabilities are so varied
- resources can be difficult to obtain in resource-poor fields such as social work

Addressing these issues is an on-going process in social work field education. To help minimize problems that can arise out of these structural problems, and to help ensure quality in substance and supervision in the students' practicum work assignments, schools utilize selection criteria for both agencies as well as for field instructors, training programs for new and tenured field instructors, and educational contracts.

Conclusion

Social work students, regardless of their particular backgrounds, academic interests, and career goals, are committed to people and social justice. They choose social work because they want some part in addressing urgent social problems.

In social work school they learn how to effectively serve and/or advocate on behalf of, or with, those who are under-served.

Though in a fundamental sense, all of social work education is service-learning, the practicum is the aspect of social work training that best exemplifies the service-learning model.

It is here, in the practicum, that students begin to transform their ideals into practice.

Chapter 17

LINKING COMMUNITY SERVICE WITH INDEPENDENT STUDIES

Toby Citrin

Background

Many university degree-granting programs grant credit for individual learning experiences designed by the student and approved and supervised by a faculty member. In the University of Michigan School of Public Health these courses are labelled "Independent Studies," the term used in this chapter. Typically these courses involve a student selecting a specific topic or problem related to his/her field of concentration, identifying and reading a list of materials, and writing a paper. The faculty member helps frame the topic, suggests readings, meets periodically with the student to discuss the readings and review progress in writing the paper, and critiques the paper. Letter grades or a "pass-fail" grade may be applied at course completion. An Independent Studies course may be designed for a single student or for a group whose members share a common interest. Typically the credit hours assigned to the course help satisfy the requirements for graduation in the program.

The Independent Studies course format provides an excellent vehicle for engaging in community service learning, but its potential in this regard barely has been recognized. It is the purpose of this chapter to explore that potential, present examples of several types of community service Independent Studies courses, explore barriers inhibiting the development of these courses, and suggest ways in which these barriers might be overcome.

Independent Studies courses focusing on community problems and linked with community-based organizations (CBOs) present a win-win curriculum strategy. If developed carefully, these courses can satisfy the desire of a growing number of university students to engage in public service while pursuing their education, provide an effective problem-based real-life mode of education, serve the needs of communities, and develop enhanced awareness among faculty of the applicability of their research to community problems.

Types and Examples of Courses

There is an infinite variety of potential Independent Studies courses linking community-based problem solving with university education. Four types of courses are highlighted here—needs assessment/program design, grant proposals, "Community Grand Rounds" seminars, and advocacy projects—to illustrate the variety of proven courses within the University of Michigan School of Public Health.

1. Needs Assessment/Program Design

This model involves students working together with a CBO to assess one or more community needs and assist in the design of programs addressing those needs. Activities carried out by students might include developing and administering a community survey, assembling data on a community problem, reporting to the community on survey results or findings resulting from the data search, review of literature on programs used elsewhere in addressing the problems and their cost and effectiveness, discussing alternative responses to the problem with the community, and assisting in the design of specific programs. A three-way interaction is desirable, with the community members providing experience and knowledge of their specific community, faculty providing their scholarly expertise, and students serving as a "bridge" between faculty and community, with each group teaching and learning at the same time.

An example of a needs assessment effort involves the Arab-American community of Southeastern Michigan. This community contains more Arab-speaking people than any area in the world outside of the Middle East. Of the approximately 200,000 Arab-Americans living in Southeastern Michigan, more than half arrived in the U.S. during the past 10 years. While located geographically in suburban and outer rim areas of Detroit, many of the recent arrivals share the health problems of inner city areas, exacerbated by language and transportation difficulties, a lack of access to medical care facilities, unemployment and poverty. On the positive side, the community has developed effective health and social service organizations, and has a group of dedicated health care professionals providing volunteer services. An impressive array of categorical programs have been put in place in response to individual grant initiatives, but there is a need to provide long-term stability to these programs and to knit them together into a coordinated, comprehensive system of health care.

A consecutive series of two Independent Studies courses are being developed to enable students working with the two major organizations serving the Arab-American community, to both carry out a needs assessment focussing on health care needs and a follow-up feasibility study assessing the potential of creating a comprehensive primary care clinic serving the population. A faculty member with expertise in health-related surveys and primary care organization will serve as instructor, and a team of students will gather data, interview existing providers and patients, write a report summarizing their findings, and present the report to the community. The student team beginning the activity includes several Arab-American students, several students of other backgrounds, and several students from the satellite campus of the University which is located near the target area. Students meet together with their instructor to discuss their findings, carry out individual work in the field, and divide up the writing of the report as a team effort.

2. Grant Proposals

Informal surveys of CBO needs which might be satisfied by the School of

Public Health disclose that assistance in the writing of grant proposals is a high priority. The typical small CBO service provider is without exclusive grant-writing staff, so that time spent by program or administrative staff in writing a proposal is taken away from the provision of valuable services. Moreover, CBO staffs often lack the expertise needed to complete at least some portions of a major grant proposal. An Independent Studies course involving the preparation of a grant proposal can provide significant assistance to a CBO in its search for foundation or government agency funding.

A grant-writing Independent Studies course can also provide a worthwhile learning experience for students. A typical CBO-oriented grant proposal involves the description of the community, definition of a problem, design of an intervention, and evaluation of its impact. Each of these proposal components offers an educational opportunity linking expertise of the faculty with a need of the community, with students serving as the bridge connecting them.

An example of a grant-writing Independent Studies course grew out of a prior needs assessment Independent Studies class. In the first class students developed a Handbook on American Indian Health in Michigan, pulling together a myriad of studies and conference and commission reports which had identified health problems and recommended solutions, few of which had been implemented. The studies to date had been specific to individual tribal organizations or urban settings. They left unclear the role of the state and local public health system in satisfying health needs of the Indian population, in view of the unique status of American Indians with both treaty and citizenship rights.

The Handbook also contained information on available resources to address Indian health problems, description of the complex organizational structure of the Indian population, the disparity of resources among the various tribal organizations and urban groups, and the health beliefs of this community which must be taken into account in fashioning effective interventions.

The process of developing the Handbook led to two further Independent Studies activities. First, it set a model for Handbooks which will now be prepared for each of the other four minority communities in Michigan (African American, Asian Pacific Islander, Hispanic/Latino and Arab American). And once the initial Handbook has been prepared for a minority group, it will be kept current by subsequent students as Independent Studies work.

The other spin-off from the American Indian Health Handbook was an Independent Studies course involving the preparation of a major grant proposal for the development of a state-wide "Action Plan" for American Indian Health in Michigan. Students working on the grant proposal are utilizing materials gathered in the previous Independent Study which developed the Handbook, designing a process for the development of a state-wide health plan, relating data on American Indian Health in Michigan with the goals and objectives for public health nationally (the "Healthy People" objectives) and interviewing health professionals who work with each of the major tribal organizations in Michigan.

If funded, the Action Plan will provide a series of further opportunities for Independent Studies courses, assisting the American Indian organizations in developing the Plan and working on its implementation.

3. "Community Grand Rounds" Seminars

These seminars, initially begun as a joint academic-practice activity betweeen the School and the local health department, involve the coming together of local health department professionals, faculty and students in the discussion of a problem faced by the health department. Once a problem has been selected and faculty and professional participants identified, students develop background materials on the problem and interview each of the participants. The background paper is disseminated to all participants, and issues it identifies are used by the seminar moderator to guide the discussion. Upon completion of the seminar, students prepare an edited transcript, highlighting the insights gained and summarizing the recommendations for future action.

The "Community Grand Rounds" seminars have been so successful that they have spawned two additional seminar series covering local health departments and CBO's. Each individual seminar provides an opportunity for development of an Independent Studies course.

The "Community Grand Rounds" seminars offer an opportunity for expertise of a multidisciplinary faculty group to be joined together with experience of practitioners working in the field in addressing a problem of common interest. Students again play a "bridge" role, and develop insight into both the theoretical and practical aspects of the problem.

4. Advocacy Projects

Advocacy efforts of CBO's and other non-profit organizations provide another vehicle for using the Independent Studies approach to community service learning. Students assisting an organization on an advocacy project can simultaneously learn about the substantive problem with which the project is related, and gain real-world knowledge of how the political process works. While direct advocacy of proposed legislation or administrative action may not be appropriate for receipt of course credit, the development of educational materials related to the project can provide valuable assistance to the community while broadening the student's educational experience.

The Independent Studies course that revolved around the proposal to double Michigan's tobacco tax provides an example of this type of advocacy-related educational project. A coalition of non-profit organizations in Michigan was formed to support the tax hike, proposed both to reduce smoking and to provide revenue for needed health and educational government programs. The course, taught by the School's Director of Community and Government Relations, involved a group of eight students assisting the coalition.

Each member of the eight-student team was assigned two specific roles in the project—to assist a specific organization or legislator, and to develop materials relating to one aspect of the tax hike (e.g. effect on the state's economy; effect on the prevalence of smoking; experience of other states dealing with similar proposals). Materials sought by any of the organizations or the coalition as a whole were assigned to students whose subject area was involved. These papers were circulated among all the students as well as presented to the coalition for use in the campaign. An electronic computer conference was used to facilitate continuing communications between the students and the instructor, providing instant sharing of information developed by students as well as information on the progress of the proposed legislation. Upon completion of the term, the students assembled all documents together into a manual which was presented to the coalition for use in its continuing activities to promote the tax hike.

This model for an Independent Studies course is adaptable to a wide variety of advocacy projects, and can provide a CBO with the kinds of research which is usually only available to well-financed lobbyists and large advocacy organizations.

Barriers and How to Overcome Them

Independent Studies courses have a number of attractive features making them suitable for community service learning. They are flexible, can be designed in a manner which best serves the interests of the CBO, provide project-based real-life learning experiences for students, and promote closer relationships between faculty and the community. But they also present formidable barriers as compared with more traditional courses.

A major threshold problem in developing community-linked Independent Studies courses is finding the intersection for the three key constituencies: organizations whose activities might form the basis for an Independent Studies course, faculty to coordinate the course, and students to enroll in the course. Ideally these functions are carried out by an office or staff established by the academic unit to develop and maintain community-related activities. At the School of Public Health, the Office of Community and Government Relations serves this function. This office elicits information from a wide variety of CBO's on opportunities for assistance, maintains a database on faculty interests and expertise, and provides an annual "menu" of community sevice activities to all students at the beginning of each academic year. The CBO, faculty and student data is then used to develop suggestions for potential Independent Studies courses, faculty so identified are contacted and encouraged to develop a course, and courses decided upon are advertised to the students. The Director of Community and Government Relations often serves as the course instructor, enlisting other faculty members to serve as consultants to students taking the course. The Community and Government Relations staff provide support to faculty in arranging the logistical aspects of the courses to minimize the demand on faculty time. Models of successful Independent Studies courses are maintained and can be used by faculty to minimize the time spent designing new courses. Community service Independent Studies courses are described in School and University periodicals, to generate continuing interest in similar activities. Faculty receive teaching credit proportionate to the number of students enrolled in the course.

Another barrier to the development of these courses is the discrepancy in timing between the term-based academic schedule and the timetable of the community in carrying out its activity. A grant proposal deadline may not coincide with the end of a term; an advocacy project might need to be closely aligned with a legislative timetable. This type of barrier can be minimized by maintaining a consecutive series of similar Independent Studies courses, enabling successive courses to continue work on a common problem or project, and by utilizing Community and Government Relations staff to continue CBO assistance after a course is completed.

Costs incurred in carrying out Independent Studies courses linked with the community present yet another barrier. Student travel, long distance telephone calls, mailing, faxing, computer communications, make most community service learning courses more expensive than traditional courses. Costs can be defrayed in some cases by having the CBO or service organization reimburse the university, by seeking foundation funding for these aspects of the entire program, or by recognizing these expenses as legitimate costs of the School's instructional program to be covered by tuition and other applicable revenue.

If the Independent Studies approach to community service learning is pursued with care and vigor, appropriate infrastructure support is provided, results are widely disseminated and models are committed to writing, the entire program can develop increased momentum from year to year. Successful Independent Studies courses can be converted to pilot courses and ultimately to permanent courses. This form of education can thus provide an exciting stimulus to the development of new educational experiences, invigorate the curriculum, present variety to the students, strengthen their motivation to learn, and at the same time enhance the ability of CBOs to address problems of their communities.

BIBLIOGRAPHY

Bibliography

Barber, Benjamin. 1992. *An Aristocracy of Everyone*. New York: Ballantine.

Beane, James et al. 1981. Long term effects of community service programs. *Curriculum Inquiry*. 11: 143-155.

Bell, D. 1992. *Faces at the Bottom of the Well: The Permanence of Racism*. New York: Basic Books.

Blumberg, Abraham. 1979. *Criminal Justice: Issues and Ironies*, 2nd edition. New York: New Viewpoints.

Boggs, G. 1993. Redefining the American Family: A 21st Century Perspective. In (Ed.) Bryant, B. *The Future: Images for the 21st Century* Ann Arbor: Office of Minority Affairs.

Boyte, Harry C. 1991a. "Community service and civic education," *Phi Delta Kappan*, 72, 765-767.

_____ 1991b. "Turning youth on to politics," *The Nation,* May 13, 1991, 626-628.

Bryant, B. 1993. The 1988 Presidential Campaign and Multicultural Education. In Schoem, D. et al. (Eds.) *Multicultural Teaching in the University*. Westport, Connecticut: Praeger.

Bryant, B. and Weahkie, L. 1991. Strategy Workshop: Education and Youth. In Lee, C. (Ed.) *The First National People of Color Environmental Leadership Summit*. New York: United Church of Christ Commission for Racial Justice.

Bryant, B. 1990. *Environmental Advocacy: Concepts, Issues and Dilemmas*. Ann Arbor: Caddo Gap Press.

Bryant, B. 1992. *Toward a Curriculum for Environmental Programs*. The Environmental Professional. Vol. 14.

Bryant, B. 1989. *Social Change, Energy, and Land Ethics*. Ann Arbor: Prakken Publications.

Checkoway, Barry. 1982. The empire strikes back: More community organizing lessons for health care consumers. *Journal of Health Politics, Policy and Law*. 7: 111-124.

Checkoway, Barry. 1991. Unanswered questions about public service in the public research university. *Journal of Planning Education*. 5: 219-225.

Checkoway, Barry. 1985. Voter participation and political change: A Michigan case study. 19: 14-17.

Checkoway, Barry and William Cahill. 1981. Student workshops and neighborhood revitalization. *Journal of Alternative Higher Education*. 6: 96-110.

Checkoway, Barry and Michael Doyle. 1980. Community organizing lessons for health care consumers. *Journal of Health Politics, Policy and Law*. 5: 213-218.

Checkoway, Barry and Janet Finn. 1992. Young People as Community Builders. Ann Arbor, Center for the Study of Youth Policy, University of Michigan.

Checkoway, Barry, Kameshwari Pothukuchi, and Rogeair Purnell. 1992. Community Youth Planner's Bookshelf. Ann Arbor: Center for the Study of Youth Policy, University of Michigan.

Coleman, James S. 1977. "Differences between experiential and classroom learning." In Morris T. Keaton, ed. *Experiential Learning: Rationale, Characteristics, and Assessment*. San Francisco: Jossey-Bass.

Collins, Donald, Barbara Thomlinson, and Richard M. Grinell, Jr. 1992. *The Social Work Practicum: A Student Guide*, Itasca, Ill: F.E. Peacock Publishers, Inc.

Commission on National and Community Service. 1993. What You Can Do For Your Country. Washington: Commission on National and Community Service.

Conrad, Daniel E. and Diane Hedin. 1991. School-based community service: What we know from research and theory. *Phi Delta Kappan*. 72: 743-749.

Conrad, Daniel E. and Diane Hedin. 1982. The impact of experiential education on adolescent development. *Child and Youth Services*. 4: 57-76.

Daly, Kathleen (forthcoming). *Gender, Crime, and Punishment*. New Haven: Yale University Press.

Dewey, John. 1938. *Experience and Education*. New York: Collier Books.

Dionne, E. J. 1991. *Why Americans Hate Politics*. New York: Simon & Schuster.

Duckenfeld, Marty and Lorilei Swanson. 1992. Service Learning: Meeting the Needs of Youth at Risk. Clemson: National Dropout Prevention Center, Clemson University.

Ellis, T. 1993. Work and Slavery: A Gaian Perspective. In (Ed.) Bryant, B. *The Future: Images for the 21st Century*. Ann Arbor: Office of Minority Affairs.

Evers, Williamsom M. 1990. *National Service: Pro and Con*. Stanford: Hoover Institution Press.

Freire, P. *Pedagogy of the Oppressed*. New York, Seabury Press, 1970.

Freire, P. *Education for Critical Consciousness*. New York, Seabury Press, 1973.

Freire, P., & Shor, I. *A Pedagogy for Liberation*. Granby, MA, Bergin & Garvey Publ., 1987.

Goldsmith, W.W. and Blakely, E.J. 1992. *Separate Societies: Poverty and Inequality in U.S. Cities*. Philadelphia: Temple University Press.

Greider, William. 1992. *Who Will Tell the People*. New York: Simon & Schuster.

Hamilton, N., and Else, J. 1983. *Designing Field Education: Philosophy Structure, and Process*, Springfield, Ill: Charles C. Thomas.

Hedin, Diane. 1989. "The power of community service," *Proceedings of the Academy of Political Science*. 37, 201-213.

Heumann, Leonard. 1988. The changing role of the workshop course in educating planning professionals. *Journal of Planning Education and Research*. 7: 135-146.

Heumann, Leonard and Lewis Wetmore. 1984. A partial history of planning workshops: The experience of ten schools from 1955 to 1984. *Journal of Planning Education and Research*. 4: 120-130.

Hooks, b. 1984. *Feminist Theory from Margin to Center*. Boston: South End Press.

Horton, M. and Freire, P. 1990. *We Make the Road by Walking: Conversations on Education and Social Change*. B. Bell, J. Gaventa, and J Peters (Eds.). Philadelphia: Temple University Press.

Kadushin, A. 1976. *Supervision in Social Work*, New York: Columbia University Press.

Kendall, J. and Associates (Eds.) 1990. *Combining Service and Learning: A Resource Book for Community and Public Service*, National Society for Internships and Experiential Education.

Kohler, Mary Conway. 1982. Developing responsible youth through youth participation. *Child and Youth Services.* 4: 5-12.

Lang, John. 1983. Teaching planning to city planning students: An argument for the studio/workshop approach. *Journal of Planning Education and Research.* 2: 122-129.

Lynch, K. 1979. The spatial world of the child. In W. Michelson, S.V. Levine, & E. Michelson (Eds.), *The Child in the City: Today and Tomorrow*, pp. 102-127.

Markus, Gregory B., Jeffrey P. F. Howard, and David C. King. 1993. "Integrating community service with classroom instruction enhances learning: Results from an experiment," *Educational Evaluation and Policy Analysis*, Winter 1994.

Meyerson, D. and Scully, M. 1993. Tempered radicalism and the politics of ambivalence: Personal alignment and radical change within Traditional Organizations. Unpublished manuscript.

Mileski, Maureen 1971. Courtroom encounters: an observation study of a lower criminal court. *Law & Society Review* 5(4): 473-538.

Miller, M.G. 1993. A student's lot. In *Progressive Architecture*, July, p. 11.

Morton, Keith. 1993. Models of Service and Civic Education. n.p., Campus Compact.

Moskos, Charles C. 1988. *A Call to Civic Service.* New York: Free Press.

Nathan, Joe and Jim Kielsmeier. 1991. The sleeping giant of school reform. *Phi Delta Kappan.* 72: 81-88.

Newman, Frank. 1985. *Higher Education and the American Resurgence.* Princeton: Carnegie Foundation for the Advancement of Teaching.

Newmann, F. M. 1989. Reflective civic participation. *Social Education*, 53 (6), 6-9.

Newmann, Fred M. and Robert A. Rutter. 1988. The effects of high school community service programs on adolescent social development: Evidence of program effects. *Journal of Adolescent Research.* 3: 65-80.

Packer, Herbert 1964. "Two models of the criminal process." *University of Pennsylvania Law Review*, CXIII (November): 1-68.

Pascarella, Edward et al. 1988. The influence of college on humanitarian/civic involvement values. *Journal of Higher Education.* Summer: 412-437.

Peterson, Virgil. 1975. Volunteering and student value development: Is there a correlation? *Synergist.* 3: 44-51.

Principles of Good Practice for Combining Service and Learning, 1988, Johnson Foundation, Inc., Racine, WI.

Purpel, D. E.(1989). *The Moral and Spiritual Crisis in Education: A Curriculum for Justice and Compassion in Education.* Granby: Bergin & Garvey.

Pyle, Richard K. 1981. International cross-cultural service-learning: Impact on student development. *Journal of College Student Personnel.* 22: 509-514.

Rabkin, E. S., & Smith, M. (1990). *Teaching writing that works: A group approach to practical English.* Ann Arbor, MI: The University of Michigan Press.

Royse, David, Surjit Singh Dhooper and Elizabeth Lewis Rompf. 1993. *Field Instruction: A Guide for Social Work Students,* White Plains: Lingman, Inc.

Rutter, Robert A. and Fred M. Newmann. 1989. The potential of community service to enhance civic responsibility. *Social Education.* 53: 371-374.

Sagawa, Shirley and Sanuel Halperin, eds. 1993. Visions of Service: The Future of the National and Community Service Act. Washington: National Women's Law Center and American Youth Policy Forum.

Schneck, Dean, Bart Grossman, and Urania Glassman. 1991. *Field Education in Social Work: Contemporary Issues and Trends,* Dubuque: Kendall/Hunt Publishing Company.

Schoem, D., Frankel, L. Zúñiga, X., and Lewis, E.A. 1993. The meaning of multicultural teaching: An introduction." In *Multicultural Teaching in the University.* Westport: Praeger.

Sennett, R. 1978. *The Fall of Public Man. New York:* Vintage Books.

Serow, Robert C. 1991. "Students and voluntarism: Looking into the motives of community service participants," *American Educational Research Journal,* 28, 543-556.

Sigmon, R. 1990. Service-learning: Three principles. In J. Kendall and associates (Eds.), *Combining service and learning: A resource book for community and public service,* 1 (pp. 56-64). National Society for Internships and Experiential Education.

Sheafor, Bradford W., and Lowell E. Jenkins. 1982. *Quality Field Instruction in Social Work: Program Development and Maintenance,* New York: Longman, Inc.

Sheafor, Bradford W., and Lowell E. Jenkins. 1981. "Issues that affect the development of a field instruction curriculum," *Journal of Education for Social Work,* 17(1): 12-20.

Shulman, L. 1991. Core skills for field instructors. Montreal Canada: McGill University. (this is a five-part video series, Library of Congress catalogue numbers 83-706438 - 83-706442.)

Smith, Marilyn W. 1992. The Effects of Service-Learning Participation on Students Who Serve: Bibliography and Annotated Bibliography of Research. Washington: Commission on National and Community Service.

Stanton, Timothy K. 1990. *Integrating Public Service with Academic Study: The Faculty Role.* Providence, RI: Campus Compact.

Walden, T., and Brown, L.N. 1985. "The integration seminar: a vehicle for joining theory and practice," *Journal of Education for Social Work,* 21(1): 13-19.

ABOUT THE CONTRIBUTORS

About the Contributors
(All Contributors teach at the University of Michigan)

Buzz Alexander is a Professor of English Language and Literature. He has taught at UM since 1971, except for a term at the University of Lima in Peru in 1985. He is the author of *William Dean Howells: The Realist as Humanist* and *Film on the Left: American Documentary Film from 1931 to 1942* and is currently working on a book about community-based theater.

Lisa Bardwell is an Assistant Research Scientist in the School of Natural Resources and Environment. Her interest in service-learning has led her to initiate several environmental Project Community courses, and to research the impact of service on student learning and community response to environmental issues.

Bunyan Bryant has his major faculty appointment in the School of Natural Resources and Environment; he is also a member of the Urban Technological and Environmental Planning Program and the Center for Afro-American and African Studies. His current research interests include developing case studies on corporate, agency, and community responses to hazardous waste sites.

Barry Checkoway is Professor of Social Work and Urban Planning, and Chairperson of the University Task Force on Community Service Learning. He is the Coordinator of Community Organization/Social Administration/Social Policy Programs in the School of Social Work, and a Faculty Associate in the Center for the Study of Youth Policy.

Mark A. Chesler is a Professor of Sociology, a core faculty member of the Program on Conflict Management Alternatives and faculty sponsor for Project Community for 18 years. He is an activist scholar, whose field-based and experiential approach to research mirrors the approach to the pedagogy discussed in this book.

Toby Citrin, J.D., is based at the School of Public Health, University of Michigan, where he serves as Director of Community and Government Relations, Executive Director of The Resource for Public Health Policy, and Adjunct Professor of Public Health Policy and Administration. Citrin's 13-year career at the University of Michigan has been devoted primarily to developing mutually productive relationships between faculty and students at the School of Public Health, community-based organizations in Michigan and public health agencies at the federal, state and local levels.

Hilary U. Cohen received her B.A. in Drama from Stanford University in 1969 and her Ph.D. in Theater from the University of Michigan in 1980. She shares her time between teaching theater courses at the University and being Artistic Director of Wild Swan Theater. She is the author of numerous articles in the area of theater and disability.

Karis Crawford holds a Ph.D. in medieval studies from the University of Toronto. She has taught composition and medieval and Renaissance literature, has worked as a lexicographer for the Middle English Dictionary, and is currently the Assistant Director of Faculty Affairs for the University of Michigan Medical School. Her own community service has centered on women's health advocacy and on economic democracy through cooperatives.

Kathleen Daly received her Ph.D. in Sociology from the University of Massachusetts at Amherst in 1983. She has taught at the State University of New York at Albany and at Yale, and is currently a Visiting Associate Professor at the University of Michigan. Her forthcoming book, *Gender, Crime, and Punishment,* examines problems of equality and justice in penal practices.

Jeffrey Howard is the Director of the Office of Community Service Learning. He has been a service-learning educator with this Office for 16 years, and is Editor of the forthcoming inaugural issue of the *Journal of Community Service Learning.* His research interests include the academic and social responsibility outcomes for service-learners, and he presently Chairs the Curriculum Development Committee of the Michigan Campus Compact.

Christina Jose Kampfner is an Assistant Professor in the School of Education at Eastern Michigan University. She has worked extensively in the Latino community in Southwest Detroit. She has taught Psychology and Women Studies at the University of Michigan, where she received her Ph.D. in Education and Psychology.

Peter B. Kaufman has been a Professor of Biology at the University for more than 30 years. His research interests are extensive, enabling him to work with environmentalists, bioengineers, biochemists, space biologists, and others. He is a devoted instructor and committed environmentalist.

Gregory B. Markus is Professor of Political Science and Research Scientist in the Institute for Social Research. He specializes in the politics of the United States, in particular the ways that citizens influence—and are influenced by—the American political process.

Wilbert McKeachie served as Chair of the Psychology Department from 1961 to 1971 and in 1965 supported the development of Project Outreach, one of the first service-learning programs on campus. He has served as President of the American Psychological Association and the American Association for Higher Education. He has taught a number of undergraduate psychology courses involving service-learning opportunities, and his book on college teaching, *Teaching Tips,* is now in its ninth edition.

Allen Menlo has been a faculty member in the School of Education since 1951. His major areas of teaching and research have been interpersonal, group, organization, and community dynamics and development. In 1981, he founded an international research partnership, the Consortium for Cross-Cultural Research in Education, with which he continues as Director as he moves to an active Emeritus status.

Jerry Miller is the Faculty Coordinator for Project Outreach in the Department of Psychology. He has been guiding students in field-based experiences for almost twenty-five years. He has served as a mental health consultant to numerous community agencies, and is currently involved in research to evaluate the impact of service¬learning experiences on students.

Lily Jarman-Rohde received her MSW in 1982 from the University of Michigan School of Social Work, where she has been director of field education since 1984. Before that, she was a public service journalist in Washington D.C. and in Philadelphia.

Shannon Sullivan is a 2nd year Ph.D. student in the School of Natural Resources and Environment. She has been a teaching assistant for an Environmental Studies class and for an Ecological Issues class. Her research interests include human interactions with nature, environmental value formation, and the impact of nature in urban areas.

Sharon E. Sutton is Associate Professor of Architecture and Urban and Regional Planning and a core faculty member of the Program on Conflict Management Alternatives. She is coordinator of the Urban Network, a nationally-recognized program that enables youth to improve their communities, and the recipient of the 1992 Regents Award for Distinguished Public Service. She holds degrees in music, architecture, and psychology, and was formerly a Kellogg National Fellow.

John E. Tropman graduated from Oberlin College and the University of Chicago (AB from the former, AM from the latter) and received his Ph.D. from the University of Michigan. He teaches nonprofit management in the School of Social Work and organizational behavior in the School of Business Administration. His areas of specialty are American values and culture, charity and philanthropy, and executive leadership. He is also a fisherman.

Mari Ziegler is an environmental educator and an avid naturalist. She teaches about nature and ecological responsibility at elementary and senior high schools, jr. colleges and universities, as well as in special programs for mentally, emotionally and physically impaired students.